The Impact of Napoleon, 1800–1815

THE MAGILL BIBLIOGRAPHIES

The American Presidents, by Norman S. Cohen, 1989
Black American Women Novelists, by Craig Werner, 1989
Classical Greek and Roman Drama, by Robert J. Forman, 1989
Contemporary Latin American Fiction, by Keith H. Brower, 1989
Masters of Mystery and Detective Fiction, by J. Randolph Cox, 1989
Nineteenth Century American Poetry, by Philip K. Jason, 1989
Restoration Drama, by Thomas J. Taylor, 1989
Twentieth Century European Short Story, by Charles E. May, 1989
The Victorian Novel, by Laurence W. Mazzeno, 1989
Women's Issues, by Laura Stempel Mumford, 1989
America in Space, by Russell R. Tobias, 1991
The American Constitution, by Robert J. Janosik, 1991
The Classical Epic, by Thomas J. Sienkewicz, 1991
English Romantic Poetry, by Bryan Aubrey, 1991
Ethics, by John K. Roth, 1991
The Immigrant Experience, by Paul D. Mageli, 1991
The Modern American Novel, by Steven G. Kellman, 1991
Native Americans, by Frederick E. Hoxie and Harvey Markowitz, 1991
American Drama: 1918-1960, by R. Baird Shuman, 1992
American Ethnic Literatures, by David R. Peck, 1992
American Theatre History, by Thomas J. Taylor, 1992
The Atomic Bomb, by Hans G. Graetzer and Larry M. Browning, 1992
Biography, by Carl Rollyson, 1992
The History of Science, by Gordon L. Miller, 1992
The Origin and Evolution of Life on Earth, by David W. Hollar, 1992
Pan-Africanism, by Michael W. Williams, 1992
Resources for Writers, by R. Baird Shuman, 1992
Shakespeare, by Joseph Rosenblum, 1992
The Vietnam War in Literature, by Philip K. Jason, 1992
Contemporary Southern Women Fiction Writers, by Rosemary M. Canfield Reisman and Christopher J. Canfield, 1994
Cycles in Humans and Nature, by John T. Burns, 1994
Environmental Studies, by Diane M. Fortner, 1994
Poverty in America, by Steven Pressman, 1994

The Short Story in English: Britain and North America, by Dean Baldwin and Gregory L. Morris, 1994
Victorian Poetry, by Laurence W. Mazzeno, 1995
Human Rights in Theory and Practice, by Gregory J. Walters, 1995
Energy, by Joseph R. Rudolph, Jr., 1995
A Bibliographic History of the Book, by Joseph Rosenblum, 1995
The Search for Economics as a Science, by the Editors of Salem Press (Lynn Turgeon, Consulting Editor), 1995
Psychology, by the Editors of Salem Press (Susan E. Beers, Consulting Editor), 1995
World Mythology, by Thomas J. Sienkewicz, 1996
Art, Truth, and High Politics: A Bibliographic Study of the Official Lives of Queen Victoria's Ministers in Cabinet, 1843-1969, by John Powell, 1996
Popular Physics and Astronomy, by Roger Smith, 1996
Paradise Lost, by P. J. Klemp, 1996
Social Movement Theory and Research, by Roberta Garner and John Tenuto, 1996
Propaganda in Twentieth Century War and Politics, by Robert Cole, 1996
The Kings of Medieval England, c. 560-1485, by Larry W. Usilton, 1996
The British Novel 1680-1832, by Laurence W. Mazzeno, 1997
The Impact of Napoleon, 1800-1815, by Leigh Ann Whaley, 1997
Cosmic Influences on Humans, Animals, and Plants, by John T. Burns, 1997
One Hundred Years of American Women Writing, 1848-1948, by Jane Missner Barstow, 1997
Vietnam Studies, by Carl Singleton, 1997
British Women Writers, 1700-1850, by Barbara J. Horwitz, 1997
The United States and Latin America, by John A. Britton, 1997
Reinterpreting Russia, by Steve D. Boilard, 1997

The Impact of Napoleon, 1800–1815

An Annotated Bibliography

Leigh Ann Whaley

Magill Bibliographies

The Scarecrow Press, Inc.
Lanham, Md., & London
and
Salem Press
Pasadena, Calif., & Englewood Cliffs, N.J.
1997

SCARECROW PRESS, INC.

Published in the United States of America
by Scarecrow Press, Inc.
4720 Boston Way
Lanham, Maryland 20706

4 Pleydell Gardens, Folkestone
Kent CT20 2DN, England

Copyright © 1997 by Leigh Ann Whaley

All rights reserved. No part of this publication may be reproduced, stored in a retrieval system, or transmitted in any form or by any means, electronic, mechanical, photocopying, recording, or otherwise, without the prior permission of the publisher.

British Cataloguing-in-Publication Information Available

Library of Congress Cataloging-in-Publication Data

Whaley, Leigh Ann.
   The impact of Napoleon, 1800–1815 : an annotated bibliography / Leigh Ann Whaley.
      p. cm. — (Magill bibliographies)
   Includes bibliographical references and index.
   ISBN 0-8108-3316-6 (alk. paper)
   1. Napoleon I, Emperor of the French, 1769–1821—Bibliography.
2. Napoleon I, Emperor of the French, 1769–1821—Influence.
3. France—History—1789–1815—Historiography. 4. France—Kings and rulers—Historiography. 5. Civilization, Modern—French influences—Sources—Bibliography. I. Title. II. Series.
Z8612.W43   1997
[DC203.9]
016.94405—dc21   97-3434
                                                                               CIP

ISBN 0-8108-3316-6 (cloth : alk. paper)

™
∞ The paper used in this publication meets the minimum requirements of American National Standard for Information Sciences—Permanence of Paper for Printed Library Materials, ANSI Z39.48–1984.
Manufactured in the United States of America.

Contents

Acknowledgments ix

Introduction xi

Chapter 1: Trends and Obsessions: Conflicting Approaches in
   Napoleonic Historiography 1
     Nineteenth Century Trends   1
     Napoleon and the French Academicians   10
     The Anti-Napoleonic Tradition   14
     University Historians   16
     Revolutionary Historians   19
     The Bicentenary of Napoleon's Birth   20
     Foreign Histories   22
     Gaps in Napoleonic Scholarship   30
     Notes   31

Chapter 2: Primary and General Source Materials 34
     Primary Sources   34
     Reference Works   48
     Histories and Historiography   53

Chapter 3: Biographies of Napoleon and His Brothers 60

Chapter 4: Internal Affairs 72
     Government and Administration   72
     The Economy under Napoleon   80
     Education during the Consulate and Empire   89
     Developments in Science and Medicine   95

Chapter 5: The Napoleonic Legend 99

Chapter 6: Military Histories 106

Chapter 7: Women during the Consulate Empire 132

Chapter 8: Society under Napoleon 137

Chapter 9: Napoleonic Colonies and Empire 145

Chapter 10: Religion 166
    General   166
    Protestantism   166
    Catholicism   167
    Judaism   173

Chapter 11: Diplomacy 176

Chapter 12: Culture 185

Author Index 199

Subject Index 205

About the Author 209

Acknowledgments

The author would like to thank Professor William Pelz of DePaul University in Chicago for approaching me in 1992 to write this book for G. K. Hall Macmillan, which subsequently canceled the Western Civilization series of which this volume was a part. In addition, the author would like to thank Professor Pelz for recommending me to Salem Press and its excellent editorial team, and in particular, its senior editor, Ms. Chris Moose.

This work has been made possible through the assistance of the interlibrary loan service at the Queen's University of Belfast library, the sources located at the Bibliothèque Nationale in Paris, France; and most important, the superb collection at the John P. Robarts research library at the University of Toronto, Toronto, Canada.

The completion of this project has been facilitated by a semester's study leave for which the author is grateful.

Introduction

According to Napoleonic expert Louis Villat, the first comprehensive biography of Napoleon dates from 1821, the year of his death, *Napoléon, sa naissance, son éducation, sa carrière militaire, son gouvernement, sa chute, son exile et sa mort*. It was published anonymously by M.C. The massive Napoleonic literature began with this relatively impartial account of Napoleons life and work. By 1821, the bibliography of Napoleonic works was already immense and was divided between pamphlets and personal eulogies. Today, the number of works about Napoleon exceeds 250,000. There are more studies about Napoleon than days since his death.

The present work is not another biography, nor is it a general history of the period. Rather it is a work of reference, designed for the interested layperson and scholar alike. It should be of interest not only to those wanting to learn about Napoleon and his tremendous impact upon his times, but, in addition, to anyone with a passion for military history and for the history of great leaders and their contributions to history. Despite the wealth of material published on Napoleon, this type of reference work, which summarizes the literature in a clear and concise manner and which provides an extended annotated bibliography of printed sources, simply does not exist. There are a number of excellent bibliographical reference tools, the most complete of which is Ronald A. Caldwells two-volume *The Era of Napoleon* (Garland, 1991). None of these guides, however, including Caldwells, provides readers with lengthy annotations.

This reference work is intended to be of aid to both senior-level university students and researchers planning to pursue further study on Napoleon and the Napoleonic era. It will direct them to the literature and inform them what is useful and why.

No author writing about Napoleon could claim to be comprehensive. For the purposes of this book, every attempt has been made to include the leading works in their field, written by the authority on the subject. This means that only the most significant works, works that have been universally recognized for their scholarly merit, for their detail, or for their contributions to the historiographical debate, have been included. In addition, the most recent studies are cited and discussed. Because this book is intended primarily for an English-speaking readership, the vast majority of citations are of English-language works. Only those important works which are unavailable in English are listed in French, Italian, and German.

This book is composed of two major parts. The first, which consists of Chapter 1, is an historiographical essay which surveys the immense literature about Napoleon and the Napoleonic era. It traces the leading works and schools of thought, focusing on the French schools, from the earliest histories to those of the present day. The essay analyzes the reasons why there have been so many divergent opinions about Napoleon from the nineteenth century onward, and examines these questions in an international context. This chapter closes with suggestions for further research.

The second part, which forms the bulk of the book, is a critical annotated bibliography composed of approximately 480 works, ranging from theses, chapters of books, and articles, to full length multivolume studies. The bibliographical chapters are divided into numerous thematically organized sections and subsections. The chosen themes reflect the numerous aspects of life upon which Napoleon had an influence during his lifetime and facets where this influence has persisted to the present day.

Chapter 2, "Primary and General Source Materials," is divided into three sections. The first covers primary sources, including the memoirs, letters, and bulletins of Napoleon and other key contemporary figures, such as major statesmen and Napoleons brothers. The editions of the memoirs and letters have been selected for their helpful introductions, notes, and commentaries. Reference works such as bibliographical guides, historical dictionaries, historical companions, and works of a historiographical and general nature, comprise the second part of the chapter. Reference works such as bibliographical guides, chronologies, historical dictionaries, and companions make up the second part of the chapter. Finally, histories of a general nature and historiographical works comprise the final section of this chapter.

Chapter 3, "Biographies of Napoleon and His Brothers," incorporates the major biographies written by international experts. Chapter 4, "Internal Affairs," is composed of subsections listing works on government and administration, the economy, education, and developments in science and medicine. Chapter 5, "The Napoleonic Legend," examines works representing both sides of the "for" and "against" debate about Napoleon.

Military histories, comprising Chapter 6, include works on the army, the navy, the various Napoleonic battles in addition to studies on the impact of war on society. Chapter 7, "Women during the Consulate Empire," treats the subject of the impact of Napoleonic policies on women. Chapter 8, "Society under Napoleon," scrutinizes works on population, social classes, cities, and institutions. Napoleonic expansion is the subject of Chapter 9. Chapter 10, "Religion," is divided into sections composed of works of a general nature, as well as more specialized studies on Judaism, Roman Catholicism, and Protestantism. Foreign affairs and international relations are the topic of Chapter 11, "Diplomacy." The final chapter, "Culture," surveys the major works on Napoleons impact on the visual arts, contemporary writers, the theater, and music.

Two indexes are provided for users of this reference work: The "Author Index" alphabetically lists all authors and editors of the works listed in this bibliography with the page numbers on which those works are cited. The "Subject Index" lists all topics of note—events, personages, institutions, locales, and concepts—which receive discussion in the annotations and hence the works themselves.

Chapter 1

TRENDS AND OBSESSIONS
Conflicting Approaches in Napoleonic Historiography

Nineteenth Century Trends

Two major trends dominated Napoleonic historiography during the nineteenth century.[1] The first was inspired by the Napoleonic myth or legend, which Napoleon inaugurated himself at the beginning of the Italian campaign in 1796 with his issuing of propaganda in the form of the newspaper, *Courrier de l'armée d'Italie*, or *La France vue de l'armée d'Italie*. This journal, followed by his *Bulletins de la Grand Armée*, provided the official version of his campaigns and promoted his glory and genius across Europe. The second school developed in opposition to the first, and it was dominated by writers such as Chateaubriand, Benjamin Constant, and most significantly, the great contemporary enemy of Napoleon, Madame de Staël. Most of this pioneering historical writing was dominated by political and personal considerations.

The ultra-royalist Chateaubriand, a precursor to the Romantic movement in literature, originally had amicable relations with Napoleon, but his relationship with the Emperor soured with the execution of the duke d'Enghien in 1804. Chateaubriand wrote an anti-Napoleonic pamphlet, *De Buonaparte, des Bourbons et de la nécessité de se rallier à nos principes légitimes pour le bonheur de la France et celui de l'Europe* (1814), which did much to foster the "black legend." In this work, he depicted Napoleon as the "ogre from Corsica," thirsty for the blood of young Frenchmen. The major themes of the "black legend": the usurper of power, the parvenu, the centralizer with a foreign policy of European domination and permanent warfare, were all present in Chateaubriand. He also judged

Napoleon harshly in his twelve-volume history of the Napoleonic years, *Mémoires d'outre tombe* (1849-1850), in which he made the years from 1800 to 1814 into a personal battlefield between himself and Napoleon.

Without a doubt, the formidable Madame de Staël was the most significant of these early opponents for she distinguished herself as the first critic whose condemnation was based on tangible events. Napoleon disapproved of her novels, *Delphine* (1802) and *Corinne* (1807), which displayed unconventional attitudes toward morality. He interpreted them as a challenge to his newly reconstructed social order. In addition, Madame de Staël refused Joseph Fouché's advice to insert flattering comments about Napoleon in her writings. Her lack of French patriotism in her study of Germany, *De l'Allemagne* (1810), also incurred his wrath. Napoleon attempted to have it destroyed. In her chronicle of Napoleon's life in Part II of the *Considérations sur la Révolution française*, published posthumously in 1818, she portrayed him as the destroyer of the republican liberties of the French Revolution with which she so strongly identified. In her words, he eradicated "republican idealism."

Madame de Staël's companion, Benjamin Constant, was an important figure in the liberal opposition during the early years of the Consulate as a member of the Tribunate from 1799 to 1802. His increasing opposition to Bonaparte's authoritarianism had him expelled, and he followed Madame de Staël into exile. Constant's *De l'esprit de la conquête et de l'usurpation dans leurs rapports avec la civilisation européenne* (1814) was instrumental in articulating the liberal position at the time of Napoleon's collapse. It was written as an attack on military dictatorships.

Napoleon's extraordinary success aroused mixed emotions among the English Romantics. For the vast majority, he was a vile figure. Published in the same year as Constant's work was Lord Byron's *Ode to Napoleon Buonaparte*, which protested against Napoleonic tyranny in favor of liberty. Written upon hearing the news of Napoleon's abdication, it is the most celebrated anti-Napoleonic poem. During this period, Byron produced his *Childe Harold's Pilgrimage* (1812-1819), which contains his protagonist's famous pilgrimage to Waterloo. Byron, who was deeply interested in Napoleon, believed they were similar men. He interpreted Napoleon from the personal side, and his comments range from condemnations to praise.[2]

To William Wordsworth, Napoleon was a tyrant who revealed the illusive nature of the universal freedoms proclaimed by the French

Revolution. The revolts in the Iberian peninsula against Napoleon were a turning point for the English in their own struggle. These events profoundly influenced Wordsworth's poetry. Percy Bysshe Shelley saw things differently. For Shelley, Napoleon was the first man in Europe to have risen to the apex of power through his own merit, rather than through privilege. His undoing and the restoration of the Bourbons to the throne constituted a defeat for the new hopes of humankind. Napoleon played a pivotal role in the formation of Samuel Taylor Coleridge's thought. A conservative politically, Coleridge had been opposed to the French Revolution. For him, Napoleon was an outlaw.[3]

Napoleon's death in 1821 provoked numerous reactions from literary writers, from the prudent *Le Cinq Mai* of the French poet and song writer Pierre-Jean de Béranger to Victor Hugo's hostile *Bonaparte* (1822). Béranger's songs and poems glorified the Empire during the Restoration.

Continuing with the Napoleonic legend were the numerous works of the French Romantic writers who succeeded Chateaubriand, Benjamin Constant, and Madame de Staël. Among these perhaps the most significant figures were Stendhal, Honoré de Balzac, and Victor Hugo. Napoleon dominated their works of literature.

Balzac's admiration for Napoleon dated from the time of Napoleon's Egyptian expedition. In Balzac's opinion, Napoleon was the greatest among great men, a genius who put an end to the anarchy of the Revolution and restored Christianity to Europe. It is possible to obtain from Balzac's series of novels, *La Comédie humaine*, a history in which Napoleon is transformed into a sort of demi-god of France. Balzac's portrayal, although laudatory, was not entirely without reproach for Napoleon. He saw Bonaparte as a bourgeois upstart. However, in the end, Napoleon represented for Balzac what he wanted to be: a great figure, larger than life itself.[4]

Victor Hugo's attitude toward life was greatly affected by the Napoleonic years. His father had worked for Joseph Bonaparte as his confidential advisor and governor of Madrid. He was converted from Royalism to Bonapartism in 1820. This was first apparent in his *Les Orientales* (1829) and burst forth in the *Ode à la Colonne* (1830), which backed Napoleon's marshals against the insults from the Austrian ambassador. Hugo idealized the Emperor.[5]

Stendhal's entire work was dominated by the figure of Napoleon Bonaparte. Napoleon's influence can be seen in his novels, particularly *The Scarlet and the Black* (1830), as well as in his nonfictional works. His *Vie de Napoléon*, written in 1817 and published in 1876, was a defense of the Emperor. He reproached Madame de Staël for misunderstanding Napoleon's strength in her *Considérations*. Although his *Mémoires de Napoléon* were written almost twenty years later, in 1836, and published in 1854, there is much similarity in the content of both works.[6]

For Stendhal, Napoleon was the greatest man since Caesar. He was more than simply a great military man: he possessed a greatness of spirit. What particularly fascinated Stendhal was the fact that Napoleon had come from humble origins and had risen to become the most powerful man on earth. Stendhal had not always admired Bonaparte. Between 1802 and 1806, he was often opposed to Napoleon's policies, which he considered to be tyrannical. Like many others, Stendhal interpreted Napoleon as the usurper of revolutionary principles, and his coronation provoked Stendhal's protest. However, in his final estimation, Napoleon received a positive press. In Stendhal's view, he had made it possible for the French people to recover their pride, partly through the institution of the Legion of Honor. Finally, Bonaparte had turned France into a country of property-owning peasants.

Other French Romantics whose writing was influenced by Bonaparte were the poets Alfred de Musset, Alfred de Vigny, Gérard de Nerval, and Alphonse de Lamartine. All applauded Napoleon as a liberal and contributed to the vogue of nostalgia for French greatness during the Restoration period.

German Romantics were tremendously affected by the behavior of Napoleon Bonaparte.[7] The reaction among them was predominantly negative. The cosmopolitan ideas of the Enlightenment had taken hold in German lands. Before Napoleon, German Romantics had not been concerned with a German identity and had supported the liberal gains of the revolutionaries. All this changed with Napoleon's overrunning of their lands. During the French Revolution, Friedrich von Schiller had been made an honorary citizen of the French republic, while Johann Gottlieb Fichte had admired the social reforms of the French revolutionaries. They saw Napoleon as a betrayer of the Revolution. Exceptions to the prevalent thinking among German writers concerning Napoleon were the poets Johann von Goethe and Heinrich Heine. Goethe remained sympathetic to both the Revolution and Napoleon. He did not become nationalistic like many of his contemporaries. For this, Napoleon bestowed upon him the Cross of the Legion of Honor in 1808. Heine praised Napoleon in his ballad *The Grenadiers* of 1816, in which he drew a parallel between Napoleon and Jesus Christ.

It was during the first half of the nineteenth century that the first memoirs and histories of Napoleon were produced. The most significant of these were the *Mémorial de Sainte-Hélène* and his private secretary Louis-Antoine Fauvelet de Bourrienne's ten-volume *Mémoires de M. de Bourrienne, ministre d'Etat; sur Napoléon le Directoire, le Consulat, l'Empire, et la Restauration* (French edition, 1829-1830; English edition, 1830). Napoleon had dictated the *Mémorial* to Comte de Las Cases at Saint Helena. In it, Napoleon is depicted as the son of the Revolution and the defender of freedom and justice. He is simultaneously the aloof and accessible Emperor. Bourrienne's memoirs glorify the Emperor. The first memoirs of the imperial era were those of Antoine-Clair Thibaudeau, *Mémoires sur le Consulat (1799-1804), par un ancien conseiller d'Etat* (1827). Contemporary accounts of military campaigns also appeared in 1827. These included Antoine Henri de Jomini's *Vie politique et militaire de Napoléon* (1841), Jacques Marquet de Norvins' *Histoire de Napoléon* (1827-1828) and the comte Maximilien Sébastien de Foy's *Histoire de la guerre de la Péninsule* (1827).

In addition to the numerous memoirs published shortly after Napoleon's death in 1821, during the Restoration there appeared the first serious histories of the French Revolution. The works of the journalist, historian, and politician Louis Adolphe Thiers, and those of the journalist, historian, and archivist François Mignet launched what has been called the "Great Tradition." It was later developed by their successors throughout the nineteenth and twentieth centuries. Their histories were intended to be contributions to the opposition against the absolutist and clerical tendencies of the Bourbon regime. Mignet produced his *Histoire de la Révolution française* in two volumes in 1824. It was essentially a political manifesto against the Restoration. For Mignet, the Revolution brought about a major transformation of society. The early years of the Constituent Assembly and the reforms proposed by the comte de Mirabeau were the zenith of the Revolution. Why did it fail? Mignet believed that the attacks of the aristocracy, and the invasion of the masses threw the Assembly off its course. The middle position of the bourgeoisie becomes very clear. Napoleon was nothing more than a self-serving soldier and a counterrevolutionary despot.

The years from 1830 to 1851, taking in the July Monarchy and the short-lived Second Republic, witnessed works primarily favorable to Napoleon. Many of these were produced under the conciliatory climate of Louis-Philippe, who had the Emperor's ashes returned to France in 1848. The year 1829 saw the publication of the first volume of Baron Louis-Pierre Edouard Bignon's *Histoire de France depuis le 18 Brumaire*. Bignon had been a diplomat during the Directory in Switzerland, under Napoleon in numerous German cities, and in Warsaw. Napoleon in his will had left Bignon 100,000 francs to write a history of French diplomacy from 1792 to 1815. Although the chief importance of his work for readers today is its information on the diplomatic service, which is based on his own papers as well as those of his contemporaries, he did not devote himself exclusively to diplomacy, as Napoleon had ordered. His fourteen volumes are a history of the epoch. Moreover, the fact that his was a commissioned work does not mean that Bignon was without independent thoughts about the Emperor. He is most critical after the Treaty of Tilsit in 1807, and of Napoleon's domestic reforms, such as those in education.

A particularly fertile year, 1845, saw the publication of the first volume of the revolutionary journalist and later Sorbonne professor Jean Charles Dominique de Lacretelle's *Histoire du Consulat et de l'Empire*. Also appearing in that year was the Napoleonic diplomat Armand Lefebvre's *Histoire des cabinets et l'Europe pendant le Consulat et l'Empire*. These were the first histories of the reign of Napoleon, and they were entirely sympathetic in tone and content. In many ways, they are similar to Bignon's books, except that Lacretelle and Lefebvre placed their works in a wider time frame, which included the French Revolution. Lefebvre began the trend in diplomatic historiography that justified Napoleon's wars as the defense of France's "natural frontiers." Later historians, including Albert Sorel, Edouard Driault, Jacques Bainville, and to a lesser extent, Georges Lefebvre, repeated this thesis.

Without a doubt, the most significant work of Napoleonic literature that appeared during the nineteenth century was the French politician Louis Adolphe Thiers' monumental twenty-volume *Histoire du Consulat et de l'Empire*, on which he began work in 1840. Thiers, as prime minister under Louis-Philippe, was responsible for the completion of the monuments Napoleon had begun himself for his glorification. Thiers viewed Napoleon's rule as the best compromise between the liberalism stemming from the French Revolution and the order required after the anarchy and chaos of the Terror. His history was published in two parts, separated by Napoleon III's coup of 1851. Volumes 1-11 were published between 1845 and 1851, while the nine remaining volumes appeared between 1856 and 1862. The separation between the two parts is marked not only by a division in time but, significantly, by a change in perspective toward the Emperor by the author. The first eleven volumes were written entirely for the purpose of glorifying Napoleon, Thiers' hero. The coup of 18 Brumaire, the Concordat, the Civil Code, the Peace of Amiens, the Coronation, Austerlitz, Iena, Tilsit, and Wagram all represent the national epic, and imperial glory. He understood the regime of the Consulate as a regime that deserved the admiration of Europeans. After Louis-Napoleon Bonaparte's coup of 2 December 1851, the tone changed. These later volumes are characterized by despondency, and a fear that the Second Empire would only bring disaster on France.

Thiers was considered by contemporaries as the "ablest and most popular living historian in Europe."[8] In the end, Thiers came down on the side of the Napoleonic myth by linking Bonapartism with liberty. The French Revolution was made incarnate by him and with him it spread across Europe. He denounced the Bourbons as illiberal and impolitic for not accepting the gains made by the French Revolution. For Thiers, Napoleon was first and foremost the greatest soldier history had ever produced. With his taste for military history, it is not surprising that many volumes of vivid descriptions of battles and the minutiae of operations resulted. Although Thiers exaggerated the greatness of Napoleon, and his work is not without its critics,[9] he did make use of various archival sources including the Archives des Affaires Etrangères, the Napoleonic papers held at the Louvre before they were published, and the correspondence of several Napoleonic ministers. In addition, he interviewed survivors from the Napoleonic years who provided firsthand accounts for his history. Some of these included Soult, Molé, Marbot, and Méneval. Thiers benefitted from the oral tradition passed on by men such as general Bugeaud, who recounted to him the siege of Saragossa. He read 30,000 of Napoleon's letters, and he visited the battlefields; he was a fanatic for facts and for simplicity. His history remains a classic vital to all studying this period.

During the reign of Napoleon I's nephew, Napoleon III (1852-1870), several more important works were published. The era saw a renaissance of interest in Napoleon, and it was during these years that the official correspondence of the Emperor was published. The publication of this important source began in 1855; it was not completed until 1870, and it constitutes 22,000 letters in thirty-two volumes. A commission was appointed to manage the publication, and initially the intention was to publish all of Napoleon's letters, but this liberal attitude changed when letters were found which were not entirely flattering to the Napoleonic regime. Hence, the second committee charged with the publication of the correspondence omitted the less laudatory letters. The *Correspondance de Napoléon* cannot be considered a definitive source for the history of the Napoleonic era, but rather its main usage is for the history of his campaigns. Today the total number of volumes in Napoleon's correspondence goes beyond sixty. Although there was scholarly representation on the commission in the person of Charles-Augustin Sainte-Beuve, a literary critic and historian, the reasons for the publication were not scholarly. Rather, the intention was to enhance the reputation of Napoleon I. When further volumes of Napoleon's correspondence appeared during the Third Republic, the one-sided nature of the official commission's editing was made clear to the public.

In addition to the Emperor's official correspondence, complimentary volumes of correspondence by members of the Bonaparte family appeared, all intended to reinforce the Napoleonic legend. These included the *Mémoires et Correspondance* of Joseph (1853-1854), of Eugène Beauharnais (1858-1860), and of Jérôme (1861-1866). Countless other primary sources were published during the Second Empire such as the memoirs of André Masséna, Pierre Louis Roederer, André-François Miot de Mélito, and Lazare-Nicolas-Marguerite Carnot.

The Second Empire was significant not simply because of the reawakening of interest in Napoleon and the wealth of primary material that it published, but it was during the final years of the reign of Napoleon III, when his popularity was waning, that the first anti-Napoleonic literature was produced. The most important critical works were written by Jules Romain Barni, *Napoléon et son historien M. Thiers* (1865), Edouard Quinet, *La Révolution* (1865), and Pierre Lanfrey, *Histoire de Napoléon Ier* (1867-1875, 1886). These men were republican writers who attacked the despotic nature of Napoleon I's regime at a time when his nephew's government was becoming increasingly tyrannical. Barni was a French politician and philosopher who lived in exile in Switzerland. Although his short work is highly polemical and not a history, he did offer a lucid critique of Thiers, and in common with Madame de Staël, and many later critics, he declared that Napoleon was not French, but an Italian with the ambition of becoming a Caesar. Quinet, who was an academic historian at the Collège de France, shared Barni's view of Napoleon as a foreigner and a Roman Emperor who had drifted into France. He believed that Napoleon could be understood only as a Corsican descended from the Ghibellines of Florence.

Of these three critics of the 1860s, the renowned journalist Lanfrey had the most impact. Writing between 1867 and 1875, Lanfrey was the first to attempt an impartial biography that was more than simply a polemical assault. His aim was to castigate the current government of Napoleon III through his uncle. Based primarily on the published *Correspondance*, it was well researched and scholarly. For the first time, a history of Napoleon furnished the facts of the Emperor's life to Frenchmen. His work did much to destroy the Napoleonic legend and was the most important uncomplimentary work of Napoleon during the nineteenth century.[10]

With the fall of the Second Empire after France's defeat in the Franco-Prussian War, interest in Napoleon waned. The debate over Napoleon resumed with the work of the philosopher and critic Hippolyte Taine. Taine's attitude was deeply affected by the humiliation of the 1870 defeat and by the anarchy of the subsequent Paris Commune. His psychological study was intended as a personal critique of Napoleon. In February and March 1887, his two articles appeared under the title "Napoléon Bonaparte." These essays, which contributed enormously to the reaction against Napoleon, were reprinted in book form under the title *Les Origines de la France contemporaine*, between 1875 and 1893. According to Taine, Napoleon—once again viewed as an Italian—descended from the *condottieri*, who during the fifteenth and sixteenth centuries had shocked Italy through their exploits and excesses. Napoleon was nothing more than a resuscitated *condottiero*, possessing all of such a figure's vigorous qualities: his brutality, his indifference to any idea of fidelity to a fatherland, and his lack of a moral conscience. In addition, Napoleon was a Corsican, imbued with a clan mentality whose allegiance remained only with himself rather than to France. Driven by an insatiable desire for power, his goal was to control first France and then Europe. Through ferocity, force, and sheer energy, Napoleon ended the French Revolution and built a new world. The end result of his regime was the defeat of France in two successive invasions.

The response to Taine from the Napoleonic camp was Prince Napoleon's *Napoleon and His Detractors* (1887), in which Taine's work was characterized as a libellous.[11] Prince Napoleon questioned the validity of Taine's major sources, Bourrienne, Madame de Rémusat, and Miot de Mélito. This was a polemical work not taken seriously by scholars. It repeated the Napoleonic legend.

Napoleon and the French Academicians

Toward the close of the nineteenth century, a new kind of Napoleonic historiography emerged. This was "academic" history, dominated by writers who held the chair of the French Academy. They wrote during the establishment of the Third Republic, when there was a resurgence in nationalism and a search for glory manifested in men like General Boulanger, whose popularity was based on revenge for the Sedan defeat and the loss of Alsace-Lorraine to the newly unified Germany, and an expansion in overseas colonies. In terms of Napoleonic historiography, the tide turned once again in favor of the Empire and historians who praised Napoleon, dominated the Academy. They did much to rekindle the legend. These writers were Arthur Lévy, Henry Houssaye, Frédéric Masson, Albert Vandal, and Albert Sorel. All inaugurated a reaction against Taine. Their works were based either on the newly opened public archives or, as in the case of Masson, on private collections. They tended to write micro-histories: detailed histories that focused on narrow topics.

Houssaye, an essayist, art critic, and historian who began his career writing histories of Greece, and who had served as an officer during the Franco-Prussian War, produced a multivolume series between 1888 and 1905. The success of the highly patriotic *1814* was enough to get him elected to the French Academy. He meticulously read every possible contemporary source available to him: memoirs, correspondence, newspapers, police reports, writings by travelers, and diplomatic papers. All of his books follow a similar format. There is no argument, but a chronicle of the "facts" set against a background of blind loyalty to the Emperor. Any mistakes made were the fault of the generals and ministers. The historical value of Houssaye remains the detail contained in his histories and the contribution they made to the revitalization of the Napoleonic legend which occurred between 1890 and 1900.

Masson, who had begun his career as a librarian at the archives of the French Ministère des Affaires Etrangères, became increasingly attracted to Napoleon through his research on diplomatic history. Consequently, he resigned his position as librarian to dedicate himself entirely to researching and writing about the Emperor. Masson was a friend and literary advisor of Prince Napoleon and Princess Mathilde. Experts agree that no Napoleonic writer was "more wholehearted in his admiration, none more passionate, more one-sided, more partisan and also more sincere, more honest, none was more convinced that he served the truth." In addition, "no writer has done more to explain

Napoleon's personality." After working on Napoleon for more than thirty years, Masson wrote: "I intoxicate myself with his glory."[12]

The result of Masson's labor was more than sixty tomes in addition to many speeches and articles. The outstanding achievement of his prodigious career and the work that represented his methodology and philosophy was his *Napoléon et sa famille*, based on private archives and consisting of thirteen volumes published between 1897 and 1919. Masson was not pleased with the tendency of previous historians to distinguish between the private and public persona of Napoleon. His aim was to unite the two aspects of the man, as to him they were inseparable. Masson interpreted history as being "human" rather than a mere "chronological arrangement of facts." It was "something which will remind you of life itself." Details such as the way in which the Emperor shaved and the type of paper he used for his correspondence were not trivial details to Masson, but revealing facts about Napoleon's character.[13]

For Masson, it was not a question of writing a general history of the life and times of Napoleon, but one of Napoleon and his relationship with members of his family and their behavior toward him. In Masson, one will not find a history of Spain under Joseph, of Naples under Murat, or of Westphalia under Jérôme. Family members are not portrayed in an entirely approving light. They are depicted as unquestionably ungrateful of everything their brother did for them. What Masson has produced is a series of biographies that simultaneously harmed the reputation of the Bonaparte clan, awakened an interest in Napoleon's personality, and inspired a more sympathetic treatment of him.

Albert Sorel underscored the continuity in French foreign relations in his eight-volume *L'Europe et la Révolution française* (1885-1904). His work in the Ministère des Affaires Etrangères from 1866 to 1875 provided him with a good knowledge of the functioning of diplomatic relations for his future publications. He spent almost thirty years writing his classic, which is based on previously unpublished documents on French diplomacy. He later printed them in *Revue historique*. According to Sorel, Napoleon continued the policy of the French revolutionary Committee of Public Safety of 1793, which was merely an enlargement of the policy of Louis XIV: to obtain France's "natural frontiers" and achieve her domination of Europe. Sorel maintained that the impediment to this goal was the actions of her enemies: Sir William Pitt and his successors in Great Britain and Prince Metternich and other adversaries on the Continent. The coalition against France was permanent because England could not accept France's acquisition of her "natural frontiers." According to Sorel, Napoleon, who merely wanted to keep France's "natural frontiers," had no other choice than to advance. His true intention was to make peace once France's "natural boundaries" were secure. Setting aside its pro-Napoleon bias, Sorel's diplomatic history of the revolutionary and Napoleonic era remains the foremost scholarly investigation of diplomatic relations.

A contemporary of Sorel, Emile Bourgeois, who was a professor at the Ecole Normale Supérieure, opposed Sorel's thesis concerning Napoleon's foreign policy. He did not accept Sorel's fatalistic interpretation, but argued that Napoleon was master of his foreign policy. The European powers did not resist a continuation of the revolutionary policy, but they did resist Napoleon's personal ambition. In that, they found a much more serious threat to their interests than the maintenance of France's borders. Bourgeois held that Napoleon had an "oriental secret" which was to dominate the east: the Mediterranean, the Ottoman Empire, and Poland.[14]

Vandal studied under Sorel and succeeded him as professor at the Ecole des Sciences Politiques, a school founded by Taine that attracted scholars with conservative politics. For Vandal, history was a drama, and the historical personages found in his drama provided color and life to history.[15] He produced two works worthy of mention here. His *Napoléon et Alexandre Ier: L'Alliance russe sous le Premier Empire*, a three-volume study published between 1891 and 1897, provides a detailed narration of the relations between the two leaders between 1807 and 1812. The work is analogous to a drama in three parts: the Alliance, the Decline of the Alliance, and the Rupture.[16] Vandal attempted to provide readers with lessons of history based on past failures. His basic theory is that Napoleon attempted to entice Alexander into a strong alliance by offering him the hope of some of the Ottoman Empire. Napoleon's major goal was to stabilize his system in Europe, and this required British acceptance. This work won for Vandal the prestigious Prix Goncourt (1893 and 1894) and led to his election to the French Academy in 1897.

His second work, *L'Avènement de Bonaparte,* which appeared from 1902 to 1907, is similar in style and method to Houssaye's work, although it is of superior quality. It does not have an argument and consists foremost of a detailed study of a short period of time and a narrowly focused topic. In the case of Vandal, it is the rise to power of Napoleon. Vandal calls his work a political history, the purpose of which is to demonstrate how Bonaparte seized power in revolutionary France. He made good use of unpublished police reports in the French archives to shed light on the plot of Brumaire. He explained Napoleon's rise to power as gradual, achieved through military victories in Egypt and Marengo, the Brumairian coup, and the development of the institutions of the Consulate. In his interpretation of the Brumairian coup, Vandal demonstrated that the Directors were incompetent and ruthless rulers who were extremely unpopular. The accession of Napoleon was therefore inevitable. Napoleon's impact was one of reconstruction and reconciliation.

Although an admirer of Napoleon, Vandal did differ slightly in his interpretation from Houssaye and Masson in the sense that he did not see Napoleon as the fulfillment of the Revolution. Nor did he consider Napoleon to be the icon of the people, yet he continued to believe Bonaparte was a genius. Contemporaries greeted his work with great praise.

The academician Arthur Lévy wrote two works about Napoleon: *Napoléon intime* (1892) and *Napoléon et la paix* (1902). *Napoléon intime*, which had great success, was written to refute Taine. Napoleon was an exceptional man, but one of mainly middle-class values. The great soldier was also a great conciliator. Before Napoleon came to power, France had been torn apart by civil war; after Napoleon, France formed a strong and proud nation galvanized by patriotism.[17] The major value of the work is that Lévy provides a good narrative of Napoleon's daily activities. Lévy's second and less successful work, *Napoléon et la paix*, deals with Napoleon's conduct of foreign policy. His thesis is similar to that held by Sorel: Napoleon defended France's natural frontiers against European powers. His goal throughout his regime was peace. The European powers are portrayed as the aggressors. Using the *Memorial* as his major source, Lévy was completely devoted to Napoleon. His blindness prevented him from understanding the historical realities.

Louis Madelin contributed numerous significant works to Napoleonic scholarship. His doctoral dissertation, completed at the Sorbonne in 1901, resulted in the biography *Fouché, 1759-1821*, based upon Fouché's letters. It is an exemplary biography still worth reading. In 1936, Madelin began work on his classic *Histoire du Consulat et de l'Empire*, in which he undertook to rewrite and modernize Thiers. Appearing in a series called the National History of France, Madelin's work presented a grand view of Napoleonic history. The sixteenth and final volume was completed in 1954 after his entry into the French Academy. Madelin remained faithful to the conservative bourgeois view of Napoleon's policies. In addition, he continued the tradition of French historians that has been mainly biographical in the sense that their histories focus on Napoleon himself. Madelin's books are written in simple narrative. He has been criticized for his ignorance of the economic problems of the Empire, for providing a narrow diplomatic view of history, for a lack of discussion of Napoleonic institutions, and for numerous factual errors. In addition, he was wrongly convinced that Napoleon's popularity among the bourgeoisie remained intact in 1814.

The Anti-Napoleonic Tradition

Beside the worshippers of Napoleon, during the early twentieth century, an anti-Napoleonic school composed of two opposing groups developed. These were the royalists and the republicans. The royalists considered Napoleon to be a usurper of power while the republicans reproached him for having confiscated to his benefit the liberties bequeathed by the French Revolution. The royalist school was represented by the writers who formed the Action Française, which began in 1898 when a group of right-wing intellectuals met around a philosophy professor, Henri Vaugeois, to search for the political basis of a French rebirth based on nationalism. They created a committee for this purpose and then in July 1899 a journal, *Revue d'Action Française*, was started to disseminate the ideas of the group. These men spoke against the republic, and attributed the harm done to the army and the weakness of the government during the Dreyfus affair, not to individuals, but to the form of government. They found it difficult to express their views in the conservative journals, which for the most part were either mildly republican or so moderately royalist as to be afraid of vigorous conclusions. This was the rationale behind the founding of their own monthly review. In 1938, Charles Maurras, the chief ideologue of the group, drew a parallel between Joan of Arc, Louis XIV, and Napoleon and was particularly unfavorable to the latter. For Maurras, the preservation of the prerevolutionary past was important.[18]

The chief historian of the group was Jacques Bainville, who was a leading royalist historian of twentieth century France.[19] His books were widely read between 1914 and 1940 and his biography of Napoleon remains one of the most popular in France to this day. One of the reasons for Bainville's success was his straightforward, concise style, which, according to the French royalist historian Philippe Ariès, was more palatable to the French than either the flowery romantic prose or the obscure academic writing of earlier

Trends and Obsessions

historians of Napoleon.[20] The purpose of Bainville's *Le Dix-huit Brumaire* (1925), which dealt with the causes of the 1799 coup, was to modify the Napoleonic legend. The coup, according to Bainville, had been "provoked in the interest of the revolution in order to reaffirm the revolution," which had reached a stalemate by 1799. He argued that revolutionary politicians decided to support the "republican on horseback" as they believed he would save rather than destroy the new republic. According to Bainville, if the revolutionaries had not decided to support Bonaparte when they had done so, then the Bourbons would have overthrown the Revolution.[21]

Bainville's purpose was to explain Napoleon's career in terms of his motivation.[22] In this sense, he wrote an early psychobiography. His depiction of Napoleon was not new and, in many ways, had much in common with that of Sorel and Vandal. Like Sorel, he often forgave Napoleon for the great destruction his wars brought to France. Bainville openly relied heavily on Vandal for his facts, and from Sorel he appropriated the theory that the Revolution was driven by France's obsession with securing her natural frontiers and the idea that Bonaparte, as a spiritual son of the Revolution, simply continued that policy after his attainment of complete power.[23]

Although Bainville's work challenged traditional interpretations of Napoleon, it was largely overlooked by academic historians. Undeterred by this lack of recognition by France's scholarly community, he continued to pursue his research on Napoleon. The result was a biography, *Napoleon* (1931), commissioned by the French Academy, which he entered four years later. It was an immediate best-seller. According to Geyl, it was "probably the most read biography of Napoleon in our time."[24] In terms of actual knowledge, Bainville told us little that was not already made known by Sorel and Vandal. This did not seem to matter to readers who were taken with the book's style rather than its content. Its wide circulation served to popularize the revisionist interpretation of the Napoleonic phenomena that Bainville had employed in his earlier monograph about the eighteenth of Brumaire.

In Bainville's *Napoleon*, one finds two different works: first, an historical study explaining the political activity of the Emperor, and second, a drama about destiny played out in several acts. Napoleon's impossible mission, bequeathed to him by the revolutionaries who had survived the Terror, was to retain France's territorial gains made during the Revolution. To accomplish such a task, Napoleon was forced to establish a new monarchy which he called an Empire. This would assure that the old one would not be reestablished. Europe and especially England, were opposed to this growth in French power, and this hostility resulted in constant warfare. Bainville's *Napoléon* is also the drama of man's internal struggle, which shows the tragic side of his hero marching toward his destiny with perfect clarity. Like a hero of Greek mythology, Napoleon is devoted to perpetual warfare, condemned to constant victory. Although he was constantly in battle, he desired peace but never obtained it. Only after a catastrophe would he have revenge on destiny. This was the legend he created for himself at Saint Helena.[25]

There is much of Napoleon which Bainville omits. For example, his administrative and judicial reforms as well as the entire restructuring of the French educational system are rarely mentioned. When Bainville does refer to achievements other than military and diplomatic, he critiques Napoleon for uniting himself to revolutionary ideals and transmitting them throughout Europe. He was an expert at the popularization of the royalist interpretation of Napoleon.

Although Bainville found much to praise in Napoleon—his strong will, his restoration of financial stability, religion, and national security to France—in the final analysis he presented a negative interpretation of Napoleon as a man who had contradictory aims. On the one hand, he attempted to bring about a peace in Europe to satisfy conservatives, but at the same time he was obsessed with the glory of France, which meant sustaining "the conquests of the revolution." Napoleon lost power because he was unable to give up the latter goal. In the eyes of Bainville, the extensive damage that Napoleon did to France in both human and material terms had simply not been worth it. He concluded that, "Except for glory, except for art, it would have been better if he had never existed."[26]

University Historians

Historians trained at French universities called themselves "scientific." A battle emerged between the scholars of the university and those of the academy. The former considered their research and writing to be of a superior quality. Scientific historians called for a close examination of the primary sources, especially parliamentary debates, memoirs, and correspondence. University historians complained that those from the Academy wrote literary history which resulted in an excess of useless works. Unlike the *académiciens*, the *universitaires* tended to interpret Napoleon and his legacy in a negative light. The Napoleonic legend had not influenced their thinking.

François-Alphonse Aulard was a pioneering university historian. In 1886, he became the first holder of the newly created prestigious chair of French revolutionary studies at the Sorbonne. Through the publication of numerous volumes of documents concerning the revolutionary and Napoleonic period, he did much to assist scholarly research. His *French Revolution* (1910) ends with Bonaparte's coronation in 1804, which in his opinion terminated the Revolution. Aulard explained Napoleon in terms of a reactionary who reintroduced many aspects of the Old Regime. Napoleon had, for example, completely destroyed the Rights of Man, which were so important to Aulard. Napoleon had effectively abolished liberty and violated equality.

Edouard Driault, a *lycée* teacher, took on the previous studies of Napoleon's foreign policy by historians of the Academy such as Sorel and Vandal. He wrote narrative histories of Napoleon's foreign policy, *La Politique extérieure du premier Consul*, and *Austerlitz: La Fin du Saint-Empire*, published in 1910 and 1912 respectively. These were the fruit of more than ten years of research in the archives of France's Ministère des Affaires Etrangères. Driault insisted that Napoleon's policies broke with those of the revolutionaries. Napoleon was something other than a successor to Georges-Jacques Danton or Lazare Carnot. It was Napoleon who refused to make peace and, in claiming to defend his Empire, compromised the gains of the Revolution. Driault argued that there were many aspects of Napoleon's foreign policy that the Continental Blockade and the struggle against England did not explain: the founding of an empire, the coronation, Austerlitz, and the Confederation of the Rhine. Driault came up with an original interpretation of Napoleon's conduct vis-à-vis foreign powers. According to Driault, Napoleon's goal was to reestablish the unity of the Roman Empire, which would realize his destiny as Emperor.

In addition to pursuing "scientific" research, the university historians founded scholarly journals dedicated to Napoleon and major theses or studies. The French journal dedicated to the enrichment of Napoleonic scholarship entitled *Revue des études napoléoniennes*, begun by Driault in 1912, marked a turning point in Napoleonic historiography.[27] In the first issue of the journal, he set out as its purpose "to release the person of Napoleon from the heroic legend in order to pursue scientific knowledge."[28] An important mandate was to systematically "organize research and to exploit unedited sources." These goals involved the publication of many documents.[29] The most outstanding Napoleonic specialists contributed to the review: Aulard, Charles Ballot, Jean Bourdon, Ferdinand Boyer, Marcel Dunan, André Fugier, Louis Hautecoeur, Léon Lanzac de Laborie, Philippe Sagnac, Evgenii Tarlé, Louis Villat, and Charles Schmidt. A summary of the works published between 1912 and 1931 under the title "Twenty Years of Napoleonic Studies" demonstrated that Driault's purpose had been realized. These years marked the journal's greatest success and contained its major contributions. Afterward, under the influence of a new editor, G. Maugen, its quality declined. Articles became briefer and much less scholarly. They were mainly anecdotal in content. The collaborators of the first years no longer contributed, and many began writing for the more scholarly periodical *Annales historiques de la Révolution française*, founded in 1924.

Driault inaugurated a new journal, the *Revue de l'Institut Napoléon*, at a general assembly of the Friends of Napoleon in 1932. It was founded on the occasion of the centenary of the death of the king of Rome and was dedicated to Napoleonic studies. From January 1943, the Institute published a trimestrial bulletin whose purpose was to establish a link between its members and disseminate the Institute's aims: "to cultivate in France, as well as outside France . . . the memory of Napoleon."[30] In 1936, its directorship was taken over by the Philippe Sagnac, who held the chair of French revolutionary studies at this esteemed institution. Under Sagnac's leadership, the review published numerous documents. Publication of the journal was interrupted by World War II, but in 1947 it resumed publishing under the presidency of Sagnac's successor as chair of French revolutionary studies at the Sorbonne, Marcel Dunan.

Dunan was instrumental in introducing research in France on the Continental Blockade. He had first attracted the attention of the scholarly community with an important article on this topic in the *Revue des études napoléoniennes* as early as 1913. This issue was at the center of his doctoral dissertation, *Le Système continental et les débuts du royaume de Bavière (1806-1810)*. In addition, he wrote *Napoléon et l'Europe: La Politique extérieure du premier consul 1800-03* (1942). It was a significant contribution to research into the foreign policy of the Empire.

Dunan's interests were not merely confined to his own research. He had numerous graduate students whose work contributed enormously to our knowledge of the Continental Blockade. Odette Viennet, in *La Crise de 1810-1811* (1946), studied the impact of the system on French industry. She examined Napoleon's role in regulating and helping business and industry. In 1955, Kirsten Heils examined the problem from a Danish perspective in *Les Rapports économiques franco-danois sous le Directoire, le Consulat et l'Empire*. England was tackled by François Crouzet in his monumental thesis, *L'Économie britannique et le blocus continental 1806-1813*, first published in 1958 and reissued thirty years later in 1988. It has remained the classic on the subject. Crouzet convincingly demonstrated how British exports were able to resist the Continental Blockade because of trade with the American market. He showed how Napoleon did not understand the importance of North America for British commerce.

Revolutionary Historians

In 1936, *Napoléon*, by the Marxist historian Georges Lefebvre, appeared. It is a general history of the period from 1800 to 1815 in the Peuples et Civilisations series, edited by Louis Halphen and Philippe Sagnac, and represents the first serious attempt at this genre of historical writing. Lefebvre's work is the result of extensive research, and even with minor weaknesses, such as its interpretation of the Continental Blockade, it remains one of the most important contributions to twentieth century Napoleonic historiography. Lefebvre viewed Napoleon as both the heir of the French Revolution and the forebear of Romanticism. Far from condemning Napoleon's dictatorship and seeing in Napoleon's ambition the cause of contemporary warfare, he qualified his judgment of the Emperor in the following manner: "The great achievement of Napoleon—the installation of a new dynasty and the erection of a universal empire—ended in failure. . . . An authoritarian government was indispensable to save the Revolution as long as its enemies were in league with the foreigner and the middle classes needed Napoleon to give this authority."[31] Lefebvre became one of the first French historians of Napoleon to stress the continuity of the Revolution and the Empire in the social sphere: "The revolution of 1789 had thrust the middle classes forward into power, but this power had then been disputed by a rising democracy. Under the protection of the Emperor, the notables succeeded in recovering it, and grew in wealth and influence."[32]

The Marxist historians on the one hand, were sympathetic to Napoleon the man, while, on the other, they condemned what he did to France. The best Marxist synthesis is that found in *Napoléon*

(1959), by Emile Tersen, who argued that Napoleon was the instrument of the bourgeois class. His economic policies served the interests of this group. Bonaparte was the man of the bourgeoisie, which abandoned him at the hour of his defeat.

After World War II, historians of the university tended to concentrate on the French Revolution, and the Napoleonic studies that did appear remained under their control. The revolutionary historian Albert Soboul, who held the chair of French revolutionary studies at the Sorbonne, opened up new perspectives on the social history of the Empire during the 13th Congrès International des Sciences Historiques, held at Vienna from 29 August to 5 September 1965. Papers by a team of international scholars, including Lewis Hertzman from the United States and A. Z. Manfred and A. L. Narotchnitzki from the Soviet Union stressed the impact of social and economic factors on European society during the Napoleonic wars.

Under the influence of Marcel Dunan, Marcel Reinhard, A. Z. Manfred, Jacques Godechot, Ernest Labrousse, and Albert Soboul, new sectors of research opened up. The new research stressed economic and demographic history, and social problems. Labrousse defended his theory that during the Napoleonic era the French economy expanded and that there was a general growth in production. The Continental Blockade did have a sluggish effect, but it did not inhibit growth. Godechot's study of Napoleonic institutions, *Les Institutions de la France sous la Révolution et l'Empire* (1851), pointed out the gaps in research in this area.

Outside the university, most writers continued their exaltation of the Emperor. Jean Thiry attempted a *Napoléon Bonaparte* in twenty-five volumes in which he devoted much space to the military operations of the Empire, while Commander Henry Lachouque also composed numerous works on the campaigns of Napoleon.

The Bicentenary of Napoleon's Birth

The year 1969, the bicentenary of the birth of Napoleon Bonaparte, marked a watershed in Napoleonic historiography. During that year, more than two hundred new works appeared, and many older studies were reprinted. The towering French work was *Napoléon et l'Empire*, which brought together, under the editorship of Jean Mistler, the most distinguished revolutionary and Napoleonic specialists. Godechot and Reinhard recounted Napoleon's accession to power, which they saw as inseparable from the French Revolution. Studying

French society under the Empire, Bertrand Gille insisted that Napoleon had effected a successful transition between the Old Regime and the modern world, by the restoration of the old nobility and the creation of a new one based on merit.

In 1969, researchers turned away from predominantly biographical, diplomatic, and military studies to social and economic history. Leading international scholars presented many papers at a conference held at the Sorbonne in October of that year. The results appeared in print form of special editions of the *Revue d'histoire moderne et contemporaine* and the *Annales historiques de la Révolution française* in 1970. Similar conferences, such as the Colloque de Bruxelles: Occupants-Occupés, 1792-1815, were held throughout Europe. Participants of each colloquium were from different nations, and papers dealt with almost all subjects, with the exception of the overdone military and diplomatic areas. The "idol" was deemphasized in favor of the institutional, legal, social, cultural, economic, and political impact of the Napoleonic years. Papers highlighted specialized topics within both France and the Empire, using the new methodology of statistics and prosopographic history. Outstanding examples of the new history are the special issues of the *Annales historiques de la Révolution française*: "L'Italie jacobine et napoléonienne" (1977), and "Education" (1981), although the latter focuses primarily on the French Revolution. The long-term consequences of Napoleon's reign were explored.

The new history that was born in 1969, converging on the underlying structures of Napoleonic society, has resulted in pioneering works by the Napoleonic historians Jean Tulard, Guy Chaussinand-Nogaret, and Louis Bergeron. These historians have moved away from the traditional "for" or "against" personal histories of Napoleon which had dominated past historiography. Bergeron's *France under Napoleon* (1972; English edition, 1981) is most representative of the new trend. It deals with the economic, financial, social, and cultural history of the Napoleonic years. Bergeron considers topics neglected by traditional histories such as the impact of Napoleon's policies on urban workers, peasants, industry, and the bureaucracy.

Tulard has been director of the Institut Napoléon since 1974, and at the sixth section of the Ecole Pratique des Haute Etudes in Paris. His *Napoleon: the Myth of the Saviour* (1977; English edition, 1984) effectively distinguishes between the myth and reality of Napoleon. Clearly influenced by the Annales school, it represents a new type of biography, which includes social and economic topics. This work compliments Tulard's many other studies, such as *La Vie quotidienne* des Français sous Napoléon (1978) and his Napoléon et la noblesse d'Empire (1979). As its title suggests, the former deals with the daily life of peasants and artisans, which, Tulard argues, did not change after 1800. Ostensibly his work on the nobility considers this group under the Napoleonic Empire, but there is much more to it. It is concerned with the nature of the society created by Napoleon, which Tulard argues was ordered and hierarchical, reversing the French Revolution's philosophy of advancement by merit. Only those who had profited from the Revolution's sale of national lands or those who were already wealthy had the chance to do well under Napoleon. Ennoblement under Napoleon was reserved for the Old Regime's nobility, holders of public office, or high-ranking officers. Lastly, the author asserts that the Napoleonic regime rapidly and irreversibly turned to caesarism, and that in the final analysis, Bonaparte's system rested on the notables, not on the people. In addition, Tulard has enhanced our knowledge about life in the French capital with his *Nouvelle Histoire de Paris: Le Consulat et l'Empire, 1800-1815* (1970), an indispensable tool for those interested in the political, social, and economic history of the city under Napoleon.

Foreign Histories

The first British studies were biographies and military histories. Those published shortly after Napoleon's death represented both sides of the "for and against camp." On the against side, Sir Walter Scott's critical nine-volume *Life of Napoleon Buonaparte* (1827) was the leading work. Scott interpreted Napoleon as a rogue. Although he professed to have written an objective history and to have consulted with the Duke of Wellington for factual accuracy, a work written so quickly cannot be taken seriously for its historical value. It was praised some contemporaries—Goethe spoke favorably of it in his letter to Scott dated 12 January 1827—while it caused much alarm among Bonapartists. The chief importance of Scott's *Napoleon* is that it enunciated the fundamental anti-Napoleonic contention for the next 150 years.

William Hazlitt was a renowned British radical, whose biography *The Life of Napoleon Buonaparte* (4 vols., 1828-1830) was written to counterbalance the English prejudices of Scott and to set forth the case against divine-right monarchy. As a supporter of the French Revolution, Hazlitt viewed Napoleon as its son and inheritor.

Napoleon was interpreted as the "great man," the "hero," and, thanks to Saint Helena, "the martyr."

John Gibson Lockhart, an English essayist published his *History of Napoleon Buonaparte* (1829) anonymously not long after he became editor of the *Quarterly Review*. Intrepreting Napoleon from the Tory perspective, his work was based heavily on Scott's, but was more balanced. Written in a pithy and graceful style, it represents an early English view of Napoleon.

On the military side, Sir William Francis Patrick Napier's *History of the War in the Peninsula* (6 vols., 1828-1840) remains the classic study of the period. It is a monumental work of literature written by a British officer who served in some of the important campaigns of the Peninsular War. This study has been praised for its literary merit but criticized for its factual inaccuracies and for its one-sidedness.

The conspicuous lacuna in early English historiography of scholarly works was partially filled with the publication in 1900 of Lord Rosebury's *Napoleon, the Last Phase*. English writers had finally begun to take a serious interest in the problem of Napoleon. Rosebury, a British statesman, was most interested in Napoleon's last years spent at Saint Helena. He was seriously disadvantaged by the lack of good sources, but nevertheless he attempted a critical comparative analysis of the Saint Helena literature, the accounts by Las Cases, Montholon, O'Meara, and Gourgaud. Rosebury's objective was to dissipate the false ideas that had accumulated over the preceding century about Napoleon. He attacked not only the memorialists but also Sir Hudson Lowe and the anti-Napoleonic leanings of previous English studies. For the first time, a relatively unbiased analysis was attempted.

The first serious biographical study of Napoleon by an Englishman was John Holland Rose's *The Life of Napoleon I* (2 vols., 1902). Rose, a professor at Christ's College, Cambridge, not only used the official correspondence but also went to the archives of the British Foreign Office, where he found diplomatic papers including reports of ambassadors. In addition, he used the archives of the British War Office and the Admiralty. Rose painted a reasonably benevolent portrait of the Emperor, although he was unshakably attached to the idea that England had rendered great service to Europe in defeating Napoleon. He was an admirer, but not a worshipper, of Napoleon. His biography became a classic work in English on Napoleon and was reissued several times.

In 1906, the ninth volume of the Cambridge Modern History series appeared under the title *Napoleon*. Here Napoleon is no longer treated as a tyrant or a despot. In the preface, the editors, all Englishmen, state that although Napoleon's hostility to Great Britain was a historical fact, it did not "blind Englishmen to his greatness."[33] The phenomena of the French Revolution and the forces that it controlled are considered from a European perspective. It is worth noting that two years before the publication of this volume, the Entente Cordiale between Britain and France was signed. Having France as an ally made it difficult for the authors of this volume to judge Napoleon too harshly. Moreover, one chapter, "France under the Empire," was written by a Frenchman, Georges Pariset.

Napoleonic studies in England suffered from a lack of interest between 1906 and the 1950s. There were English translations of foreign studies, such as Tarlé's in 1937 and Bainville's in 1938. H. A. L. Fisher wrote a short biography, *Napoleon*, in 1912, covering the man himself and internal reforms. However, it was not until J. M. Thompson's biography, *Napoleon Bonaparte: His Rise and Fall*, which appeared in 1951 (reissued in 1990), that a work of importance appeared in England. An Oxford University history professor, Thompson produced a work that is scholarly and well balanced. He focused on the political aspects of Napoleon's rule: he criticized Napoleon's autocracy but was less condescending toward him than were his predecessors. He viewed Napoleon as one of history's greatest egoists, and from that premise wrote what remains one of the most outstanding biographies of all time. Thompson tended to be Anglo-centric, calling the Ecole Militaire the French Sandhurst, the French Senate a kind of House of Lords, and Toulon the French Portsmouth.[34] Despite these minor shortcomings, the facts that Thompson's work was reissued in 1990 and that very few scholars have challenged his balanced interpretation prove that this biography has weathered the test of time. It remains a standard reader on undergraduate syllabuses.

The next major work by an English historian was Felix Markham's *Napoleon*, published in 1963. In the years between Thompson's and Markham's works, several new primary sources had been discovered, including the memoirs of Henri-Gratien Bertrand and Marie Louise's letters, and several secondary works of outstanding quality, such as Godechot's *Institutions* and Crouzet's *L'Economie britannique*, had appeared. Markham made use of all of these. It was no longer a question of justifying English policies vis-à-vis Napoleon after 150 years since Waterloo; Markham's was the first English biography to be free of national prejudice. His interpretation of Napoleon was that of the inspirer for a modern Europe rather than a usurper of power.

American work on Napoleon has not been plagued by the same prejudices as that of the English. This is evident in the comparison of two contemporary nineteenth century biographies: *A Short History of Napoleon the First* (1886), by the Englishman and Cambridge professor of history John Robert Seeley, and *The First Napoleon: A Sketch, Political and Military* (1885), by the American John Codman Ropes. Although both are scholarly, well written, and based on documents, Seeley is negative while Ropes is positive.

Geoffrey Bruun's *Europe and the French Imperium, 1799-1814* (1938) is an attempt to get beyond the traditional confines of political and military history without entirely neglecting them. These are discussed in conjunction with developments in the economic, financial, social, religious, cultural, and artistic spheres. Bruun neither idolizes nor detests Napoleon.

In keeping with the American tradition of balanced accounts of Napoleon is Robert B. Holtman's *The Napoleonic Revolution* (1967). Holtman states in clear terms that his book is not about the "for or against" debate. For this reason, it remains one of the best English-language surveys on Napoleon's lasting achievements. Holtman is concerned to investigate the ingredients of the "Napoleonic revolution" and their origins. His work demonstrates how Napoleonic practices combined components from the Enlightenment and the French Revolution.

Owen Connelly's *Napoleon's Satellite Kingdoms* (1965) continues to be the best introductory study of this subject, providing an excellent comparative analysis of the five Napoleonic kingdoms: Italy, Naples, Holland, Spain, and Westphalia. The background to the establishment of each kingdom is discussed, as is the relationship between Napoleon and the members of his family placed on the thrones. In addition, Connelly, the leading American scholar of Napoleon, is chief editor of the *Historical Dictionary of Napoleonic France 1799-1815*. The dictionary is wide-ranging in its coverage, although military affairs do not figure fully. The major emphasis is on the Empire. As Connelly states in his preface, the dictionary is more concerned with the history of the period than with the man, and in this light, biographical details about Napoleon have been kept to a minimum. Finally, Connelly has produced a fine military history, *Blundering to Glory* (1987), in which he challenges many of the views of Napoleon as a great military commander. For Connelly, Napoleon won his wars through the skill of his subordinates, luck, and his own scrambling.

The early years of the early twentieth century produced many excellent non-English-language studies on Napoleon which remain classics. The leading Russian expert is Evgenii Tarlé, a Russian soldier who held the chair of history in the Leningrad Historical Research Institute. His speciality was the Continental System, and his use of Russian sources enabled him to expound Russian policy effectively and to treat the Russian side of the campaign in a manner superior to that of most French and British writers. For him, Napoelon was the son of the Revolution; without it, his rise to power is inconceivable. From the Revolution, he received his army, and an understanding of war and its tactics. At the same time, Napoleon was the liquidator of the French Revolution. In the end, Tarlé concluded that Napoleon was a military genius.

For a more recent Russian view of Napoleon, there is Albert Manfred's *Napoléon Bonaparte* (1971). It was translated into French in 1980 but has yet to find an English translator. It is good on the general history of the Consulate and Empire, and on Franco-Russian relations, using the press and the Russian archives of the Foreign Ministry. More than half the book is concerned with Napoleon's formative years, the period up to the coup of 18 Brumaire. Manfred argues that from the start Napoleon possessed neither a clear vision of what he was to become nor a determined ambition. This view contrasts with what many previous historians have posited. Only the taste for risk and for a gamble explain Napoleon's rise to power.

F. M. Kircheisen is the all-time German authority, having produced a nine-volume work, *Napoleon: Sein Leben und seine Zeit* (1911-1934). Kircheisen worked from printed sources, chiefly German and Austrian. His work is especially good for the campaigns in which these two nations were engaged against the French. Napoleon is not idolized, as he had been in many early French accounts; rather, a balanced view is presented. Kircheisen is also unfavorable to Great Britain.

Emile Ludwig's early psychobiographical portrait, *Napoleon* (1926), was written like a novel and was widely read. A history of the personality of Napoleon, it examines the inner nature of Napoleon, his feelings and thoughts through his words, written and spoken. Political acts and events are also used to illustrate Napoleon's character. Military and diplomatic events are not covered. The author is not entirely positive about Napoleon and is not afraid to discuss his faults.

The Austrian Auguste Fournier's biography, *Napoleon I. Eine Biographie,* was first published in 1895, translated in 1903, and appeared in an expanded form in 1904-1905. It is one of the best and most highly regarded of the early biographies, with a special emphasis on military history. The only defect is that the author, as an Austrian, attempted to defend the policy of Austria, and in doing so he tended to distort the events.

Military histories have occupied a central place in Napoleonic historiography. Histories of the Napoleonic wars have been well served in English. A thorough early military history is Colonel Francis Loraine Petre's five-volume series covering five campaigns: *Napoleon's Conquest of Prussia*, *Napoleon's Campaign in Poland*, *Napoleon and the Archduke Charles*, *Napoleon's Last Campaign in Germany*, and *Napoleon at Bay*, published between 1901 and 1913 and reprinted between 1974 and 1977. Ramsay Phipps wrote an extensive study of the campaigns beginning in 1926 and completed twelve years later. Jean Thiry has produced more than thirty volumes on the military operations of Napoleon since 1939.

The most comprehensive Napoleonic military history remains David Chandler's work of more than one thousand pages, *The Campaigns of Napoleon* (1966). Chandler describes and analyzes Napoleon's battles in great detail. He thoroughly explores arms and tactics. Owen Connelly's *Blundering to Glory* (1987) is a good recent account for its balanced interpretation. Gunther Rothenberg's *The Art of War in the Age of Napoleon* (1977) is a study of European wars rather than simply those dealing with France and Britain. It surveys of each of the revolutionary and Napoleonic wars and is held to be a commendable survey. It is not surprising that Rothenberg, a former soldier, focused on the realities of warfare rather than military theory or the impact of warfare on society. In the traditional sense of military history, arms, equipment, and tactics provide the primary subjects.

Some historians have been more innovative in their approach to the Napoleonic wars, concentrating on their social impact. Alan Forrest's *Conscripts and Deserters: The Army and French Society during the Revolution and Empire* (1989) examines the response of villages to the military conscription imposed on them by the state. He tells the fascinating tale of the struggle between the French state, determined to obtain the necessary recruits for war, and a rural population that did everything to resist this pressure. Isser Woloch has also studied the impact of warfare on French society in his works on the veteran and war widows. Geoffrey Best's survey, *War and*

Society in Revolutionary Europe 1770-1870 (1982), is a superb example of a sociomilitary history, which includes a chapter on Napoleon. Best declares that a new style of warfare was accomplished by Napoleon and attempts to answer at what cost to society this was achieved. It is an intelligent, lively, and innovative work on the social aspects of war. Lastly, John Tone's *The Fatal Knot: The Guerrilla War in Navarre and the Defeat of Napoleon in Spain* (1994), which investigates the resistance of the Spanish guerrillas in Navarre to Napoleon's attempt to integrate Spain into the Empire, is the latest example of the new military history. Tone tells his account from the perspective of the guerrillas of Navarre, who were the most effective guerrilla army in the Iberian peninsula.

Nevertheless, the attraction to traditional military history, to the study of battles, has in no way vanished. Reassessments of Waterloo, by Alan Schom (1992) and by David Hamilton-Williams (1993), of Trafalgar, by Schom (1990), and, most recently, Robert M. Epstein's *Napoleon's Last Victory and the Emergence of Modern War* (1994) testify to this rekindling of interest in conventional military history. Epstein, in his study of Napoleon's last victorious campaign, is interested in restoring military history to its roots: the management of warfare. The social and economic consequences of warfare are not under consideration here. He attempts to place the Franco-Austrian War in the context of the emergence of modern warfare.

Many of the most outstanding recent studies of the impact of Napoleon outside France have been written in neither English nor French. They reveal the progress that has been made in the field of Napoleonic scholarship, particularly true of the works studying the impact of Napoleon's policies on the conquered territories of the Empire. On Italy, the most important of these include R. Davico's *"Peuple" et notables (1750-1816): Essais sur l'Ancien Régime et la Révolution en Piédmont* (1981) and Pasquale Villani's *Italia napoleonica* (1978), which summarizes his earlier, more specialized monographs on Naples. Davico stresses economic and social aspects and looks at subjects such as demography, price movements, agricultural production, industry, metallurgy, and industry. With the exception of two articles in French—"Les Majorats français dans le duché de Varsovie (1807-1813)" (*Annales historiques de la Revolution française*, 1964) and "Le Duché de Varsovie" (*Occupants-Occupés*, 1969)—M. Senkowski-Gluck's studies on Poland are written in Polish. What all of these works have in common is their emphasis on the impact of Napoleon's policies on the local population in general and the elites in particular. The best German works of this genre are Elisabeth Fehrenbach's *Traditionale Gesellschaft und revolutionäres Recht. Die Einführung des Code Napoléon in den Rheinbundstaaten* (1974) and H. Berding's *Napoleonische Herrschafts- und Gesellschaftspolitik im königreich Westfalen 1807-1813* (1973). Fehrenbach examines both the circumstances leading to the introduction of the Napoleonic Code in the Confederation of the Rhine and its reception there. Berding's brief but informative study examines the social consequences of Napoleon's practice of rewarding his subordinates with Crown domains in the German satellite state of Westphalia. Finally, the recent work of Thomas Nipperdey, *Deutsche Geschichte 1800-1866: Bürgerwelt und Starken Staat* (1983), studies Germany from 1800 to 1866 and stresses the modernizing impact of Napoleon on this region.

An informative survey of German-language studies of German lands under France is contained in the first section of John Breuilly's article, "State-Building, Modernization and Liberalism from the Late Eighteenth Century to Unification: German Peculiarities" (*European Historical Quarterly*, April 1992). Of special significance is H. P. Ullmann's study about financial reforms in Bavaria and Baden, *Staatsschulden und Reformpolitik: Die Entstehung moderner öffentlicher Schulden in Bayern und Baden 1780-1820* (2 vols., 1986), which Breuilly states will be the standard text for some time.

The few English-language works of this type are by the American Jeffrey Diefendorf, who studied the bankers, merchants, and manufacturers in Cologne, Aachen, and Crefeld, and their association with Prussian and French regimes, and by T. C. W. Blanning, whose *The French Revolution in Germany: Occupation and Resistance in the Rhineland, 1792-1802* (1983) provides an excellent examination of the French in the Rhineland, although it ends only two years into the Consulate. Geoffrey Ellis' excellent work on Alsace, *Napoleon's Continental Blockade: The Case of Alsace* (1981), and the relevant chapters in Stuart Woolf's general work, *A History of Italy, 1700-1860* (1979) are two outstanding English works on the Empire. Ellis' *The Napoleonic Empire* (1991) has the merit for the English reader of providing an excellent synthesis of this latest German, Polish, and Italian socioeconomic research of the official Empire and the annexed lands. In addition, Stuart Woolf's general text, *Napoleon's Integration of Europe* (1991), is based on several non-English-language sources. It examines the Napoleonic impact on Europe from the perspecitve of the bureaucrats and soldiers. Without these innovative works, this new information would be unavailable to the average anglophone student of Napoleon.

Gaps in Napoleonic Scholarship

A field of study in which good histories are lacking is international relations. The standard French text is André Fugier's *La Révolution française et l'Empire napoléonien* (1954), but it is a survey and offers nothing new. In English, there are several specialized studies of Napoleon's opponents, such as Alan Palmer's work on Tsar Alexander. Worthy of mention is Hugh Ragsdale's *Détente in the Napoleonic Era* (1980). Ragsdale argues that Napoleon's foreign policy was governed by his relations with Russia. The title and subtitle are misleading, as the book does not deal with "détente" and covers only three years rather than the whole period.

Despite the progress made in the social and economic history of the Empire, no detailed history of education covering the Napoleonic era on its own has been written. What is available to the reader consists of articles or of chapters in surveys covering hundreds of years. A work treating in-depth interaction between schools, state, and society has yet to be written. With the exception of Rebecca Rogers' *Les Desmoiselles de la Légion d'Honneur: Les Maisons d'éducation de la Légion d'Honneur au XIXe siècle* (1992), which studies the schools founded by Napoleon in 1807 for the daughters of members the Legion of Honor, nothing has been written about the education of women. Indeed, studies of women in general during the years from 1800 to 1815 are scarce.

It is apparent that—although an extraordinary amount of work has been done on Napoleon and much progress has been made in recent years away from simply focusing studies on the life and personality of Napoleon—several gaps in our knowledge, particularly in English language, remain. An attempt to fill this gap and to present the period in a new light is the most recent general history of Napoleon, Martyn Lyons' *Napoleon Bonaparte and the Legacy of the French Revolution* (1994). In his introduction, Lyons points out that too much Napoleonic historiography has centered on Napoleon's life and death, and as a result, researchers remain ignorant about many aspects of the Napoleonic era. Lyons' purpose is not to repeat the details of the Emperor's life or to march through the well-trodden ground of military history but to "examine the importance of the Napoleonic period from the social, economic, political and cultural history of France." In a word, his objective is to get away from the *petite histoire*, or personalized history, which has so dominated the writing of Napoleonic history. What he has produced is an excellent study that introduces Bonapartism as an influential social system.

Lyons posits that the reason Napoleonic studies—particularly those written by English scholars—have been overwhelmingly personality-oriented is that, under the influence of the renowned French revolutionary historian Richard Cobb, scholars have opted for the chaos of the French Revolution and have treated the bureaucratic order of the Napoleonic period with contempt. In addition, as a period the Napoleonic years, during which popular protest of any kind was stifled, does not offer much scope for social historians. Although Lyons' book is not based on new research but relies heavily on the work of French historians Louis Bergeron and Jean Tulard—who have done so much to open up new inroads in Napoleonic scholarship—it is a watershed in English-language studies for its lack of emphasis on biography and the military. Lyons has made a noble attempt to place Napoleon within his historical context and proves that, as great and larger-than-life as he was, it is impossible to understand Napoleon outside the forces of his time, which included the French Revolution.

Each generation has produced its version of Napoleon and Napoleonic history. The current one, with its emphasis away from personality and the new propensities in military history, is doing much to fill the gaps which remain in our comprehension of these significant years in world history.

Notes

1. For an informative survey of nineteenth century historiography of Napoleonic studies, see George Matthew Dutcher, "Le Développement et les tendances actuelles des études napoléoniennes," *Revue des études napoléoniennes* 11 (janvier-juin 1919): 87-128.

2. For an expansion of this topic, see John Clubbe, "Byron and Napoleon 1814-1816," *Littera Pragensia* 3, no. 5 (1993): 42-57.

3. The most recent thorough treatment of Napoleon's impact on the English Romantics is Simon John Julian Bainbridge, "The 'Master Spirit' of the Age: Napoleon Bonaparte and English Romanticism," Ph.D. dissertation, University of York, England, 1992. This thesis has now been published as a book, *Napoleon and English Romanticism* (Cambridge: Cambridge University Press, 1995).

4. See André Wurmser, "Napoléon et Balzac," *Europe* 480-481 (1969): 138-153.

5. Andrew Martin, "Three Representations of Napoleon," *French Studies* 43 (January 1989): 31-46.

6. See Dennis Porter, "Stendhal and the Lesson of Napoleon," *PMLA* 85 (1970): 456-462.

7. See *Napoléon et la littérature: Europe* 480-481 (avril-mai 1969).

8. "Thiers' Revolution of the Hundred Days," *The Edinburgh Review* 114 (October 1861): 487.

9. See, for example, the contemporary work by Victor Chauffour-Kestner, *M. Thiers, Historien: Notes sur l'histoire du Consulat et de l'Empire* (Paris: Librairie International, 1863).

10. For an evaluation of Lanfrey's importance, see G. P. Gooch, *History and Historians of the Nineteenth Century* (New York: Peter Smith, 1949), pp. 255-258, and Pieter Geyl, *Napoleon: For and Against* (London: Jonathan Cape, 1949).

11. For a contemporary analysis of Taine's and Prince Napoleon's works, see the essay by Gustave Bord, "Napoléon et ses derniers historiens," *La Revue de la Révolution* 10 (1887): 385-417.

12. Pieter Geyl, *Napoleon: For and Against*, p. 177; Gooch, *History and Historians*, p. 260.

13. Frédéric Masson, *Napoléon et sa famille* (Paris: Ollderdorf, 1897-1919), introduction to vol. 5.

14. See Emile Bourgeois, *Manuel historique de politique étrangère*, vol. 2: *Les Révolutions 1789-1830* (Paris, 1898).

15. See the article on his historical methodology, Gabriel Monod, "Albert Vandal," *Revue historique* 105 (1910): 348-352.

16. *Ibid.*, p. 352.

17. Arthur Lévy, *Napoléon intime* (Paris: Nelson Editeurs, 1892), p. 546.

18. Maurras was not an historian, but he did use historical examples to substantiate his political beliefs. For the fullest statement of his these ideas, see his *Enquête sur la Monarchie* (Paris: Nouvelle Librairie Nationale, 1909).

19. William Keylor, *Jacques Bainville and the Renaissance of Royalist History in Twentieth Century France* (Baton Rouge: Louisiana State University Press, 1979), pp. xiii-xiv.

20. See Philippe Ariès, *Le Temps d'histoire* (Monaco: Editions du Rocher, 1954).

21. *Le Dix-huit Brumaire* (Paris: Hachette, 1925), pp. 7, 69.

22. Jacques Bainville, *Napoléon* (Paris: Arthème Fayard, 1931), p. 7.

23. Keylor, *Jacques Bainville*, pp. 240-241.

24. See Geyl, *Napoleon: For and Against*, p. 376.

25. Cited in Jean Montador, *Jacques Bainville: Historien de l'avenir* (Paris: Editions France-Empire, 1984), pp. 103-104.

26. Bainville, *Napoléon*, p. 581.

27. See Jean Tulard, "L'Historiographie napoléonienne française au XXe siècle," *Rivista italiana di studi napoleonici*, no. 27, anno ix (ottobre 1970): 168.

28. E. Driault, "Les Etudes napoléoniennes depuis Napoléon," *Revue des études napoléoniennes* 1 (janvier-juin 1912): 5.

29. Driault, "Les Etudes napoléoniennes en France et hors de France," *Revue des études napoléoniennes* 21 (juillet-décembre 1923): 10.

30. Jean Tulard, "L'Institut Napoléon historique et table," *Revue de l'Institut Napoléon* 96 (juillet 1965): 129.

31. Georges Lefebvre, *Napoleon*, vol. 2, p. 368.

32. *Ibid.*, p. 369.

33. Preface to *Cambridge Modern History*, vol. 9, *Napoleon*, edited by A. W. Ward, G. W. Prothero, and Stanley Leathes (London: Macmillan, 1906), p. vi.

34. J. M. Thompson, *Napoleon Bonaparte* (Oxford: Basil Blackwell, 1951), pp. 9, 30, 148.

Chapter 2

PRIMARY AND GENERAL SOURCE MATERIALS

Primary Sources

Arnold, Eric A., Jr. *A Documentary Survey of Napoleonic France.* Foreword by Harold T. Parker. Lanham, Md.: University Press of America, 1994.
The focus of this anthology of seventy complete sources is Napoleon as the first successful modern dictator. The chosen texts are all from the public domain and the selection includes treaties, laws, decrees, policy statements, constitutions, and legislation on the limitation of public opinion. Arnold's expertise in police affairs is clear in his selection of documents. They are arranged chronologically rather than thematically. A brief commentary precedes each document. A welcome addition to the printed primary literature in the English language, which remains surprisingly scarce. Index and bibliographical references.

_____. *A Documentary Survey of Napoleonic France. A Supplement.* Lanham, Md.: University Press of America, 1995.
This volume is composed of an additional twenty-five laws, letters, decrees, treaties, and policy statements to Arnolds original volume of seventy documents. These documents are intended to be illustrative of Napoleons administration. The new collection begins with "Napoleons Recollection of the Storming of the Tuileries Palace; August 10, 1792," and closes with "Napoleons Response to François-Just Rayounard and Other Deputies of the Legislative Body; January 1, 1814." Arnold notes in his introduction to this supplement that it is intended to fill gaps in his aim of providing a collection of the most important government-related documents.

Of significance are the documents concerning Napoleons creation of the Council of State on 26 December 1799, and the Sénatus-Consultus concerning judicial tenure on 12 October 1807.

Anderson, Frank Maloy, ed. *The Constitutions and Other Select Documents Illustrative of the History of France 1789-1904.* New York: Russell and Russell, 1967.
An English translation of the constitutions, laws, decrees, and treaties of the Consulate and Empire. Strongest on foreign policy. Documents concerning domestic changes are organized thematically. Under religion, he includes a copy of the Concordat and the Organic Articles for both Catholics and Protestants. Documents on education include the Law of Public Instruction and the Decree for Organizing the Imperial University. Governmental documents consist of those on the Senate, the Tribunate, the law for organizing the administrative system, and the various constitutions. Each section is preceded by a short commentary and a bibliography. A valuable collection of documents which brings together material scattered in printed collections such as the *Histoire parlementaire*, the *Archives parlementaires*, the *Moniteur*, Napoleon's *Correspondance*, and other sources.

Aulard, François-Alphonse. *Paris sous le Consulat: Recueil de documents pour l'histoire de l'esprit public à Paris.* 4 vols. Paris: L. Cerf, 1903-1909.
An excellent collection of documents concerning life in Paris during the Consulate. The major documents are administrative and police reports from the Prefecture of Police, the Police Ministry, and the Central Bureau of the Canton of Paris. His stated purpose is to monitor the regular changes in the public's activities and in public opinion toward the regime. His daily reports focus on newspaper articles, the theater, activities of priests and workers, and food provisioning in the capital. A major source for the internal history of the Consulate in Paris.

_____. *Paris sous le Premier Empire: Recueil de documents pour l'histoire de l'esprit public à Paris.* 3 vols. Paris: L. Cerf, 1914-1923.
Similar in presentation and purpose to the collection concerning the Consulate (cited above). The documents are taken from the archives of the Ministry of Justice, Ministry of Police, and the Prefecture of Police. Aulard refers to the lack of press freedom,

but he has done his best to provide political news from the only official paper, the *Moniteur*, and has included extracts from other papers that provide information on cultural activities, commerce, and religion. The police reports are particularly useful for political data. Aulard has done for Paris what d'Hauterive has done for the provinces in his collection of police bulletins (cited below).

Beugnot, Jacques Claude, comte. *Mémoires du comte Beugnot, ancien ministre (1783-1815), publiés par Albert Beugnot.* 2 vols. Paris: Dentu, 1866, 3d ed., 1889.

———. *Mémoires du comte Beugnot, publiés avec une introduction et notes par R. Lacour-Gayet.* Paris: Hachette, 1959. Beugnot was one of Napoleon's great prefects. He organized the Kingdom of Westphalia and administered the Duchy of Berg. Written during the Restoration, his memoirs first appeared in contemporary journals: the *Revue française* from 1838 to 1839 and the *Revue contemporaine* in 1852. The history of the Empire begins with Beugnot's nomination as administrator of the Grand Duchy of Berg. The eight chapters on this topic are an essential source for the subject. Four chapters deal with the first Restoration.

Bonaparte, Joseph. *Lettres inédites ou ésparses de Joseph Bonaparte à Naples (1806-1808).* Edited by Jacques Rambaud. Paris: Plon, 1911.

These letters complement Rambaud's major work on Joseph Bonaparte, *Naples sous Joseph Bonaparte, 1806-1808* (see Chapter 3). This critical collection consists of an analysis of about five hundred letters and reproduces 214 in addition to some of Joseph Bonaparte's speeches. The majority of these letters were found in Naples and form an important source of information for his reign there. Some concern war events, details of the administration (particularly financial), and information concerning the execution of laws. The letters assist in elucidating Joseph's character.

Bonaparte, Lucien. *Lucien Bonaparte et ses mémoires, 1775-1840.* Edited by Th. Iung. 3 vols. Paris: Charpeniter, 1882-1883. Translated as *Memoirs of the Private and Political Life of Lucien Bonaparte, Prince of Canino*, 2 vols. London: H. Colburn, 1818, 2d ed. 1835.

Lucien Bonaparte was the most intransigent of Napoleon's brothers and the only one who did not receive a title from the Emperor. Iung's is the best edition of Lucien's memoirs, providing a commentary. The most valuable of the three volumes is the third, which deals with Lucien's term as minister of the interior. Covers the period from 1804 to 1840. The English edition is listed for those unable to read French.

Bourdon, Jean, ed. *Napoléon au Conseil d'Etat: Notes et procès-verabux inédit de Jean-Guillaume Locré, secrétaire général du Conseil d'Etat.* Paris: Berger-Levrault, 1963.
There are fifty-four documents in this collection, comprising the extant notes of the minutes of discussions in the Council of State. The discussions are all introduced, summarized, and well documented with notes. Most are from the years between 1809 and 1813. Carefully arranged by subject, the documents include the interpretation of laws, the police, prisons, politics, finance, justice, religion, economics, war, and foreign policy. A fundamental resource for Napoleonic administration.

Bourrienne, Louis-Antoine Fauvelet de. *Mémoires de M. de Bourrienne, ministre d'Etat; sur Napoléon le Directoire, le Consulat, l'Empire et la Restauration.* 10 vols. Paris: Ladvocat, 1829-1830. Translated as *Private Memoirs of Napoleon Bonaparte during the Period of the Directory, the Consulate, and the Empire*, 4 vols. London: H. Colburn and R. Bentley, 1830.
When they were published in 1829, the memoirs of Bourrienne, a childhood friend, loyal diplomat, and private secretary of Napoleon, created quite a commotion. Since that date, they have been used many times by historians of Napoleon. Because the memoirs are entirely worshipful of their subject, they must be used with caution. Based upon incomplete notes and written (with the exception of the first two volumes) by Maxime de Villemarst, an unsuccessful diplomat who became a journalist when Bourrienne was unwell, they are full of inaccuracies. Bourrienne's editors used their own notes, supplied by the publisher. Most valuable for Napoleon's youth.

Cambacérès. *Cambacérès and the Bonapartes: Unpublished Papers of Jean-Jacques-Régis Cambacérès, Second Consul and Later Arch-Chancellor Relating to the Emperor Napoleon and His Circle, a Calendar by Richard Boulind.* New York: H. P. Kraus, 1976.
A volume composed of 168 letters belonging to Hans P. Kraus of Ridgefield, Connecticut. Section I consists of a collection of Cambacérès' letters to Napoleon between 1805 and 1814, while

Section II is composed of papers relating to his role as Napoleon's lawyer. The letters clearly show how the administration was virtually concentrated in Bonaparte's hands, while the papers document the personal history of the Empire. This collection complements Tulard's volumes, which, Boulind noted, opened up a new era in Napoleonic historiography.

_____. *Lettres inédites a Napoléon, 1802-1814*. Notes by Jean Tulard. 2 vols. Paris: Klincksieck, 1973.
A collection of the drafts of Cambacérès' letters previously held in the private collection of the Baron Guido Zerilli-Marimò, an Italian industrialist and writer, who donated them to the Archives Nationales. In this collection are the letters written by Napoleon to his treasury minister, Mollien. They were subsequently published by Jean Tulard, who provides a useful commentary, which includes the identification of less well-known figures. All letters were addressed to Napoleon when he was away from Paris. They are useful for elucidating the workings of the administration, the evolution of public opinion, and Cambacérès' competence in judicial affairs.

Caulaincourt, Armand-Louis-Augustin, marquis de. *Memoirs of General de Caulaincourt, Duke of Vicenza*. Edited by Jean Hanoteau. Translated by Hamish Miles, 2 vols. London: Cassell, 1935-1938.
An excellent edition of memoirs which includes an introduction of 234 pages. Caulaincourt, who served Napoleon as duke of Vicenza, ambassador to Tsar Alexander I, and his final foreign minister, organized the daily notes that he took during the Empire from 1822 to 1825. When reading these memoirs, one should keep in mind that they were written in self-defense at a time when the author was the object of attacks by the Emperor. They concern the last six years of the Empire and are useful for the Russian campaign, the tsar's character, the Chatillon Congress, important developments between Napoleon and the allies, Napoleon's attitude, his abdication, and his attempted suicide.

Chaptal, Jean-Antoine. *Mes souvenirs sur Napoléon, par le comte Chaptal, publiés par son arrière petit-fils*. Paris: Plon, 1893.
Chaptal's personal memoirs, written between 1756 and 1804, form the first part of the book, while the second half consists of Chaptal's memoirs of Napoleon. These memoirs, full of anecdotes, have often been used by historians. They are generally hostile to

the Emperor, and are written from the perspective that while Chaptal was minister, Napoleon was a liberal. As soon as Napoleon became Emperor, the year Chaptal lost his post, he alleges Napoleon turned into a despot. An important chapter considers Napoleon's economic views. A record of personal judgments about Napoleon by the minister of the interior, an important contribution to the literature.

Chateaubriand, René. *De Buonaparte, des Bourbons et de la nécessité de se rallier à nos principes légitimes, pour le bonheur de la France et celui de l'Europe.* Paris: Le Normand, 1814. 2d ed. Paris: Mame, 1814.
Considered one of the most important of the "black" legend works. Napoleon is considered a destroyer of the younger generation, an adversary of the freedom of thought, and an enemy of writers. Should be read with Chateaubriand's other works.

_____. *Mémoires d'outre tombe.* 12 vols. Paris: Penaud, 1849-1850. Translated by Robert Baldick as *The Memoirs of Chateaubriand*, 6 vols. London: Hamish Hamilton, 1961.
Chateaubriand decided to write his memoirs as early as 1803, and by 1829 he had completed the research for the chapters about Napoleon. The work first appeared in the journal *La Presse*. These memoirs are autobiographical, political, rhetorical, and social in that they deal with Chateaubriand's career, relationships, and his times—with much attention to the Consulate and the Empire. The author interpreted these years in terms of a huge duel between the Emperor and himself. The memoirs are most useful for their literary rather than historical merit and their contribution to the formation of the black Napoleonic legend. Index.

Choderlos de Laclos, Etienne. *Le Fils de Laclos: Carnets de marche du commandant Choderlos de Laclos (an XIV-1814), publiés avec une préface et des notes par Louis de Chauvigny.* Lausanne: Payot, 1912.
Often forgotten, these four notebooks, written by a Napoleonic commander, provide details on various campaigns. The first summarizes the battle of Austerlitz; the second covers the Prussian campaign to the Battle of Eylau; the third deals with Friedland and Tilsit. Finally, the fourth notebook provides details on the French and German campaigns to 1814.

Constant de Rebecque, Benjamin. *Journaux intimes: Edition intégrale des manuscrits autographes, publiée pour la première fois avec un index et des notes par A. Roulin et C. Roth.* Paris: Gallimard, 1952.

――――――. *Mémoires sur les Cent Jours. Préface, notes et commentaire d'O. Pozzo di Borgo.* Paris: Pauvert, 1961.

The intimate journals comprise the period from 1803 to 1816. Their interest is considerable for the history of ideas under the Empire and for the opposition to the regime. The best edition of the memoirs is that of Pozzo di Borgo, who provides helpful notes and comments. He states that Constant's memoirs were a justification of his attitude in 1815.

Gaudin, M. M. C. *Mémoires, souvenirs, opinions et écrits du duc de Gaete, ancien ministre des finances.* 2 vols. Paris: Baudouin, 1826. Reprint. Paris: A. Colin, 1926.

Gaudin was Napoleon's minister of finance from 1799 to 1814 and during the Hundred Days in 1815. There are two parts to Gaudin's memoirs: notes on his life and an historical essay on French finances from 1800 to 1814. Mainly technical in nature, these memoirs were written to justify Gaudin's ministry and financial reforms and were the object of criticism during the Restoration. An important source of information for the financial history of the Empire.

Gourgaud, Gaspard, baron. *Campagne de dix-huit cent quinze: Ou, Relation des opérations militaires qui ont eu lieu en France et en Belgique pendant les Cent Jours écrite à Saint-Hélène par le général Gourgaud.* Paris: P. Mongie Aîné, 1818. Translated as *The Campaign of 1815; or, A Narrative of the Military Operations Which Took Place in France and Belgium.* London: J. Ridgway, 1818.

――――――. *Mémoires pour servir à l'histoire de France en 1815 avec le plan de la bataille de Mont-Saint-Jean.* Translated by B. E. O'Meara. Paris: Barrois l'Aîné, 1820.

These two volumes, consisting of two successive dictations by Napoleon at Saint Helena, provide details on Napoleon's interpretation of the political and military history of his reign. The particulars of the Italian campaigns are especially vivid. This statement of Napoleonic ideas, if at times deceptive, reveals the fruitfulness of Napoleon's imagination and most accurately reflects the Emperor's thinking.

Hauterive, E. d', ed. *La Police secrète du Premier Empire: Bulletins quotidiens adressés par Fouché à l'Empereur, 1804-1810*. 5 vols. Paris: Perrin, 1908-1964.
An important annotated collection for problems of law and order, notably military conscription. Police reports were presented every evening to the Emperor by the minister of Police, Fouché, and later Savary. Today they are located in various archives in Paris: the Archives de la Police, the Archives Nationales, and the Secrétaire d'Etat Impériale. These bulletins are an enormous source of information for the internal workings of the Empire, and the editor has made them more accessible to historians by publishing five volumes of them. Each bulletin is in the form of a pamphlet and consists of ministerial correspondence, extracts or summaries of letters, reports, secret notes addressed to the minister concerning foreigners, military judgments, conscription, emigrants, priests and their "abuses," and news from foreign and enemy countries. An essential source for the internal history of the First Empire.

Herold, J. C. *The Mind of Napoleon: A Selection from His Written and Spoken Words*. New York: Columbia University Press, 1955.
An intelligent anthology of documents containing the thoughts of Napoleon grouped by subject in chronological order. The documents include his correspondence, orders, addresses and proclamations, and the memoirs he dictated. Herold is committed to the essence of the Napoleonic legend in that he considers the Emperor to be a hero. This work is mainly directed to the nonspecialist reader, but much remains for the specialist. Generally considered a thoughtful, if brief, introduction, with well-done translations. Bibliography.

Las Cases, Emmanuel, comte de. *Memorial de Saint-Hélène: Journal of the Private Life and Conversations of the Emperor Napoleon at Saint Helena*, 4 vols. London: H. Colburn, 1823. Reprinted as *Le Mémorial de Saint-Hélène: Première édition intégrale et critique, établie et annotie par Marcel Dunan*, 2 vols. Paris: Flammarion, 1951.
The crucial work in the formation and dissemination of the Napoleonic legend throughout the nineteenth century. Las Cases accompanied Napoleon to Saint Helena, where he became the latter's secretary until he was expelled by the English governor in 1816. Although at times rambling and incoherent, the *Memorial* contains information on Napoleon's political views, interesting

recollections, and vivid portraits. The best French edition is that of Marcel Dunan, whose accompanying notes are excellent.

Marbot, Baron de. *The Memoirs of Baron de Marbot*. Translated by A. J. Butler, 2 vols. New York: Longmans, Green, 1892.

These memoirs of a Napoleonic general portray Napoleon's soldiers in such a favorable light that it is difficult to believe them. They were among the most popular of the imperial period. However exaggerated the battles depicted may be, the narrative does give the reader a sense of military life under Napoleon. The French Mercure edition is the most complete. It shows that Marbot's testimony is less whimsical than previously believed. Index and bibliographical references.

Marchand Louis. *Mémoires de Marchand, premier valet de chambre et exécuteur testementaire de l'Empereur, publiés d'après le manuscrit original par Jean Bourguignon*. 2 vols. Paris: Plon, 1952-1955.

The first volume consists of memoirs by Napoleon's valet, Marchand. They begin in 1811, Marchand's first year of service. The first part was published immediately after the embarkment following the abdication of 1814. Part II recounts the stay in Elba, and Part III deals with the Hundred Days. Marchand took daily notes, which were intended for his daughter, and experts believe that these memoirs are accurate. The notes by Bourguignon and Henri Lachouque enrich the collection. Illustrations.

Metternich, Clement-Wenceslas-Lothaire, prince. *Memoirs of Prince Metternich, 1775-1815*. 5 vols. New York: Charles Scribner's Sons, 1880.

Appearing simultaneously in German, French, and English, the first part which comprises the first two volumes, consists of documents concerning Metternich's mission to Berlin, the Austrian embassy in Paris, the mission of 1810, and the events between 1814 and 1815. This is a fundamental source for the foreign policy of the Empire. Unfavorable to the Emperor, it was the source of much criticism by Napoleon III (see pages 59-104 of Prince Napoleon's *Napoléon et ses détracteurs*).

Miot de Mélito, André-François, comte. *Mémoires du comte Miot de Mélito, ancien ambassadeur, conseiller d'Etat et membre de l'Institut (1788-1815)*. 3 vols. Paris: Michel Lévy, 1873-1874.

Miot served as Joseph's minister of the Interior in Spain. These are the papers of Miot which were published by his son-in-law, General Fleischmann. Hostile to Napoleon, they were written from daily notes and consider political subjects during the Consulate, and life at Naples, Corsica, and Spain. A fundamental source for the study of life during the Napoleonic era.

Mollien, F. N. *Mémoires d'un ancien ministre du Trésor public de 1800 à 1814.* 4 vols. Paris: H. Fournier, 1837.

Mollien was the treasury minister from 1806 to 1814 and during the Hundred Days. In these memoirs, written in 1817 as a justification of his ministry, he provides a picture of the financial situation of France at Napoleon's ascension to power. All questions of a financial nature are discussed, including an examination of the financial principles followed by Mollien, a study of his budgets, the effects of the Continental System, the financing of the wars, and the public's attitude toward taxes. A very detailed work, including interviews and correspondence with the Emperor, this is an indispensable source of information for the internal history of the Empire.

Napoleon I. *Correspondance de Napoléon Ier publiée par ordre de l'empereur Napoléon III.* 32 vols. Paris: Imprimerie Impériale, 1855-1870.

The official, authoritative edition of Napoleon's letters, published by the director of the administration of Napoleon III. Generally considered to be, if not the most important, certainly the most definitive collection of Napoleon's correspondence. Contained here are the proclamations to the French people and the army, the bulletins of the Grand Army, and an immense collection of Napoleon's political and military orders. Napoleon III edited and eliminated some of the letters that were not complimentary to the family. The years 1800-1815 begin with Volume 6.

_____. *The First Napoleon: Some Unpublished Documents from the Bowood Papers.* Edited by Henry Lansdowne earl of Kerry. London: Constable, 1925.

A collection of published manuscripts from the Bowood archives, the archives of the editor's family. The count of Flahault, an aide-de-camp of Napoleon in his later campaigns, was also a relation of the earl of Kerry through marriage. The papers concern mostly the later years of the Emperor's life, including contemporary notes of conversations with Napoleon, the letters and journals of Admiral Viscount Keith (who was in charge when Napoleon arrived at Plymouth in the Bellerophon), and various papers of Hortense Beauharnais and her husband, Louis Bonaparte. A substantial addition to the mass of primary material, although none of these documents altered opinion about Napoleon. Genealogical table, map, and portraits.

_____. *Letters and Documents of Napoleon 1769-1802*. Vol. 1, *The Rise to Power*. Edited and translated by J. E. Howard. London: Cresset Press, 1961.

A valuable collection of 750 letters, more substantial than are Herold's (cited above) and Thompson's (cited below), including the supplementary collections to the official correspondence. The first volume goes to the Peace of Amiens in 1802. The emphasis is on Napoleon as a soldier. The editor attempts to reveal the "true" Napoleon through these letters. Each section contains a useful introduction. Illustrations and bibliographical references.

_____. *Lettres au comte Mollien ministre du trésor public du 16 mars 1803 au 9 juin 1815*. Edited by J. Arnna, C. Gay. Rochecordon: C. Gay, 1959.

These letters reveal a good deal about Napoleon's financial policy. They demonstrate the extent to which he wished to modernize the French economy, to increase France's trade, and to enhance domestic production through the development of credit in expanding the role of the newly created Bank of France. His views clashed with those of his contemporaries, especially those who were in charge of the bank, who were much more conservative. The publication of these letters enlightened researchers on a subject about which little was previously understood. Illustrations.

_____. *New Letters of Napoleon I, Omitted from the Edition Published under the Auspices of Napoleon III*. Translated by (Lady) Mary Lloyd. New York: Appleton, 1897.

Leonce de Brotonne collected and published 1,500 of Napoleon's letters which are not contained in the official correspondence. The originals may be found in various archives, such as the archives of the Ministère des Affaires Etrangères and the Archives Nationales. This collection includes letters written from 1793 to 1815. They deal with official matters—military, administrative, and foreign affairs—and are addressed to Fouché, Talleyrand,

Chaptal, Gaudin, and numerous generals, including Mathieu, Dumas. Most are very short and unedited, and many concern orders.

_____. *Napoléon à Sainte-Hélène*. Texts prefaced, chosen, and edited by Jean Tulard. Paris: Robert Laffont, 1981.
Napoleon dictated his memorial to his exiled companions, Las Cases, Gourgaud, Montholon, and Bertrand. For the first time, Tulard has brought together in a single volume extracts from the most important texts of four "evangelists" of Saint Helena, and the testimonial of Marchand. In addition, Tulard has written short biographies of Napoleon's entourage at Saint Helena. He stresses the historical reliability of these texts as opposed to the memoirs. A detailed index, a chronology, and a glossary of names facilitate the use of this volume.

_____. *Napoleon's Letters*. Selected, translated, and edited by J. M. Thompson. London: Dent, 1934, 1954.
A selection and translation of three hundred letters from the official correspondence from 1784 to 1815. This well-balanced work demonstrates the many facets of Napoleon's mind. The author's intention is to illustrate the versatility of Napoleon, and to this end he includes letters the Emperor wrote encouraging poetry and scientific theories. An introduction and useful notes accompany the letters.

Oeuvres littéraires et écrits militaires publiés par Jean Tulard. Preface by Marcel Dunan. 3 vols. Paris: Société Encyclopédie Française, 1967-1968.
In honor of the bicentenary of Napoleons birth, Jean Tulard has published two volumes of Napoleons literary works (1786-1789) and (1789-1796) and one volume of his military writings (1797-1815). The military writings, composing Volume 3, comprise articles from the *Moniteur* (the only official newspaper, to which the Emperor contributed many articles), reports to the Directory, proclamations to the Armies of the Republic, and bulletins to the Grand Army. Tulard notes the difficulty in ascertaining the authenticity of the more than 30,000 letters, notes, and bulletins because most were not signed. Napoleon dictated his orders to his secretaries. Méneval, one of his principal secretaries, wrote that it was impossible to write word for word what the Emperor dictated; thus the reader is left with a summary of the main points.

The three volumes are bound in leather; the pages are on a fine parchment and contain a beautiful gold edging. They are accompanied by a leather portfolio, which contains a printed silk scarf, copies of documents stamped "Premier Consul," including a map of the Russian campaign with notes by Napoleon. A bibliography composed of printed primary sources from 1821 to 1964 and an index are located at the back of Volume 3. Several color plates accompany this beautiful collection. This is the first critical edition of Napoleons literary and military writings.

_____. *Proclamations, ordres du Jour: Bulletins de la Grande Armée.* Introduction by Jean Tulard. Paris: Union Générale d'Histoire, 1964.

In his preface to Napoleon's proclamations, daily orders, and the bulletins of the Grand Army, Tulard shows what were the models and inspiration for the Napoleonic harangues. He characterizes the style of the proclamations and orders, determining their influence on the soldiers, and discusses the bulletins' impact on public opinion. The work is divided into three parts that consider (1) the armies of the republic, where one finds the most famous proclamations and orders from the Army of Italy and the Egyptian expedition; (2) the Grand Army, which contains a selection of texts published between 1805 and 1809; and (3) the defeats of the Grand Army based on a selection of bulletins and proclamations. All bulletins and proclamations are extracts from Napoleon's official *Correspondance.*

Noailles, Marquis de. *Le Comte Molé (1781-1855): Sa vie, ses mémoires.* 6 vols. Paris: Champion, 1922.

_____. *Souvenirs d'un témoin de la Révolution et l'Empire (1791-1803). Pages inédites retrouvées en 1939, publiées et présentées par la marquise de Noailles.* Genève: Le Milieu du Monde, 1943.

In his biography of Molé, who served in various official capacities during the Consulate and Empire (including Minister of Justice from 1813 to 1814), Noailles reproduced fragments of his journal. However, he noticed that the period was missing a section at the beginning of the Consulate. This was found in 1939. It forms the most interesting part of the journal and consists of a psychological portrait of Molé and information on England after the Peace of Amiens, on the salons, on the reorganization of France, and on his entry into the Council of State. The first volume of the 1922 edition provides valuable information on the debates of the Council of State and on the Great Sanhedrin. Also covered are the events from 1814 to 1815. If one keeps in mind that Molé was justifying his political acts in this journal, it furnishes a very useful source of information.

Pasquier, E. D. *Histoire de mon temps: Mémoires du chancelier Pasquier, publiés par M. le duc d'Audiffret-Pasquier.* 6 vols. Paris: E. Plon Nourrit, 1893-1894.

_____. *Souvenirs du chancelier Pasquier. Introduction et notes de R. Lacour-Gayet.* Paris: Hachette, 1964.

Pasquier, a former member of the Paris Parlement, became a chancellor and then a police prefect under Napoleon. He was well situated to observe the workings of the state, and it is this which makes his memoirs interesting. Taine considered Pasquier to be the best and most informed witness for the first part of the eighteenth century. These memoirs are most useful for their insight into the functioning of the Council of State, the Great Sanhedrin, the Malet plot, and the imperial police. A requisite source for the internal history of the Empire.

Pelet, Jean Jacques Germain. *The French Campaign in Portugal, 1810-1811: An Account of J. J. Pelet.* Edited, annotated, and translated by Donald D. Horward. Minneapolis: University of Minnesota Press, 1973.

Pelet was a general on Massena's staff who was sent to Napoleon by Massena to expose the events of the Portuguese campaign: Ney's disobedience of Napoleon's orders and Massena's retreat. Pelet's interview with Napoleon is of much interest. He provides an invaluably detailed firsthand description of the French side from April 1810 to March 1811. The text is generously detailed and includes an annotated biography of Pelet and statistical information about the army. Illustrations and bibliography.

Roederer, Pierre Louis. *Journal du comte P. L. Roederer, ministre et conseiller d'Etat. Notes intimes et politiques d'un familier des Tuileries. Introduction et notes par Maurice Vitrac.* Paris: Daragon, 1909.

_____. *Mémoires sur la Révolution, le Consulat et l'Empire, présentés par Octave Aubry.* Paris: Plon, 1942.

The daily notes intended for the memoirs of one of the most influential people of the new regime. They were written between

1799 and 1806, and are an accurate report of Bonaparte's remarks concerning the internal affairs of the Consulate: plots, institutions, and assemblies. Roederer's journal is full of valuable information on his work as Director of Public Instruction. The memoirs are also a good source of information on the Kingdom of Naples and Spain.

Staël-Holstein, A. L. G. Necker, baronne de. *Mémoires: Dix ans d'exil. Oeuvre posthume publiée par M. le duc de Broglie et le baron de Staël.* Paris: Treuttel, 1821.

——————. *Dix années d'exil. Edition nouvelle d'après les manuscrits avec une introduction, des notes et un appendice par Paul Gautier.* Paris: Plon, 1904.

The story of Madame de Staël's conflict with Napoleon. These are not her memoirs, but fragments from seven years of her life from the years 1800 to 1804, and 1810 to 1812. Her intention was to denounce Napoleonic tyranny, and to immortalize resistance to despotism. Napoleon is portrayed as a monster. The edition published by Gautier in 1904 is better than the original of 1821, as there are many inaccuracies which needed rectifying. Index and a useful appendix composed of excerpts from Madame de Staël's papers at Coppet château, Switzerland.

Thibaudeau, Antoine-Clair. *Mémoires sur le Consulat (1799-1804), par un ancien conseiller d'Etat.* Paris: Ponthieu, 1827. Translated as *Bonaparte and the Consulate* by G. K. Fortescue. London: Methuen, 1908.

In these excellent memoirs, Thibaudeau provides many details on his administration of the prefecture of the Gironde, his passage to the Council of State, his nomination to the prefecture of the Bouches-du-Rhône, and the difficulties he encountered there with the clergy, the royalist opposition, and in feeding the local population during the economic depression. The memoirs also increase our knowledge of the administration and legislators during the Hundred Days.

Reference Works

Bergeron, Louis, and Guy Chaussinard-Nogaret, eds. *Grands Notables du Premier Empire: Notice de biographie sociale.* 21+ vols. Paris: Editions du Centre National de la Recherche Scientifique, 1978.

As of 1994, there were twenty-one volumes in this collection of short biographies of the most significant notables of each department. Each department comprises a separate monograph and is written by an expert in the field who has conducted firsthand research in the local public and, if possible, family archives. The books vary in quality and length. Among the departments completed are Vaucluse and Ardèche, Loire, Mont Blanc, Leman, and JuraMaritimes. When the series is completed, it will constitute a tool indispensable to research on the notables of the First Empire.

Bertaud, Jean-Paul. *Histoire du Consulat et de l'Empire: Chronologie commentée 1799-1815*. Paris: Perrin, 1992.
The stated purpose of this brief reference work is to serve as a "practical instrument of indisputable knowledge." It consists of a chronological summary of important dates concerning Napoleon from 9 November 1799 to 1990. The closing entry states that 700,000 people visited Napoleon's tomb at the Invalides that year, and more than half this number were foreign. The volume also includes a biographical dictionary of the major figures of the epoch, a short annotated bibliography, and list of films about Napoleon.

Caldwell, Ronald J. *The Era of Napoleon: A Bibliography of the History of Western Civilization, 1799-1815*. 2 vols. New York: Garland, 1991.
Considered the most comprehensive bibliography on Napoleon. It includes not only monographs but also scholarly articles and theses from the United States, Canada, and Europe. More than half the 48,000 bibliographic entries cover France, and the majority are not in English. French biographical works and local histories make up more than 14,000 entries. The commanding influence of Napoleon is clear in the remaining entries, which encompass the rest of Europe (including many neglected countries, such as the countries of eastern Europe and Scandinavia) and the Americas. Index.

Chandler, David G. *Dictionary of the Napoleonic Wars*. New York: Macmillan, 1979.
Contains 1,200 short articles on persons, places, and topics of the Napoleonic period, not just the military. Several lengthy articles cover large topics including military commanders, infantry, artillery, battles, and armaments. Much attention is paid to the

British side of the wars. Probably the best English-language dictionary of the Napoleonic wars. Illustrations, maps, chronological table, appendix entitled "Napoleon's Military Movements, 1796-1815," and bibliography.

Connelly, Owen, ed. *Historical Dictionary of Napoleonic France 1799-1815.* Westport, Conn.: Greenwood Press, 1985.
A useful research tool with many good bibliographies at the end of each article. Articles are written by many American and French specialists of the period including Jane Burton, Harold Parker, Jacques Godechot and Jean Tulard. The amount of material on the military has been deliberately limited in order not to repeat Chandler. The best articles are those on the satellite kingdoms, the editor's specialty, and the elite of the bureaucracy. Entries vary in length and cover most aspects of Napoleon's life and Napoleonic society. Index and bibliography.

Emsley, Clive. *The Longman Companion to Napoleon.* New York: Longman, 1993.
The latest in a growing number of reference books on Napoleon, this handy guide provides easily accessible factual information on most aspects of the Napoleonic era. It is composed mainly of a series of chronologies, focusing on military and international affairs, and major political events. Included are twelve maps, genealogical tables of rulers, short biographical notices of major figures of the period, information about Napoleonic codes, a glossary of technical terms, decrees, and declarations. Social, economic, and cultural history are dealt with in only cursory fashion. Well organized, this is a useful and easy-to-use reference tool. Bibliographical references and index.

Henri-Robert, Jacques. *Dictionnaire des diplomates de Napoléon: Histoire et dictionnaire du corps diplomatique consulaire et impériale.* Paris: Henri Veyrier, 1990.
Based on national, departmental, and private archives, this handy and informative dictionary of Napoleon's ambassadors gathers information about their family backgrounds, their wealth, and their public and private lives during the Consulate and the Empire. Numerous bibliographical references direct the reader to further sources. The only work of its kind on this topic, Henri-Robert's dictionary is indispensable for understanding the diplomatic history of the period. Bibliographical references.

Horward, Donald D. *Napoleonic Military History: A Bibliography.* New York: Garland, 1986.

Cites more than 7,000 works in fourteen languages. The military theme is stressed, but works on social, political, intellectual, and economic subjects are also included, along with primary materials such as most of Napoleon's own printed works. There are no annotations, but each chapter contains a bibliographical essay providing brief comments on the sources cited. Encompasses material published through 1983.

Kircheisen, Friedrich M. *Bibliographie du temps de Napoléon, comprenant l'histoire des Etats-Unis.* Genève: 1908-1912. Reprint. New York: Burt Franklin, 1968. English ed.: *Bibliography of Napoleon: A Systematic Collection Critically Selected.* London: Sampson Low, Marston & Co., 1902.

The principal bibliography for works published in the nineteenth century, including primary sources, this is a model of organization and accuracy. A total of 5,147 books and major articles are listed, including works of general history, national biographies, memoirs, correspondence and biographies of the Bonapartes, and items on the states of Europe, the United States, and the Napoleonic wars subdivided by campaigns and battles. The English edition is shorter. Although dated, Kircheisen's bibliography remains useful for primary material, older works, and publications on Germany. No annotations.

Meyer, Jack Allen, ed. *An Annotated Bibliography of the Napoleonic Era: Recent Publications 1945-1985.* Westport, Conn.: Greenwood Press, 1987.

Covering the years from 1799 to 1815, this volume lists 1,745 books. It is intended to be used in conjunction with Owen Connelly's *Historical Dictionary.* Although the brief annotations are not critical, they do furnish information such as call numbers and chapter titles. The book is divided into sections under the headings of research, primary sources, general works, biographies of Napoleon, biographies of the Bonapartes, France (domestic and foreign affairs), and warfare on land and at sea. The best guide to books published in English and Western European languages during the past four decades. Index.

Palmer, Alan. *An Encyclopaedia of Napoleon's Europe.* London: Weidenfeld and Nicolson, 1984.

The author is an experienced compiler of historical dictionaries. This one covers the period from 1797 to 1815 and embraces all of Europe, including Great Britain. Entries include the arts, religion, science, economic and military developments, and biography. The average article is brief, about 150 to 300 words, and some are as short as one sentence. Bibliographical references.

Tulard, Jean. *Dictionnaire Napoléon.* Paris: Fayard, 1987.
Jean Tulard, president of the Institut Napoléon, has provided researchers with the dictionary of the Napoleonic era *par excellence*. Without a doubt it is the best research tool in the field, conposing 3,228 articles of differing lengths written by overwhelmingly French Napoleonic scholars. All subjects are covered. Many articles are quite long and have extensive bibliographies. These include essays on agriculture, peasants, the Continental System, the bourgeoisie, and the Council of State. It also covers significant events connected with Napoleon's career and all major institutions, such as the Legion of Honor, the Bank of France, and the Imperial University. Thematic index.

_____. *Napoléon et la noblesse d'Empire. Avec la liste complète des membres (1808-1815).* Paris: Tallandier, 1979, rev. ed. 1986.
A description and list by title, in alphabetical order of the imperial nobility. As Tulard shows, it was only the old nobility, those holding high public office and high-ranking military officers, who could hope to be ennobled under Napoleon. Includes a discussion of Napoleon's attitude toward the nobility. The most accessible reference work of its kind, complete with critical annotations. Bibliography.

_____. *Nouvelle Bibliographie critique des mémoires sur l'époque napoléonienne écrits ou traduits en français.* Genève: Librairie Droz, 1991.
An annotated bibliography of the memoirs of the Napoleonic era written or translated into French. Although the author modestly states in his preface that he does not claim to provide an exhaustive list, this is the most complete in print. An extremely useful reference tool, this work is composed of more than 1,500 annotated entries. The author lists every edition of the memoirs under consideration and indicates which is the preferable one from the scholarly perspective. A handy index located at the back of the

book organizes the memoirs thematically under the headings of Concordat, police, prefects, various battles, the Spanish war, churches, and so on.

Histories and Historiography

Aulard, François-Alphonse. *The French Revolution: A Political History 1789-1804*. 4 vols. New York: Scribner, 1910. Reprint. New York: Russell & Russell, 1965. Vol. 4, *The Bourgeois Republic and the Consulate, 1797-1804*.

Aulard was one of the most important historians of the French Revolution at the turn of the century. He held the first chair of French revolutionary history at the Sorbonne in Paris. His work is a classic history of the revolutionary and Napoleonic eras. Just over 200 pages of Volume 4 cover the period from Brumaire to Napoleon becoming Consul for life. This volume is very informative on circumstances that led to Napoleon's rise to power, the reasons for his popularity, the Constitution of Year VIII, internal pacification, and religious policy. Aulard maintains that upon becoming Consul for life, Napoleon completely separated himself from the liberals of 1789, who had foolishly allowed the coup to take place. From this point onward, Napoleon proceeded to make himself a dictator. In doing so, Napoleon effectively abolished the French Revolution.

Crawley, Charles W., ed. *War and Peace in an Age of Upheaval 1793-1830*. The New Cambridge Modern History, Vol. 9. Cambridge, England: Cambridge University Press, 1965.

A volume of essays written by experts in the field. On the Napoleonic period, the main chapter is Felix Markham's, "The Napoleonic Adventure." In addition, E. V. Gulick provides an excellent chapter on the Congress of Vienna, and Geoffrey Bruun's "Balance of Power, 1793-1814," is a survey of international relations. More than half the volume is devoted to chapters concerning regional or local history. Chapters on the army and the navy, economic change in England and Europe, education, music, painting, and literature are also offered. A worthwhile reference work with a fine introduction by Crawley. Index and an appendix containing the republican calendar.

Godechot, Jacques. *L'Europe et l'Amérique à l'époque napoléonienne (1800-1815)*. Novelle Clio: L'Histoire et Ses Problèmes, no. 37. Paris: Presses Universitaires de France, 1967.

A survey of French and American history, centering on economic, political, military, and institutional changes. The Americans are not examined in any great detail. Godechot is concerned mainly with the impact of the French Revolution and Napoleon and the First Empire's influence on the history of modern Europe. He concludes that both were profound, particularly in terms of politics, society, and administration. The brief volume provides the reader with worthwhile judgments about Napoleon and his policies. Bibliographical footnotes and bibliography.

──────────. *Napoléon, portrait*. Paris: Albin Michel, 1969.

Published in honor of the bicentenary of the Emperor's birth, this monograph is divided into two parts. In Part I, Godechot is not once again undertaking a history of the Napoleonic years, but rather supplies readers with a balance sheet and, at the same time, a portrait of the man. Part II is composed of personal reflections about Napoleon from several of his contemporaries, such as Metternich. The author also leads us to a conclusion to which historians almost unanimously have subscribed: The Napoleon portrayed in the Napoleonic myth, which Napoleon himself created and which is the best known, is not the authentic Napoleon. Godechot's Napoleon is an intelligent, hard worker, an ambitious head of the army, who carelessly sacrificed his men. Godechot does not see Napoleon as an innovative tactician. In the political sphere, the Emperor founded institutions devoted to equality before the law and the abolition of the feudal system, but he also restored certain aspects of the Old Regime. In sum, Napoleon was one of the worlds first modern dictators. Illustrations, appendix, footnotes, and bibliography.

Godechot, Jacques, Beatrice F. Hyslop, and David L. Dowd. *The Napoleonic Era in Europe*. New York: Holt, Rinehart and Winston, 1971.

Intended for publication in 1969, the bicentenary of Napoleon's birth, this splendid brief synthesis contains a helpful annotated bibliography. It is based on Godechot's work on institutions under the Empire, which has never been translated into English. At the time of its publication, it incorporated the latest research. The introductory chapter, written by Hyslop, concerns France and

Europe to 1799. The remainder of the book, which is organized thematically, focuses on the internal pacification of France, the religious settlement, and the military, economic, cultural, scientific, and social aspects of the period. A concluding chapter analyzes the importance of Napoleon and the Napoleonic myth. A clearly written book equally serviceable to the researcher and general reader. Illustrations, genealogical table, and maps.

Lanfrey, Pierre. *The History of Napoleon the First*. 4 vols. London: Macmillan, 1886.
Written fifteen years after Thiers' monumental history, and a reply to it, Lanfrey's work is based upon the published correspondence of Napoleon. Volumes 2-4 cover the years from 1800 to 1811. Since Lanfrey died in 1877, his work remains unfinished. It is a lengthy, scholarly, and bitterly negative polemic; his goal was to destroy the Napoleonic legend. A contemporary reviewer, writing in the *Westminster Review*, stated that Lanfrey was the first French scholar to portray Napoleon and his achievements objectively. Index at the end of Volume 4.

Latreille, André. *L'Ere napoléonienne*. Paris: A. Colin, 1974.
Considered at the time of its publication the best synthesis of the Napoleonic era. The importance of this work, according to Jacques Godechot, lies in its conclusions and analysis, as well as in its research. Written by a scholar who spent his life studying the Empire, it is primarily about Western Europe and Great Britain. The United States is dealt with rather briefly, receiving the same amount of space as the Caribbean. The emphasis is on Napoleon's power and its significance for the Western world. Tilsit is considered the height of Napoleon's reign, as it permitted Napoleon to dominate the Empire. Bibliography.

Lucas-Dubreton, Jean. *La France de Napoléon*. Paris: J. Tallandier, 1981.
A well-regarded general work which surveys the major changes in French life between 1800-1815. Lucas-Dubreton sees Napoleon as ending the chaos and rebuilding the edifice. Napoleon remodeled all sectors of French society, from its institutions to its economy. The book is valuable for institutions and cultural life. Although praising Napoleon's achievements and his legacy, the author does not conceal the weaknesses of his regime. The end of the Empire

and the legend receive special attention. Illustrations and bibliography.

Lyons, Martyn. *Napoleon Bonaparte and the Legacy of the French Revolution.* London: Macmillan, 1994.
An amalgamation of social history and biography, this excellent study introduces Bonapartism as an influential social system. Lyons rejects the great man of history theory. The subjects discussed include the regime's political identity, the long-term importance of the Napoleonic code, the creation of the Imperial University, and the feeble effort at opposition. He provides an interesting, if original, slant on Bonaparte and his relationship to the French Revolution. Plates, maps, tables, documents, index, and bibliographical footnotes. The twelve translated documents survey Napoleon's impact in France and in Europe.

Madelin, Louis. *Histoire du Consulat et de l'Empire.* 16 vols. Paris: Hachette, 1937-1954. Translated by E. F. Buckley as *The Consulate and the Empire.* 2 vols. New York: Putnam's Sons, 1934-1936.
Originally published in French in sixteen volumes, with Volumes 4-16 covering the years from 1800 to 1815. This major work of historical literature was the leading multivolume publication on this subject in the last half century. Napoleon is praised as the savior of the French Revolution. Any mistakes or failures were caused by forces other than the man himself. The English edition is an abridgment of the more detailed French original. Bibliography at the end of most chapters.

Mistler, Jean, ed. *Napoléon et l'Empire.* 2 vols. Paris: Hachette, 1969.
Remains one of the more significant of the two-hundred-odd books that appeared in 1969, the bicentenary of the Emperor's birth. This collective work contains contributions by the major French specialists in the field, and it covers the entire period to the Congress of Vienna. In the first volume, Godechot and Marcel Reinhard describe Napoleon's rise to power, which they argue was inseparable from the French Revolution. Jean Tulard, Charles Durand, and Mgr. Leflon are concerned with the internal pacification of the country during the early years of the Consulate. Examining French social classes, Bertrand Gille argues that Napoleon achieved a compromise between the Old Regime and the modern world which began with the Revolution. Financial

questions are competently analyzed by Jean Bouvier and Robert Lacour-Gayet. André Thot discusses the imperial economy in the light of a new "Colbertism." Among the best chapters are those on arts and letters, by Jean Mistler and René Huygle, and on the sciences, by André George. The second volume is less original and concerned with military affairs. This is a fundamental work which includes a chronology of the period and a good bibliography.

Mousnier, R., E. Labrousse, and M. Bouloiseau. *Le XVIIIe Siècle: Révolution industrielle, technique et politique (1715-1815)*. Paris: Presses Universitaires de France, 1953.
This volume—which appeared in a series by leading French scholars on the history of world civilization—concentrates on developments in revolutionary and Napoleonic France. It tends to stress the economic and social changes during the late eighteenth century. The military and ideological impacts of the Revolution and Napoleon are summarized with great care. Bouloiseau's account of Napoleonic Europe has been generally recognized as a tour de force in terms of analysis and balanced judgment. Illustrations, maps, and bibliography.

Soboul, Albert. *Le Premier Empire*. Paris: Presses Universitaires de France, 1973.
Soboul is one of the most respected historians of the French Revolution. As a Marxist, he interprets Napoleon as the promoter of the dominance of the bourgeoisie, an inevitable and necessary stage in the evolution of the capitalist state. A competent synthesis of the Empire. Begins with a survey of its economic and demographic foundations, continuing with an examination of the increase in warfare made possible by the imperial conquests. The administrative organization and social structure of the Empire are also discussed. Finally, the growth of opposition to Napoleon and his policies and the Napoleonic legend are sketched. Bibliography.

Sutherland, D. M. G. *France 1789-1815: Revolution and Counter-revolution*. London: Fontana, 1985.
Sutherland's chapters on the Napoleonic years are among the finest of the most recent syntheses available. Although the author assumes some general knowledge of the period, his book provides the reader with a well-written reexamination of some well-trodden ground. The economy, government and society of the Consulate and Empire are considered from the perspective of a historian of

the French counter-revolution and countryside. The Empire is understood as a dictatorship that became more arbitrary and harsh as time went on. Some attention is devoted to the constant wars of the era. An excellent bibliography directs the reader to more specific reading. Maps and index.

Taine, Hippolyte Adolphe. *Le Regime moderne*. Vol. 5 in *Les Origines de la France contemporaine*, 6 vols. Paris: Hachette, 1876-1893. Translated by John Durand as *The Modern Regime*. New York: Henry Holt, 1890.

Taine was a nineteenth century writer who had a theory to illustrate and a history to prove. His theory was that Napoleon as an Italian warrior from the fifteenth century who was born in the wrong century; owing to the impact of the French Revolution, the safeguards of society that normally hold such people in check had been swept away. The major significance of this work is that it produced strong protests from Napoleon's defenders at the time of its publication, and it sparked a new debate on the historical interpretation of Napoleon. It was published immediately after the Franco-Prussian War. The volumes attempt to analyze the causes of the failures of contemporary France. John Durand, an American, who translated Taine's six volumes, was a close friend and an excellent translator. The Holt edition was reprinted in 1931 by P. Smith.

Thiers, Louis Adolphe. *History of the Consulate and the Empire of France under Napoleon*. Translated by D. Forbes Campbell, 20 vols. London: Colburn, 1845-1862.

A huge work of modern historical literature, this detailed narrative was the central publication of nineteenth century Napoleonic historiography. On the whole, glorifies the Emperor. The perspective changes as the political situation in France alters. Originally a supporter of Napoleon, Thiers turned against him during the period of the Second Empire. The first popular history of Napoleonic era, this work is, above all, a study of Napoleon as a soldier. If Thiers did not create the Napoleonic tradition, he at least established it.

Thiry, Jean. *L'Avènement de Napoléon*. Paris: Berger-Levrault, 1959.

A classic political history of the Consulate and the Empire. The first volume encompasses topics such as the signature of the Concordat and the organization of the government. The second is dedicated to the disintegration of international relations after the revival of war and the royalist plots against Napoleon from 1803 to 1804. The viewpoint of the author is that Napoleon was a pacifist, and it was in spite of himself that war was renewed in 1804. The work is based on original material in both the Archives Nationales and the British Library. Maps and bibliography.

Vandal, Albert. *L'Avènement de Bonaparte*. 2 vols. Paris: Plon Nourrit, 1902-1907.

The first serious study of the Consulate since Thiers' monumental work. Vandal called his work a political history, the purpose of which was to demonstrate how Bonaparte seized power in revolutionary France. Described by reviewers as an elaborate piece of work, this history made good use of unpublished police reports in the French archives to shed light on the plot of 18 Brumaire. Vandal explains Napoleon's rise to power as gradual, achieved through military victories in Egypt and Marengo, the Brumaire coup, and the development of the institutions of the Consulate. In his interpretation of the Brumairian coup, Vandal demonstrates that the Directors were incompetent and ruthless rulers who were extremely unpopular. The accession of Napoleon was therefore inevitable. Napoleon's impact was one of reconstruction and reconciliation. Bibliographical references.

Wright, D. G. *Napoleon and Europe*. London: Longman, 1984, 5th impression 1990.

An excellent introductory survey of Napoleon's life and times, including a varied selection of relevant documents and an admirable, briefly annotated bibliography. The book is divided into five parts, beginning with a succinct account of Napoleon's youth, education, and career as a young officer. The most substantial section treats the Consulate and Empire. All aspects are given attention, from internal affairs to Napoleon's wars. Part III chronicles his "decline and fall," Part IV provides an excellent introduction to the legend, and finally the work closes with thirty relevant documents taken from a wide assortment of sources, including memoirs, newspapers, and letters. Index and chronological summary.

Chapter 3

BIOGRAPHIES OF NAPOLEON AND HIS BROTHERS

Atteridge, A. Hilliard. *Napoleon's Brothers*. London: Methuen, 1909.
Atteridge's intention is to sketch the Napoleonic era from the viewpoint of Napoleon's brothers. He is generally sympathetic to them, vindicating them against charges of disloyalty made by historians such as Masson. He blames their failures on Napoleon, who refused to take his brothers seriously and considered them to be rulers of provinces whom he could control at will. A good English work on the topic. Notes providing some sources.

Bainville, Jacques. *Napoleon*. Translated by Hamish Miles. London: Jonathan Cape, 1938.
Bainville was a well-known conservative writer. First published in French in 1936, his work remains the most widely read biography in France. Napoleon is considered from a legitimist royalist perspective. Although he based his biography entirely on secondary sources, Bainville has synthesized an amazing amount of material. Napoleon is depicted as an opportunist, and the author is generally sympathetic to those holding that France would be better off if Napoleon had never lived. Bibliography.

Barnett, Corelli. *Bonaparte*. London: Allen and Unwin, 1978.
As a distinguished military historian, Barnett focuses on Napoleon's military career. He interprets Napoleon's military victories in a very critical light. Although he recognizes Napoleon's military genius, he argues that Napoleon made many tactical errors that ultimately led to his defeat. Napoleon's victories are explained in terms of luck. Barnett puts forward the view that the Napoleonic legend is little more than skillful propaganda on the part of

Bonaparte. Strongly recommended for students of history. Illustrations, index, and bibliography.

Butterfield, Herbert. *Napoleon*. Great Lives Series. London: Duckworth, 1939. Reprint. New York: Collier, 1962.
Butterfield provides a useful summary of Napoleon's major achievements during the Consulate and Empire. He understands Napoleon as the heir to the Revolution in the sense that he continued the efficient, highly organized, and wide-ranging state that the revolutionaries had created. An admirable short biography combining the factual evidence with intelligent commentary. Chronological table and bibliographical note.

Chandler, David G. "Napoleon as Man and Leader." *Consortium on Revolutionary Europe, 1750-1850: Proceedings* 19, Part I (1989): 582-605.
An insightful analysis of the abilities, talents, and guiding principles of Napoleon's career. Chandler convincingly shows how Napoleon's career as commander and statesman was based on his abilities as a natural leader. He examines Napoleon's personality and intellectual abilities, which, he asserts, brought him the personal loyalty of his men. He concludes that Napoleon was the most powerful individual before the twentieth century. It was Napoleon's failure to institutionalize his position that led to his collapse.

Connelly, Owen. *The Gentle Bonaparte: A Biography of Joseph, Napoleon's Older Brother*. New York: Macmillan, 1968.
The only full-length biography in English. Connelly describes Joseph as a hardworking and sophisticated man, dedicated to his work, and chronicles his career from his reign as king of Naples (1806-1808) to his reign as king of Spain from (1808-1814). Much space is devoted to the Spanish years. Connelly clearly exhibits Joseph's influence on the Emperor. Well written and scholarly, this monograph is based on a Ph.D. dissertation, "Joseph Bonaparte, King of Spain, 1808-1813" (University of North Carolina, 1960). Maps, portraits, and bibliography.

Cronin, Vincent. *Napoleon*: London: Collins, 1971.
In his preface, Cronin defends writing yet another biography of Napoleon on the grounds that he has discovered new material: the notebooks of Alexander de Mazis, Napoleon's best childhood

friend; the letters of Desirée Carey, an early lover; the memoirs of Louis Marchand, Napoleon's valet; and General Bertrand's Saint Helena diary. Based upon these and other primary sources, Cronin has written an intimate portrayal of Napoleon's personal life. Topics covered include his love affairs, his diet, and his innermost thoughts. Written in a very chatty and informal style which is easy to read. Index, appendices, and bibliographical references. The appendices comprise "Memoir-Writers and Napoleon," is a useful statement on the reliability of the various memoirs written by contemporaries, and "Clisson et Eugénie," an excerpt in French from Napoleon's manuscript for a novel.

Fabre, Marc-André. *Jérôme Bonaparte, roi de Westphalie*. Paris: Hachette, 1952.
One of the few biographies of Jérôme Bonaparte, a competent narrative of his long life. He was the Emperor's favorite brother. Fabre argues that Napoleon's youngest brother was never very effective. After he had renounced his American wife, Napoleon showered him with favors and made him king of Westphalia. In spite of a dissolute private life and less than glorious conduct in the Russian campaign, Napoleon was always more indulgent to Jérôme than he was to his other brothers. Bibliography.

Fisher, H. A. L. *Napoleon*. Oxford, England: Oxford University Press, 1912.
A brief yet comprehensive biography written by a celebrated English historian. In this outline of Napoleon's career, Fisher provides a mostly positive account of the Emperor's life and achievements. The author praises Bonaparte's internal reforms, providing little on the military aspects. The slim volume includes an appendix of Napoleon's maxims, an index, a genealogical table, three maps, and a bibliography.

Fournier, August. *Napoleon the First: A Biography*. Translated by A. E. Adams, 2 vols. New York: Holt, 1911.
First published in 1895, appearing in an expanded form in 1904-1905, Fournier's is one of the best and most highly regarded of the early biographies. It is bright and readable, and contains a mass of material, including printed contemporary sources. A chronological narrative provides many details on military history. The only defect is that the author as an Austrian who attempted to defend the policy of Austria, and in doing so, tended to distort

the events. Index, chapter bibliographies, and maps. Appendices composed of letters, such as those of Napoleon to Talleyrand, 1799-1806, and Talleyrand to Champigny, 1807-1808, at the end of each volume.

Jones, R. Ben. *Napoleon: Man and Myth*. London: Hodder and Stoughton, 1977.
A short biography in which the author has attempted to demonstrate the peculiar conditions that allowed Napoleon's career to take place. The work opens with a survey of the historical context and continues with a summary of Napoleon's career as general, administrator, and diplomat. Jones concludes with reflection on the reasons for the Emperor's demise and a brief discussion of his impact in the 150 years succeeding his death. Jones has produced a very readable and concise account of Napoleon's life, achievements, and significance. The work includes an index, maps, a bibliography of recent works, and chronologies at the end of each chapter.

Kircheisen, Friedrich M. *Napoleon*. Translated by Henry St. Lawrence. New York: Harcourt, Brace and Company, 1932.
An abridgment of a monumental nine-volume work first published in German: *Napoleon I. Sein Leben und seine Zeit* (Munich: A. Langen/G. Muller, 1911-1934). Kircheisen worked from printed sources, but used many German and Austrian sources. His work is especially good for the campaigns in which these two nations were engaged against the French. Napoleon is not idolized, as he had been in many early French accounts; rather, a balanced view is presented. No notes or appendices. The translation is excellent and reads as though the work had originally been written in English. Although dated, it is still valuable for its details.

Lefebvre, Georges. *Napoleon*. Vol. 1, *From 18 Brumaire to Tilsit, 1799-1807*. Translated by Henry F. Stockhold. New York: Columbia University Press, 1969.
Lefebvre, Georges. *Napoleon*. Vol. 2, *From Tilsit to Waterloo, 1807-1815*. Translated by J. E. Anderson. New York: Columbia University Press, 1969.
Originally published in 1936 in the *Peuples et Civilisations* series, this study of Napoleon by French Marxist historian Lefebvre, has accurately been described by most reviewers as a "classic" and a "masterpiece." It is not intended as a biography per se, but as

a general survey of the Napoleonic period. Lefebvre is at his best discussing the material aspects of French life, such as the economy and the Continental System. Remains an important work. Index and footnotes.

Lévy, Arthur. *Napoléon intime.* Paris: Nelson, 1892. Translated by Stephen Louis Simeon as *The Private Life of Napoleon*, 2 vols. New York: Scribner, 1894.
In this highly positive view written to retaliate negative interpretations, the author purposely ignored all unfavorable evidence. The material he has used is judiciously organized. A personal life, this work was written with the intention of refuting Taine's history. Part of the "for" literature contributing to the Napoleonic legend.

Lockhart, John Gibson. *The History of Napoleon Buonaparte.* 2 vols. London: Murray, 1829.
An early nineteenth century British viewpoint of the Emperor. Originally published anonymously, Lockhart's is a modest corollary to the more flamboyant biography by Sir Walter Scott. Like Scott, Lockhart wrote from the Tory position, but he is markedly less violent and anti-Bonaparte. Although he drew largely from Scott for his information, he also relied heavily on the Saint Helena material, which accounts for the less severe attitude. Unfortunately, he was unable to use either the Napoleonic correspondence or the Wellington dispatches, as they had not yet been published. Maintains that Napoleon had a profound impact on destroying the Old Regime but that he was a despot. A work glorifying England. Contains numerous inaccuracies, many of which are pointed out by John Holland Rose in his 1916 edition.

Ludwig, Emile. *Napoleon.* Translated by Eden and Cedar Paul. New York: Liveright, 1926.
An eloquent, widely read dramatic work. The history of the man rather than the epoch, this biography is based on a wide assortment of documents and constitutes an early critical psychobiography. It examines the inner nature of Napoleon, his feelings and thoughts, through his words, written or spoken. Political acts and events are also used to illustrate Napoleon's character. The author is not entirely positive about Napoleon and is not afraid to discuss his faults. Index.

Manfred, Albert. *Napoléon Bonaparte*. Translated by Patricia Champe and Geneviève Dupont. Moscow: Editions du Progrès, 1980.
Considered one of the best Marxist biographies. Originally published in Russian in 1971, its originality lies in the discussion of Napoleon's intellectual development. Early writings are analyzed with great care. Argues that Napoleon did not become a dictator until after the Marengo victory. Concludes that Napoleon was a great statesman, strategist, and a person of singular destiny. Index and bibliographical references.

Markham, Felix Maurice. *The Bonapartes*. New York: Taplinger, 1975.
Sketches the history of the Bonaparte family from their eighteenth century Corsican roots to the death of Empress Eugénie in 1920. Should be considered primarily an introductory text to the brothers' lives and careers, as it contains much about the relationships between them. Not a scholarly work in the same sense as Markham's biographies of Napoleon, this book is intended for the layperson. Illustrations, genealogical table, index, and bibliography.

_____. *Napoleon*. London: Weidenfeld and Nicolson, 1963.
Markham has produced two worthwhile studies, both of which are based on primary sources, including Napoleon's *Mémoires* and *Correspondance*. His *Napoleon* is a scholarly study of its subject's political and military career. Markham provides the reader with a balanced and comprehensive examination of Napoleon's achievements, both domestic and foreign, and is especially good on Napoleon's later years. Interesting details on the state of Napoleon's health and personality add a personal touch. Markham tends not to regard Napoleon as a military dictator but as an "enlightened despot." Interesting and carefully chosen illustrations enhance the attraction of this very readable biography. Generally considered the best of the older texts.

_____. *Napoleon and the Awakening of Europe*. London: The English Universities Press, 1965.
This short work is more of a biography than its title suggests. It is the story of an adventurer, "a great man of history." The Emperor is portrayed as the last of the Enlightened despots and a typical child of the Romantic movement. Interesting details concerning Napoleon's life in exile on Saint Helena shed light on his character. A splendid piece of work. Index, footnotes, and bibliography.

Martineau, Gilbert. *Lucien Bonaparte, Prince de Canino.* Paris: Editions France Empire, 1989.

Sketches a lively portrait of Napoleon's brother, who became a Roman prince. Contends that Lucien Bonaparte was the only brother who dared to stand apart from the rest. Jacobin, minister, ambassador, and, lastly, Roman prince, he was an opportunist, possessing a strong business sense that made him the richest of the Bonapartes. Discussion of his contests with the rest of the Bonaparte clan gives readers insight into the family and the Emperor's government. Based on a wide variety of printed primary and secondary sources. Illustrations and bibliographical references.

Martinet, André. *Jérôme Napoléon, roi de Westphalie.* Paris: Société d'Éditions Littéraires et Artistiques, 1902.

One of the principal biographies, although it is now dated. Based almost entirely on Napoleon's correspondence, this narrative account is generally favorable to Napoleon. The introduction provides information on Jérôme's early years to 1807. The remainder of the book is concerned with his reign and its problems, which were mainly financial, resulting from Jérôme's lavish expenditures. Jérôme Bonaparte's personal influence over the governing of the kingdom is demonstrated to be great: it was he who was responsible for the reforms carried out there.

Masson, Frédéric. *Napoléon et sa famille.* 13 vols. Paris: Ollerdorf, 1897-1919. New ed., 3 vols. Paris: Albin Michel, 1927.

This enormous and erudite tour de force has yet to find an English translator. It provides a detailed depiction of Napoleon's private life. Historiographically it is in the "for" camp, as it glorifies the Emperor; any weaknesses and shortcomings are blamed on others. Generally considered the leading work on the person of Napoleon, Masson should be consulted by all serious scholars. Although there is no index, a very detailed table of contents may be found at the end of Volume 13.

Melchior-Bonnet, Bernardine. *Jérôme Bonaparte: Ou, L'Envers de l'épopée.* Paris: Perrin, 1979.

A competent biography of Jérôme, Napoleon's youngest brother, whom he made king of Westphalia. It is based on archival and printed primary sources. The author provides many details of his life and administration and presents a balanced interpretation of his character. Melchior-Bonnet is neither too complimentary nor too critical of her subject. She states that although he had the capacity to become a competent leader, he had neither the drive nor the taste for intellectual pursuits. In Westphalia, all he saw was a land to exploit. Illustrations and bibliography.

Murat, Inès. *Napoleon and the American Dream*. Translated by Frances Frenaye. Baton Rouge: Louisiana State University Press, 1981.
An examination of Napoleon's relations with the United States, including the sale of Louisiana and the experiences of several Frenchmen in America, primarily his brothers Joseph and Lucien. Murat relates many details concerning members of Napoleon's family, former army generals who, after 1815, moved to America. Joseph took up the comfortable life of a country gentleman in New Jersey, while Lucien married an American. Murat's work delves into the mutual fascination and misunderstanding which have characterized Franco-American relations for two centuries. She argues that "Napoleon's epic and the American myth represent two contradictory dreams by which men escape from history and are alternatively haunted." Index and bibliography.

Piétri, François. *Lucien Bonaparte*. Paris: Plon, 1939.
Before this scholarly biography appeared, the literature about Lucien Bonaparte had been entirely and unfairly negative. This biography of Lucien Bonaparte presents a sympathetic portrait of Napoleon's most intelligent and independent minded brother. All aspects of his life are examined in a new light, free from the prejudice of writers (such as the Memorialists and Iung) who edited Lucien's *Mémoires*. In addition to the printed sources, the author makes use of archival correspondence.

Pietromarchi, Antonello. *Lucien Bonaparte, prince romain*. Translated by René Carducci. Paris: Perrin, 1985.
Originally published in Italian in 1981 as *Luciano Bonaparte, principe romano*, this biography was written by an Italian diplomat who admirably reveals the complex personality of Lucien. He was always more of an orator than a statesman. Unlike his brothers, he was able to oppose Napoleon. Curiously, he became a friend of Pope Pius VII and his title was granted by the Pope rather than by his brother. He was intelligent and courageous, but incapable of following through on a task. Considered the leading work on its topic, this well-documented source replaces the older

Piétri. Plates, genealogical tables, and bibliographical references in notes.

Rambaud, Jacques. *Naples sous Joseph Bonaparte 1806-1808*. Paris: Plon, 1911.
Based on a French doctoral dissertation of 1910, this exhaustive and scholarly book is drawn from documents in the Neapolitan archives as well as French documentary and printed sources, resulting in a comprehensive study of the region and its relations with the French. Rimbaud states that southern Italy, because of its vast differences from the rest of the Empire, presented complex political, economic, and social problems. Napoleon vested much confidence in Joseph in granting him this region to govern. The author also published a critical edition of Joseph's letters. Rambaud stresses the French contributions in Naples. His book remains the definitive work on the subject. Includes sources and bibliography at the beginning, and bibliographical references in footnotes.

Rocquain, Félix. *Napoléon Ier et le roi Louis, d'après les documents conservés aux Archives nationales*. Paris: Firmin-Didot, 1875.
A combination of a history of Holland under Louis Bonaparte from 1806 to 1810, and a collection of letters and other documents. A valuable contribution on Louis, Holland, and Napoleon's relations with Holland during these years. Rocquain narrates the activities of the two brothers in great detail. He approaches the relationship between the two brothers from the perspective of international relations. Louis, he argues, acted entirely in the interest of the Dutch, which did not please Napoleon. Correspondence between Louis and Napoleon occupies pages 1-292, while pages 292-357 provide documents on Louis and Holland. This provides the first comprehensive printed collection of documents concerning Louis and Holland.

Ropes, John Codman. *The First Napoleon: A Sketch, Political and Military*. Boston: Houghton, Mifflin & Co., 1885.
Based on a series of lectures delivered at the Lowell Institute in Boston in March 1885, this work was written by an American authority who was not only an admirer but also a promoter of Napoleon. Centering his work on military affairs, Ropes contends that Napoleon was a gambler, and it was this gambling spirit that was the greatest weakness in his character. On the political side, the author sees Napoleon as upholding the liberal gains made by

the revolutionaries, although the French people were denied the political power that Napoleon considered them unfit to use. Ropes's work is free from the bias often found in French and British works from the same period. It is useful for an early American interpretation. Maps. Complements Seeley's biography.

Rose, J. Holland. *The Life of Napoleon I*. 11th ed. London: G. Bell, 1934.
A classic work which first appeared in 1902. When published, it was regarded as the best biography of Napoleon by an English scholar. Well organized, well written, and fully documented, it is a good example of historical literature. Based on what were, at the time, new diplomatic documents, including reports from ambassadors held at the Foreign Office, papers from the War Ministry, and Napoleon's correspondence published during the Second Empire. Provides a fairly balanced view of the Emperor. The first ten chapters cover the years before 1800; this edition also supplies a chronology of events during the era and a genealogical table of the Bonapartes.

_____. *The Personality of Napoleon*. London: Bell, 1912.
The printed version of eight lectures delivered in Boston in March 1912, based on an extended study of the Napoleonic period by the English expert of his generation. Topics deal with Napoleon the man, the Jacobin, the lawgiver, the thinker, and the world ruler. Rose repeats his view that Napoleon's genius as a military leader declined because of his growing megalomania rather than because of his failing health. Continues to admire Napoleon the lawgiver throughout. At the time it was written, this work was considered a significant contribution to the growing number of interpretations of Napoleon's character. Detailed table of contents for each of the eight lectures, maps, and index.

Ross, Michael. *The Reluctant King: Joseph Bonaparte, King of the Two Sicilies and Spain*. London: Sidgewick & Jackson, 1976.
The most recent English-language biography of Joseph, this is an adeptly written piece of work. The author warns his readers that it is not based on original archival research but on printed sources both primary and secondary. Noncommittal, Ross hesitates about Joseph's character, but he presents a lively portrayal of the relationship between Joseph and Napoleon, and also of the tragic Spanish affair. Stresses his diplomatic abilities. Joseph established

friendly relations with the United States in 1798, and he negotiated the Treaty of Lunéville before his brother appointed him king of Naples and the Two Sicilies in 1806. Illustrations, index, endnotes, and bibliography.

Seeley, John Robert. *A Short History of Napoleon the First*. London: Seeley & Co., 1890.
Appearing at roughly the same time as the American biography by John Codman Ropes, this brief life is generally considered to be a pioneer in English studies of Napoleon. The author sketches the Emperor's life and is generally critical of him. He acknowledges that Napoleon was a man of extraordinary ability, who rose to power because of the turmoil of the French Revolution. The internal reforms are considered more significant than the territorial conquests. In his review of Seeley, Lord Acton contends that this biography and that of Ropes are superior to contemporary French works.

Tarlé, Evgenii Viktoro. *Bonaparte*. Translated by John Cournos. New York: Knight Publications, 1937.
Tarlé, a Russian soldier, was a specialist in the Continental System. In his very clear biography of Napoleon, he made use of sources unavailable to the Western historian. This enabled him to expound Russian policy effectively and to treat the Russian side of the 1812 campaign in a manner superior to that of most French and British writers. A complete and scholarly biography. Bibliographical endnotes and bibliography.

Tersen, Emile. *Napoléon*. Paris: Club Français du Livre, 1959.
Although this work is not based on original sources, it represents a clear attempt to write an impartial account of the life of Napoleon. Tersen's conclusions are considered to be remarkably balanced and equitable. He attempts to escape from the burden of events and to show that in 1804 as much as in 1799, most French people had little reason to doubt the sincerity of Napoleon's republicanism.

Thompson, J. M. *Napoleon Bonaparte: His Rise and Fall*. Oxford, England: Basil Blackwell, 1990.
First published in 1951, this volume is a must for undergraduates. Thompson is a leading authority on the French Revolution, and it is in the light of the French Revolution that he interprets the career of Napoleon. He is interested in the Napoleon who codified

the laws and institutions created during the Revolution. Beautifully written in classical style, his work is a brilliant piece of scholarship not intended for the beginner. Thompson relies for the most part on the famous *Correspondance* published by order of Napoleon III between 1858-70. Illustrations, index, endnotes, and appendix.

Tulard, Jean. *Napoleon, the Myth of the Saviour.* Translated by Teresa Waugh. London: Weidenfeld and Nicolson, 1984.
The most recent biography to appear in English is Teresa Waugh's translation of Tulard's *Napoleon*. Tulard, a well-known scholar of the period, sees Napoleon as a talented outsider. His thesis is that the real beneficiaries of Napoleon's sixteen-year rule were the notables: the bourgeoisie who had purchased church lands. They created the "savior" on 18 Brumaire, and they withdrew their support in 1814, when Napoleon overstepped their plans for France. Included is a useful discussion of the current historiographical debates. Tulard is a master of his subject; however, he is best in the original French rather than this mediocre translation. Index, map, illustrations, bibliographical references at end of each chapter and an impressive annotated bibliography of ninety-seven pages.

Chapter 4

INTERNAL AFFAIRS

Government and Administration

Arnold, Eric A., Jr. *Fouché, Napoleon and the General Police.* Washington, D.C.: University Press of America, 1979.
Arnold summarizes the administrative organization of the police under Napoleon. Provides a detailed analysis of how the police functioned during the years of the Consulate and Empire. Arnold demonstrates that although Fouché ran the police ministry, Napoleon was still the man in charge, and he did not hesitate to intervene personally, as in the case of destroying the English spy system. In addition, Arnold proves that despite the great powers of the police, it was impossible to enforce conscription laws. Index, bibliography, and chapter notes.

Aucoc, Léon. *Le Conseil d'Etat avant et depuis 1789: Ses transformations, ses travaux et son personnel.* Paris: Imprimerie Nationale, 1876.
The purpose of this book, by a president of his section in the Council of State, is to summarize the history of this institution before and after the French Revolution of 1789. Aucoc discusses its changes, including those in the Council's personnel, work, and achievements. Using documents, lists, and bibliographies, the author provides a vast amount of information on the numerous sections and functions of the Council. As a reference tool, this book should be used in conjunction with Durand's and Piétri's works on the same subject.

Beck, Thomas D. *French Legislators, 1800-1834: A Study in Quantitative History.* Berkeley: University of California Press, 1974.

A quantitative analysis of French legislative personnel from Napoleon to the July Monarchy. Although the book focuses on the Revolution of 1830, it contains relevant information on the legislators under Napoleon, and it is the only study of its kind. In his examination of Napoleonic legislators, Beck's results confirm the view that initially Napoleon depended on the support of the revolutionary bourgeoisie, and as time went on, he increasingly relied on traditional elites, whose roots lay in the Old Regime. Maps, index, bibliography, tables, graphs, and charts.

Bourdon, J. *La Législation du Consulat et de l'Empire.* Vol. 1, *La Réforme judiciaire de l'an VIII.* Paris: Rodèz Carrère, 1942.

A collection and commentary of previously dispersed documents concerning the proposition of legislative reforms by publicists, their preparation, and the discussion and vote of each law. Bourdon states that the new judicial institutions were established by two reforms: the first demanded by the Constitution of the Year VIII and realized by the two laws of 27 Ventôse Year VIII, and the second by the Criminal Instruction Code of 1808 and realized by the of law 20 April 1810. The first reform was the most significant and the subject of study of the volume. An important work in this area.

Bourguet, Marie-Noelle. *Déchiffrer la France: La Statistique départementale à l'époque napoléonienne.* Paris: Editions des Archives Contemporaines, 1990.

In this examination of the statistics compiled by Napoleon's prefects, Bourguet attempts to determine why the prefects viewed France as they did in the Year IX, or 1801. In her endeavor to answer this question, she studied the content of the reports submitted by the prefects to the governments, and the correspondence between prefects and central government officials. The book includes a sketch of the history of statistics during the Old Regime and the Revolution. The most original part of the book deals with the examination of how the prefects collected statistics and the assumptions that underlay their presentation of the data. Bourguet provides a thorough analysis of their reports. Bibliography and indexes.

Bury, J. P. T. "The End of the Napoleonic Senate." *Historical Journal* 9 (1948): 165-189.

The title of this article is somewhat misleading, as there is much more to it than the role played by the Napoleonic Senate in April 1814 in bringing about the change from the Napoleonic regime to the Restoration. The origins, functions, powers, significance, and personnel are discussed, as well as the Senate's use by Talleyrand and Alexander in transforming it into the new Chamber of Peers. Based almost entirely on primary sources, this is a good introduction to the subject and the only work in English.

Church, Clive. *Revolution and Red Tape: The French Ministerial Bureaucracy*. Oxford, England: The Clarendon Press, 1981.

An indispensable and well documented study of the origins of French bureaucracy, the only work in English on the topic. Church demonstrates that Napoleon inherited more than he created, arguing that the Directors who preceded Napoleon were the true founders of the modern French bureaucracy. Chapter 8, which concerns Napoleon and the bureaucracy, is particularly good. Index, bibliography, endnotes; statistical tables in text on the growth of ministerial personnel, 1770-1850, the geographical origins of civil servants, and their dates of birth.

Collins, Irene. *Napoleon I and His Parliaments, 1800-1815*. London: Edward Arnold, 1979.

As a political historian, Collins is fully qualified to provide the first comprehensive study of how the parliaments functioned during the Consulate and Empire. Both their structure and their power are described. Collins' goal is to summarize the constitutional system and chronicle the activity of the two consultative bodies, the Legislative Body and the Tribunate until its suppression in 1807. The operation of the primary assemblies of the canton and the electoral colleges in the departments is also briefly discussed. Chronologically organized, the book takes the reader through the various changes in government under Napoleon. Collins argues that there was more room for opposition during the Consulate than during the Empire. In a brief but informative section on the individual legislators, she analyzes their backgrounds. An excellent chapter is devoted to the two sessions of 1813. The best work in English on this topic. Index, bibliography, and footnotes.

Coppolani, Jean-Yves. *Les Elections en France à l'époque napoléonienne*. Paris: Albatros, 1980.
This notable work grew from the author's doctoral thesis and is based on a rich documentation from departmental and national archives. Departments studied were chosen on a regional basis and include the Seine, Nord, Bouches-du-Rhône, Charente-Inférieure, Aude, Doubs, Moselle, Ariège, Cantal, Alpes-Maritimes, and Corsica. Few studies have been devoted to elections during the Napoleonic period, and this one is therefore a welcome contribution. Contains meticulous detail, including much material on election participation and results. Coppolani refutes previous arguments that elections contributed nothing to political life during this era. Bibliography, index, and endnotes.

Durand, Charles. *Etudes sur le Conseil d'Etat napoléonien*. Paris: Presses Universitaires de France, 1949.
_____. *Le Fonctionnement du Conseil d'Etat napoléonien*. Gap: Louis-Jean, 1954.
_____. *Les Auditeurs au Conseil d'Etat de 1803 à 1814*. Aix-en-Provence: La Pensée Universitaire, 1958.
The author is the acknowledged expert on the institutions of the Empire. This is a three-volume set on the Council of State. Durand describes the role of this body and argues that discussion in the council concerned implementation of decisions already made and current events. Diverse issues debated include the marriage of priests, grain control, foreign affairs, judicial reform, and the organization of the military. Arguably the most important definitive study of the Council of State. Each volume contains an index and bibliography; footnotes are in the bibliographic references. Lists of the personnel of the Conseil d'Etat and the auditors are found in the appendices to Volumes 1 and 3.

Emsley, Clive. "Policing and the Streets of Early Nineteenth Century Paris." *French History* 1 (1987): 257-282.
Based on documents including those of the Paris Prefecture of Police, this article provides a detailed depiction of the Paris police from 1800 to 1830, including its membership and function. Offers a good analysis of the multitudinous duties of the police, such as maintaining order, investigating crimes, and surveilling the general population. Emsley challenges the idea that the only troubles facing the police were of a political nature or were to hunt down refractory conscripts and army deserters. 126 notes.

Gobert, Adrienne. *L'Opposition des assemblées pendant le Consulat, 1800-1804*. Paris: E. Sagot, 1925.

A well-documented study, based on a doctoral dissertation at the University of Paris, Gobert provides the best introduction to the topic. She describes considerable opposition, especially in the first two years, holding that the "ideologues," who saw Bonaparte as the son of the Revolution and the definite defense against the return of the Bourbons, rallied to his support. One of the most important contributions to the political history of the Consulate. Bibliography.

Hauterive, E. d'. *Napoléon et sa police*. Paris: Flammarion, 1943.

A detailed examination of the Napoleonic police force, from its creation under Fouché to the fall of the Empire. The author attempts to discover the nature of Napoleon's relationship with the police, to understand how it operated, and finally to examine Napoleon's personal influence on the functioning of the force. He explores every aspect of life on which the police had an impact, including the press, theaters, and individuals such as emigrants, the clergy, and foreigners. An excellent work by the scholar who edited and published Napoleonic police bulletins between 1908 and 1964 in several volumes.

Holtman, Robert B. *Napoleonic Propaganda*. Baton Rouge: Louisiana State University Press, 1950.

A demonstration of Napoleon's use of propaganda in France and in the occupied states. The author argues that Napoleon was the first dictator who talked directly and frequently to his subjects and that he pioneered the use of the government as the official center of propaganda. Although published more than forty years ago, this work is still a leading study. Index, bibliography and footnotes.

Mansel, Philip. *The Court of France 1789-1830*. New York: Cambridge University Press, 1988.

Built on fifteen years of archival research, Mansel's is the definitive work in English on the French court from Louis XVI to Charles X. It is a comparative study of the different types of courts under the various monarchs, including much useful information on the court during the Empire. Mansel stresses the importance of the court in establishing the monarch's greatness, especially in the case of Napoleon, who, he argues, used the positions of court to reward his supporters. Illustrations, index, and bibliography.

_____. *The Eagle in Splendour: Napoleon and His Court*. London: George Philip, 1987.
Complementing Mansel's work on the court of France, this competently researched text is intended to investigate the role of Napoleon as courtier rather than general or politician. The author examines the revival of the court after the Revolution and contends that there was little difference between the Bourbon court and that of Napoleon. In addition, he deals with the courtiers, whom he interprets as concerned primarily with their own promotion. The courts of Napoleon's relatives, modeled on his own, are also considered. Mansel stresses the increasing exclusivity of Bonaparte's courts and courtiers. Illustrations, bibliography, and index.

Périvier, Antonin. *Napoléon journaliste*. Paris: Plon, 1918.
A summary of the journalistic activities of Napoleon written by a former director of the newspaper *Le Figaro*. Périvier reveals the Emperor as the able and industrious director of a press bureau and, in fact, a journalist, as he founded newspapers, directed their policies, and contributed to them.

Piétri, François. *Napoléon et le parlement: Ou, La Dictature enchaînée*. Paris: Fayard, 1955.
A scholarly and detailed study of Napoleon's relationship with his elected assemblies, especially the Legislative Body. A well-regarded survey covering the entire period from 1799 to 1815. The author argues that the so-called absolutism of Napoleon is nothing more than a myth and that Napoleon's ascent to power was a tumultuous but normal constitutional change. Offers good descriptions of the functions of the Council of State, the Tribunate, and the conservative Senate. This study should be read in conjunction with the work of Irene Collins on the same topic in English. Bibliography.

Ponteil, F. *Napoléon Ier et l'organisation autoritaire de la France*. Collection Armand Colin, Section d'Histoire et des Sciences Economiques, no. 307. Paris: Armand Colin, 1956, 1965.
A study of the evolution of institutions under Napoleon during the Empire from the point of view that one of the fundamental characteristics of the regime was the complete submission to an

absolute and vigorous authority. He posits that the Napoleonic regime repudiated the tenets of liberty and equality proclaimed by the revolutionaries rested on two essential principles: the hierarchical nature of the regime, in which the creation of an imperial nobility became increasingly conspicuous, and the centralization which demanded complete obedience. A serviceable monograph on the principles and structures of the Napoleonic state. Bibliography.

Régnier, Jacques. *Les Préfets du Consulat et de l'Empire.* Paris: Editions de la Nouvelle Revue, 1907.
The subject is treated briefly, but the author demonstrates how the prefects were appointed during the Consulate and discusses their role during the Empire. The work closes with a chapter on the itinerant subprefects, whose creation was proposed by one of the most important prefects, Albert Lézay-Marnesia. Finally, the author discusses what became of the prefects after the fall of the Empire. A good summary. Bibliography.

Rigotard, Jean. *La Police parisienne sous Napoléon: La Préfecture de Police.* Paris: Tallandier, 1990.
An important study of the police prefecture, based on archival sources. The prefecture was originally created by Louis XIV and revived by Napoleon in 1800. The role played by three of Napoleon's police prefects—Dubois, Pasquier, and the former Jacobin Réal—is examined, as is the daily life of Parisians under the Empire. Major events, such as the Cadoudal affair, Malet's plot, and problems encountered by the administration, are explained. The author clearly demonstrates the revival of the Old Regime both in the work carried out by the police and in the sheer responsibility of the prefect. Index and bibliography.

Savant, Jean. *Les Ministres de Napoléon.* Paris: Hachette, 1959.
Based on primary sources from a number of French archives, this informative work focuses on the individuals who formed the essential collaborators of the Napoleonic regime. The ministers are examined on an individual basis, with the longest chapters on the chief ministers: Fouché, Talleyrand, and Chaptal. Basic biographical details, as well as information about their responsibilities and significance, are provided. Although some entries are brief, this remains a useful introductory survey on the topic of

Napoleon's ministers. Bibliography, appendix composed of lists of ministers, arranged both alphabetically and by department.

——————. *Les Préfets de Napoléon*. Paris: Hachette, 1958.
The prefects were key administrators in Napoleon's France. This short survey discusses their recruitment and their principal activities and responsibilities which included public works and the recruitment of the army. Also contains a discussion of Napoleon's relationship with these key men and a study of the more significant prefects: André Jean Bon Saint-André, Albert Lézay-Marnesia, Jacques-Claude Beugnot, and Louis-Mathieu Molé.

Tulard, Jean. *Paris et son administration, 1800-1830*. Paris: Ville de Paris, Commission des Travaux Historiques, 1979.
A detailed scholarly study based on a 1977 thesis on the history of the municipality of Paris during the first thirty years of the nineteenth century. The first 403 pages concern Paris under Napoleon. Topics include the new institutions, such as prefects, mayors, and the Prefecture of Police. Also contains a thorough discussion of commerce, health care, industry, demography, and economic problems facing the city. An excellent examination of the internal history of Paris. Maps and bibliography.

Villefosse, Louis de, and Janine Bouissounouse. *The Scourge of the Eagle: Napoleon and the Liberal Opposition*. Translated and edited by Michael Ross. New York: St. Martin's Press, 1972.
The Napoleonic regime was not without opposition, as this important study demonstrates. The authors chronicle the development of the opposition of the liberal intellectuals to Napoleon and his reaction to it, explaining that this group—including Madame de Staël, Chateaubriand, and the Ideologues—were initially supportive of Napoleon and the coup d'état of 18 Brumaire, as they believed it would save rather than destroy the republic. Much of the opposition was centered at the French Institute, which Napoleon altered in 1803 to reflect his policies. Index, bibliography, and references in footnotes.

Welschinger, H. *La Censure sous le premier Empire avec documents inédits*. Paris: Perrin, 1887.
An excellent scholarly study, based entirely on original sources, of the censorship of newspapers, books, and the theater during the Empire. Topics include the creation of censorship, its organi-

zation and administration, Napoleon's plans for censorship, and specific measures taken against journalists, writers, and directors of theaters. The censors themselves, Fouché and his entourage, are also examined. A special appendix, located at the back of the book (pages 261-377), contains sixty-nine documents drawn mainly from the Archives Nationales and the Comédie Française concerning Madame de Staël, orders, letters, and police reports.

Whitcomb, Edward A. *Napoleon's Diplomatic Service*. Durham, N.C.: Duke University Press, 1979.
In focusing on one branch of the Napoleonic bureaucracy, Whitcomb provides a much-needed contribution to the history of Napoleonic administration. He argues that the Napoleonic diplomatic service became more effective during the years 1800 to 1814. Napoleon built upon the foundations of the Old Regime and the Revolution and developed the French bureaucracy. Meticulously researched and based on archival sources, the work also clearly demonstrates that the diplomatic service continued to improve in quality even when the regime was floundering. Index, bibliography, and appendices.

_____. "Napoleon's Prefects." *American Historical Review* 79 (1974): 1089-1118.
A useful examination of the origins and careers of these administrators, who, for various reasons, have not been thoroughly studied. Based primarily on the personal dossiers of the prefects in the French Archives Nationales, this valuable social analysis with much data on the prefectorial corps. The author contests the idea that the administration deteriorated with the decline of Napoleon's regime. On the other hand, he contends that it improved with time. Eight useful tables provide statistical information on the social, political, and functional backgrounds of the prefects; fifty-nine bibliographical notes.

The Economy under Napoleon

Ballot, Charles. *L'Introduction du machisme dans l'industrie française*. Comité des Travaux Historiques et Scientifiques. Notices, Inventaires et Documents, IX. Paris: F. Rieder, 1923.
Ballot spent many years collecting material for this work before he was killed at Verdun in 1917. His colleague and friend Claude

Gével took his notes and prepared the manuscript for publication. The work extends from the mid-eighteenth to the early nineteenth century, concentrating on the years between 1780 and 1815. Organizing his data around the different industries—cotton, wool, linen, silk, and chemicals—the author reveals the efforts to secure knowledge of inventions in England and to induce English artisans to settle in France. Napoleon himself made numerous trips to factories in England to secure men and machinery. This lengthy, detailed, and well-written account, drawn from original sources, remains the leading work on the technical development of industry during the period. Bibliographical references.

Barker, Richard J. "The Conseil Général des Manufactures: Business Leaders and the State Economic Administration During the Empire and Restoration." *Consortium on Revolutionary Europe, 1750-1850: Proceedings* 19, Part II (1989): 47-66.
Expanding an earlier article, the author scrutinizes the membership, accomplishment, and restrictions of the Council within the context of the economic administration. Based on sources in the French Archives Nationales, including the *Recueil de débats législatifs et politiques des chambres françaises* and other published primary sources, the study follows the Council to the period of the Restoration, when the Council's power and status increased. It was abolished in 1830. Two figures and forty-two notes.

_____. "The Conseil Général des Manufactures under Napoleon (1810-1814)." *French Historical Studies* 6 (Fall 1969): 185-213.
The article is concerned primarily with state sponsorship of industry in France under Napoleon. The Council, an advisory body created by Napoleon in 1810, is outlined in Part III and given only cursory treatment. The author states that the Council was not very influential in economic policy and that further research is required to determine its real impact. This first English treatment of the subject serves as a useful introduction to the author's second article, cited above. Based on the Council's papers found in the Archives Nationales. Ninety-eight notes.

Bergeron, Louis. *Banquiers, négotiants et manufacturers parisiens du Directoire à l'Empire*. Ecole des Hautes Etudes en Sciences Sociales, Centre de Recherches Historiques. Civilisations et Sociétés, 51. The Hague: Mouton, 1978.

A welcome contribution to a neglected aspect of the history of the Empire, this exhaustive study of bankers and manufacturers in Paris stresses the innovative role of Parisian bankers and entrepreneurs throughout a difficult period, making extensive use of business letters, inventories, and bankruptcy statements. Illustrations, map, index, and bibliography.

Bossenga, Gail. "La Révolution française et les corporations: Trois exemples lillois." *Annales, Economies, Sociétés* 43 (1988): 405-426.

An examination of the attempt by three guilds—those of the bakers, the dry-goods merchants, and the linen thread spinners—to reimpose guildlike regulations on the economy of Lille. Bossenga suggests that the abolition of guilds during the French Revolution did not always serve the needs of the local elites. Those promoting the return of guilds included members of the Napoleonic Chamber of Commerce as well as the mayor and prefect. The laissez-faire stance of the central government conflicted with the more protectionist aims of local officials. Based on documents from departmental and municipal French archives and secondary sources. Seventy notes.

Chabert, Alexandre. *Essai sur les mouvements des revenus et de l'activité économique en France de 1798 à 1820.* 2 vols. Paris: Librairie des Médicis, 1949.

A concise but thorough treatment of French economic development, valuable for its discussion of the effects of state policies and wars on economic progress. Pages 361-397 are devoted to the Napoleonic period and include the analysis of such topics as the rapid growth of the textile factories and the improved circumstances of the manufacturing and trading classes. Experts in the field consider Chabert's work to be a significant contribution to the economic history of the time. Illustrations and maps.

Crouzet, François. *L'Economie britannique et le blocus continental 1806-1813.* 2 vols. Reprint. Paris: Economica, 1988.

When it was first published in 1958, this thesis-based monograph filled a major gap in studies of the Continental Blockade, and it remains the definitive work on the topic. A thorough account of the Napoleon's Continental Blockade on Great Britain's foreign trade and domestic economy, it focuses on the maritime aspect on the system. The thesis posits that at times when the blockade was employed, it was successful in effecting economic depression in Britain. Nevertheless, throughout these years, Britain prospered and her economy grew. The book was reissued in 1988 with a new preface of 114 pages. Index in Volume 2, bibliography, and appendix of sixteen tables and eighteen graphs.

_____. "Wars, Blockade and Economic Change in Europe 1792-1815." *Journal of Economic History* 24 (1964): 567-590.

Because his book (cited above) has yet to be translated into English, those who cannot read French will have to rely on the article. Crouzet considers the influence of the Napoleonic wars on continental development, focusing on three themes: the British sea blockade, the French Continental Blockade, and the rewriting of the map of Europe. Richard Tilly, in a commentary after the article, is not entirely persuaded by Crouzet's arguments due to a lack of evidence, and sees further research as the solution.

Dufraisse, R. "Régime douanier, blocus, système continental: Essai de mise au point." *Revue d'histoire économique et sociale* 44 (1966): 518-543.

An historiographical paper that evaluates the advancement of research on the Continental System since 1913. Dufraisse states that valuable sources have become available through the publication of documents and archival guides. The research of Georges Lefebvre, Marcel Dunan, and André Fugier has corrected the misguided tendency to lump together French tariff policy, the Continental Blockade, and the Continental System. François Crouzet, E. F. Hecksher, and Bertrand de Jouvenal have also contributed to new insights into Napoleonic economic policies and their impact. Dufraisse specifies the literature on the subject in the French Archives Nationales and lists secondary sources.

Girnius, Saulius Antanas. "Russia and the Continental Blockade." Ph.D. dissertation. Chicago: University of Chicago, 1981.

A study of the impact of the Continental Blockade on Russia. Girnius contends that this subject has been inadequately dealt with by both Western and Russian scholars, and his goal is an attempt to redress this gap. The thesis focuses on the Russian economy before and during the blockade. It examines all aspects of the economy during this period, including currency values, trade, the prices of domestic and imported products, and the development of Russian industry. A valuable contribution to a neglected subject. Bibliography.

Grab, Alexander, and Charles F. Delzell (commentator). "The Kingdom of Italy and Napoleon's Continental Blockade." *Consortium on Revolutionary Europe, 1750-1850: Proceedings* 18 (1988): 587-604.
A paper delivered at this conference which sketches the legislative origins and implementation of Napoleon's economic war against Great Britain and examines the controversy among historians over the impact of the Continental Blockade on Italy. Grab attempts to disprove Tarlé's argument from *La vita economica dell' Italia eta napoleonica* (1951) that the effects were negative. More recent research demonstrates that the Italian economy developed and that the overall impact from 1806 to 1814 was beneficial. The essay is based primarily on the correspondence in the Commercio section of the Milan State Archives. Forty-nine notes.

Hecksher, E. F. *The Continental System: An Economic Interpretation.* Edited by Harald Westergaard. Oxford, England: The Clarendon Press, 1922.
The title of this work is misleading, as it is virtually an economic history of the period covering all of Europe with a focus on Britain and France. Hecksher is critical of the Continental System and believes it had little success. A scholarly and well-written survey, although dated, it remains the leading work in English on the subject.

Higby, Chester P., and Caroline B. Willis. "Industry and Labor under Napoleon." *American Historical Review* 53 (1947-1948): 465-480.
A study of the Conseil de Prud'hommes, a Napoleonic institution which has been neglected by historians. It was a committee of manufacturers and workers in assorted industries. Committee members were elected by their peers, and the role of the Council was to restore differences between management and labor. Higby states that the council is of interest, since it was an example of nascent democracy at work in industry, and filled a gap between the guilds of the Old Regime and modern labor unions. Having a council of this type meant that France was the first modern nation to possess a court for industry. Seventy-four notes.

Hueckel, Glenn Russell. *The Napoleonic Wars and Their Impact on Factor Returns and Output in England, 1793-1815*. British Economic History Series. New York: Garland Press, 1985.

A study, based on the author's Ph.D. dissertation, which argues that the Napoleonic wars had a profound influence on the transformation of the English economy at the beginning of the nineteenth century. This transformation, according to the author, was significant enough to be termed an "Industrial Revolution." His purpose is to isolate the impact of the war against the French on changes in the returns of factors of production and the distribution of output between sectors in the English economy. Bibliography, statistical tables, and graphs.

Jouvenal, Bertrand de. *Napoléon et l'économie dirigée: Le Blocus continental*. Brussels: Editions de la Toison d'Or, 1942.

An extensive and well-documented study, including the publication of unedited documents, concerning the Continental Blockade to 1810. The author demonstrates that Napoleon did not successfully execute a system of blockade and that the attempt was abandoned after 1810. A crucial work, indispensable for the subject. Bibliographical note.

Latour, F. *Le Grand Argentier de Napoléon, Gaudin, duc de Gaete*. Paris: Editions du Scorpion, 1962.

A scholarly and deftly researched biography of Napoleon's finance minister between 1799 and 1814. Latour begins with a discussion of the financial situation at the end of the Convention, setting the stage for Napoleon's reforms. The book examines in detail the financial changes implemented by Gaudin, including the creation of the Bank of France, the "Cour des Comptes," and the restoration of various taxes. This is the only biography of an important functionary, which should be read with his memoirs.

Marion, Marcel. *Histoire financière de la France depuis 1715*. Vol. 4, *1799-1818: La Fin de la Révolution, le Consulat et l'Empire, la libération du territoire*. Paris: Arthur Rousseau, 1925.

Written by a professor at the Collège de France, this competently researched and thorough work covers the financial history of the period. Marion praises Napoleon for his reparations in this area and discusses the burden of taxation placed on the public to achieve a balanced budget. The author excuses Napoleon for his bankruptcies and his sumptuous spending because he consolidated the wealth of the elites. Remains the authoritative work on the subject. Bibliographical references.

Melvin, Frank Edgar. *Napoleon's Navigation System: A Study of Trade Control during the Continental Blockade*. New York: D. Appleton, 1919.

An outstanding work based on the author's doctoral dissertation. Melvin has used documentary sources from France, America, and England for his study of the development of the Continental Blockade from the Berlin Decrees to the fall of the Empire. Melvin explains what the Continental Blockade meant, with special reference to the licensing and permit system. He holds that the Continental Blockade started as a blockade against British trade and industry and only later, in 1810, with the development of French navigation, commerce, and industry, did it become the dominant policy. An indispensable work on this subject. Bibliographical references.

Menais, Georges Paul. *Napoléon et l'argent*. Paris: Editions de l'Epargne, 1969.

A fully researched examination of the role played by Napoleon in restoring stability to the French public finance and the monetary system. Deals with the establishment of the Bank of France. Much of the book is devoted to the work of Napoleon's ministers of finance and of the treasury. The author argues that money and finance played an extremely important role in Napoleon's life. Appendix of transcripts of documents, and a list of the governors of the Bank of France.

Ragsdale, Hugh A. "A Continental System in 1801: Paul I and Bonaparte." *Journal of Modern History* 42, no. 1 (1970): 70-89.

A detailed analysis of Napoleon's attempt at rapprochement with Russia with the intention of peace. The author posits that this short-lived continental arrangement, which closed the Continent to England in 1801, was more harmful to the English economy than the later Continental Blockade, because the English harvest had been poor and because there were fewer opportunities to circumvent the restrictions. Based on Napoleon's *Correspondance* and a variety of printed primary sources. Ninety-three notes.

Ramon, Gabriel. *Histoire de la Banque de France, d'après les sources originales*. Paris: Grasset, 1929.

The first complete history of the Bank of France, based on several archival sources, including the bank's own archives. The first part covers the creation, functions, activities, and problems of the Bank of France during the Napoleonic era. As a historian, the author integrates the history of the bank with the general financial and economic history of the nineteenth century. An indispensable source for its topic. Bibliography.

Rose, John Holland. "Napoleon and British Commerce." *English Historical Review* 8 (1893): 704-725. Reprinted in Rose, *Napoleonic Studies*. London: Bell, 1914, 166-223.
Although published before World War I, Rose's article still provides useful information on a subject poorly served in the English language. He demonstrates that by employing the Continental Blockade of England by the continent of Europe, Napoleon was merely continuing the policies the French revolutionaries had adopted in 1793. The French had been mistaken in thinking that Britain was entirely dependent on foreign trade. Rose examines the impact of both the Berlin Decrees and the British Orders in Council on the French Empire. A useful survey of this subject.

Ruppenthal, Roland. "Denmark and the Continental System." *Journal of Modern History* 15 (1943): 7-23.
Although dated, Ruppenthal's remains the best study of the effects of the Continental System on Denmark, containing a wealth of detail. The author claims that although Denmark attempted to remain neutral, that goal proved to be impossible, given the important role played by Schleswig and Holstein in introducing goods into Europe. Denmark's fate was decided by the Treaty of Tilsit, which forced the Danes into the system. Drawn from printed primary sources and relevant papers from the Danish and English archives. 119 notes.

Stourm, René. *Les Finances du Consulat*. Paris: Guillaumin, 1902.
Based on primary sources, this well-organized and clearly written study, concentrates on finances, but it is valuable for all economic aspects of the Consulate. Stourm is critical of the Consulate's polices and argues that too much power was placed in the hands of the First Consul. Although written in 1902, this remains a leading work on the subject.

Tarlé, Eugène. *Le Blocus continental et le royaume d'Italie: Situation économique de l'Italie sous Napoléon Ier, d'après des documents inédits.* Paris: Félix Alcan, 1928.

Tarlé, better known for his work on Russia during the Napoleonic era, has written an excellent monograph on the effects of the Continental Blockade on the Kingdom of Italy. Based upon documents in both the French and Italian archives, it is full of details, including many statistics. The author commences with a general depiction of Napoleon's administration of the Kingdom of Italy and local economic conditions before examining the effects of the Continental Blockade. Includes bibliographical references. For an up-to-date evaluation of Tarlé's study, see P. Villani, "Quelques aspects de la vie économique italienne à l'époque napoléonienne," *Annales Historiques de la Révolution Française* 49 (1977): 587-617.

Thuillier, G. "Pour une histoire monétaire du XIXe siècle: La Crise monétaire de l'automne 1810." *Revue historique* 238 (1967): 51-84.

A survey of the financial crisis that preceded the economic crisis of 1811. Examines the causes of the monetary crisis and its consequences for the entire country. This article is valuable because it studies an aspect of the 1810-1811 French economic crisis from on which sources are difficult to find, as the archives of the Ministry of Finance and the Mint were destroyed. Based on both primary and secondary sources.

Viennet, Odette. *Napoléon et l'industrie française: La Crise de 1810-1811.* Paris: Plon, 1947.

Viennets is the standard work on the economic crisis during the years 1810 to 1811. It is essentially a study of the depression which briefly considers Napoleon's role in regulating and helping business and industry. The author explains how Napoleon attempted to develop industry and business, and outlines reasons for the crisis, such as the problem of overproduction. A significant contribution to the literature. Index, bibliography, and appendix.

Woronoff, Denis. *L'Industrie sidérurgique en France pendant la Révolution et l'Empire.* Paris: Ecole des Hautes Etudes en Sciences Sociales, 1984.

Based on a French doctoral dissertation of the same title, a thorough and well-documented study of the iron and steel industry, a great war industry in revolutionary and Napoleonic France. Woronoff argues that although there was a great demand for iron and steel, productivity rarely met the needs of wartime France. He provides numerous reasons for this including structural and attitudinal, and concludes that, although profound changes occurred in the iron industry, these changes were neither linear nor sudden. An excellent treatment of the subject. Maps, indexes, and bibliography.

Education during the Consulate and Empire

Artz, Frederick B. *The Development of Technical Education in France 1500-1850*. Cambridge, Mass.: Society for the History of Technology and M.I.T. Press, 1966.
Artz summarizes developments made in technical education at the elementary and secondary levels and within specialized institutions. The Napoleonic discussion found in Chapter 3, "The Era of the French Revolution, 1789-1815," is concerned mainly with reforms made by Napoleon in secondary education: the closing of the revolutionary *écoles centrales* and their replacement by the *lycées* in 1802, and the *écoles secondaires*, or preparatory schools for *lycées*, in 1803. Also under discussion are the *écoles des arts et métiers* (trade schools), the Conservatoire des Arts et Métiers (industrial museum), the Ecole Polytechnique, and finally naval and military education. In a very readable and interesting chapter, the author clearly demonstrates the considerable changes made by Napoleon to technical education which made France a leader in the training of engineers and related technicians. Index and bibliographical footnotes.

Aulard, A. *Napoléon Ier et le monopole universitaire: Origines et fonctionnement de l'Université Impériale*. Paris: Armand Colin 1911.
An accomplished work detailing the reforms in education during the Consulate and Empire. All aspects of education are covered, from the primary schools to the establishment of the Imperial University in 1808. Sources include both primary and secondary. Although dated, Aulard's book remains the most complete study of Napoleon's education policies. Index and bibliographical references.

Barnard, Howard C. *Education and the French Revolution.* Cambridge, England: Cambridge University Press, 1969.

Chiefly a survey of educational reforms carried out during the revolutionary years, but two useful chapters (14 and 15) concern the Consulate. Barnard surveys the Chaptal report of 1800, which made proposals for state-controlled education, and the Fourcroy law of 1802, and he compares Napoleon's changes with those made by the revolutionaries. For example, revolutionary schools excluded religious teaching, while Napoleon's did not. Napoleon viewed education as yet another means of extending state control. Bibliographical appendix.

Bradley, Margaret. "Scientific Education versus Military Training: The Influence of Napoleon Bonaparte on the Ecole Polytechnique." *Annals of Science* 32 (1975): 415-449.

Bradley posits that Napoleon's efforts to make the Ecole Polytechnique much more militaristic, with the goal of training citizens to serve an autocratic state, were met with much resistance by the polytechnicians. She has made excellent use of material in both the archives of the Ecole Polytechnique and the Archives Nationales of France. Incorporated into the article are the texts of Napoleon's plans for changes in the Ecole (dated 1807) and his letters and decrees pertaining to the Ecole. Through the use of these and other original documents, the author shows how Napoleon attempted to use the school for his own purposes.

Chevalier, Jean-Claude. "Philologues et linguistes dans leurs institutions." *Communications* 54 (1992): 149-159.

An investigation into the developments of research on the French language and dialects in France after the Revolution. Research under Napoleon was conducted within the framework of statistical studies on the state. The best-known was the 1807 study carried out by the prefects. In addition, Napoleon used the Institut and the Collège de France for the encouragement of teaching and research. The Restoration period accentuated the characteristics of the Imperial University established by Napoleon. Learned societies were founded under Napoleon to encourage research. Bibliography.

Dooley, Edwin L., Jr. "Military Education at the Ecole Polytechnique, 1789-1815." *Consortium on Revolutionary Europe, 1750-1850. Proceedings* 20 (1990): 239-246.

This article focuses on a neglected part of the Ecole Polytechnique's education, the military facet. Courses on subjects as diverse as descriptive geometry, fortification, and topography prepared future engineers and officers with practical knowledge. The military curriculum of the Ecole and the standards it established lasted until well into the nineteenth century. Sources used for this paper include the Ecole's own archives and works by the professor of fortification and director of studies, Colonel Simon François Gay de Vernon, including his 1805 *Traité elémentaire d'art militaire et de fortification*, unpublished theses, and secondary sources. Fifteen notes.

Fourcy, A. *L'Ecole Polytechnique*. Introduction by Jean Dhombres. Paris: Librairie Classique Belin, 1987.
A reprint of Fourcy's history of 1828, written only thirty years after the school's creation, this remains the leading work on the subject. It was reissued for the bicentenary of the French Revolution. Unfortunately for Napoleonic scholars, the book is most detailed up to 1800, each year receiving one chapter. The next five years are discussed in one chapter, and the years from 1806 to 1827 constitute the final chapter. The lengthy introduction reviews the literature on the Ecole.

Frijhoff, W., and D. Julia. "Les Grands Pensionnats de l'ancien régime à la restauration: La Permanence d'une structure éducative." *Annales historiques de la Révolution française* 53 (1981): 153-198.
From the end of the Old Regime to the Restoration, private boarding schools, dominated by military academies, contributed greatly to the formation of French elites. This article stresses the stability of these establishments and postulates that these institutions maintained their reputation after the Revolution, although the numbers of students decreased and there were fewer nobles' sons than previously. Napoleon's creation of the Imperial University in 1808, a body that regulated education, did not substantially change the statute governing private education nor the type of teaching in the old military schools. For the most part, pedagogical methods did not change until the Bourbon Restoration. Eighty-three notes.

Gontard, Maurice. *L'Enseignement primaire en France de la Révolution à la loi Guizot (1789-1833): Des petites écoles de la monarchie d'Ancien Régime aux écoles primaires de la monarchie bourgeoisie*. Paris: Belles Lettres, 1959.

An examination of the regulation of primary education from 1789 to 1833. Gontard considers the changes in education legislation under the various regimes during this period. Part III, (pages 189-264) deals with the Napoleonic era. The author begins with an examination of the new legislation of 1802 and continues with an analysis of the role of Imperial University and the *petites écoles*. This scholarly, well-regarded examination is full of useful information on the topic. Bibliographical references.

_____. *L'Enseignement secondaire en France de la fin de l'Ancien Régime à la loi Falloux, 1750-1850*. Aix-en-Provence: Edisud, 1984.

Similar in format to Gontard's work on primary education, this study deals with the impact of the various governments from the end of the Old Regime to the Falloux law of 1850 on secondary education. Chapter 3, "The Napoleonic Reconstruction from the *Lycées* of 1802 to the Imperial University of 1808," summarizes education policy under Napoleon. The chapter begins with an outline of legislative developments under Chaptal during the Consulate and closes with the creation of the Imperial University in March 1808. Details such as curriculum, salaries of teachers, and the day-to-day operation of the *lyceés* are provided. Both books are fundamental surveys of education under Napoleon. The author is especially interested in the impact of politics on education. Bibliography.

Léon, Antoine. "Promesses et ambiguités de l'oeuvre d'enseignement en France, de 1800 à 1815." *Revue d'histoire moderne et contemporaine* 17 (1970): 846-859.

Léon sketches the developments of professional and technical education in France during the years from 1800 to 1815. He describes the contradictions between Chaptal's modern educational ideas and the infrastructures of the Old Regime which continued to exist during the Napoleonic years. Based on archival and secondary works.

Palmer, R. R. *The Improvement of Humanity: Education and the French Revolution*. Princteon, N.J.: Princeton University Press, 1985.

A clearly written and useful survey of education during the revolutionary and Napoleonic periods. Chapter 7 concerns the changes that took place under Napoleon. Palmer examines the types of schools, primarily the *lycées* and *collèges*, as well as the body which controlled them, the Imperial University. He argues that these schools did not differ substantially from the schools of the Old Regime. Although these schools of Napoleon made the sciences the most important subjects, they did not neglect the humanities. Index, appendix of expenditures of the central government for public instruction, higher learning, and the arts from 1789 to 1812; and bibliographical references.

_____. "Le Prytanée français et les écoles de Paris (1798-1802)." *Annales historiques de la Révolution française* 53 (1981): 123-152.

The French *prytanée*, a precursor to the Napoleonic *lycée*, was organized in 1798 and lasted until 1802. Using numerous documents from the French Archives Nationales, Palmer provides an informative account of the workings of this establishment, which was founded as a boarding school intended predominantly for students, mainly from bourgeois families, attending secondary schools. Topics discussed include the scholarships students received from the state, the curriculum, student numbers, educational background of teachers, social origins of students, and finally their transformation under Napoleon into *lycées*. Forty-two bibliographical notes.

Ponteil, Félix. *Histoire de l'enseignement en France: Les Grandes Étapes, 1789-1964*. Paris: Sirey, 1966.

The first detailed study on the topic of educational legislation in France. Approximately one-quarter of the book deals with the revolutionary and Napoleonic eras. Describes laws passed under the successive revolutionary governments and the Napoleonic administration. Although it does not make for exciting reading, this study contains a wealth of information for any student of the history of educational legislation. Index and bibliographical essay.

Schmidt, Charles. *La Réforme de l'Université Impériale en 1811*. Paris: G. Bellais, 1905.

This slim volume, based on a University of Paris doctoral dissertation, deals with Napoleon's attempt to reform the Imperial University in 1811. During the previous year, he perceived that the university was not sufficiently protected from the competition from ecclesiastical and private schools. In order to discover the extent of their influence, Napoleon had the police conduct an investigation into the situation of education in the realm. The second half of the book reproduces the results of the inquiry from prefects and police commissioners. Schmidt shows how the "university blockade" was as inefficacious as the Continental Blockade. Bibliographical references.

Shinn, Terry. *L'Ecole polytechnique, 1794-1914*. Paris: Presses de la Fondation Nationale des Sciences Politiques, 1980.
Meticulously written and skillfully researched, this work is based on the archives of the school and makes excellent use of the correspondence of the school's students. Founded in 1794 to replace the Old Regime's technical schools, the Ecole was militarized under Napoleon and had become a school for members of the upper bourgeoisie, who used it to maintain their dominant position in society. Bibliography.

Weill, Georges. *Histoire de l'enseignement secondaire en France (1802-1920)*. Paris: Payot et Cie, 1921.
Not intended to be the final word on secondary teaching of boys in France, but an outline of the major stages in its evolution, this study begins with Napoleon's 1802 law, which closed the revolutionary *écoles centrales* and, in Weill's opinion, marked the beginning of a new period in French education, or at least a turning point. A good discussion of the workings of the Imperial University. Bibliography.

Williams, Pearce L. "Science, Education and Napoleon I." *Isis* 47 (1956): 369-382.
This brief yet informative paper examines the impact on modern France of Napoleon's reforms in science education. After a succinct summary of the state of education following the turmoil of the revolutionary years, Williams persuasively argues that Napoleon did far more than restore order to the system. He fundamentally changed the philosophy of education upon which the revolutionary *écoles centrales* rested. Included in the analysis of Napoleon's influence on education and science is a discussion of the *lycée* curriculum, the faculties of letters, science, theology, and medicine in major cities in France and the Empire, and the Ecole Polytechnique. Williams successfully demonstrates Napoleon's lasting

influence on the French educational system. Based on contemporary documents in the Archives Nationales and printed primary sources. Seventy-five notes.

Developments in Science and Medicine

Ackerman, Evelyn Bernette. *Health Care in the Parisian Countryside 1800-1914.* New Brunswick, N.J.: Rutgers University Press, 1990.
This book, which concerns the management and understanding of disease in the department of the Seine-et-Oise from Napoleon to the beginning of World War I, is a mine of information on medicine and disease in one region of France. The first section of the study provides a discussion of the Napoleonic years in the old Isle-de-France. It was Napoleon who established educational and organizational standards for health maintenance in 1803. The focus of the analysis is on diseases such as smallpox, cholera, and typhoid. Illustrations and bibliography.

Ackernecht, Erwin Heinz. *Medicine at the Paris Hospital, 1794-1848.* Baltimore: Johns Hopkins University Press, 1967.
Written by a pioneer of the history of medicine, this work covers the historical aspects of the period of change and development in medicine from the later 1790s. Ackernecht provides much detail about the lives of the Paris doctors Pinel, Brovissario, Corvisart, and others. An invaluable research tool in the study of the history of medicine in Paris. Illustrations, index, and bibliography.

Beaver, D., and R. Rosen. "The Professional Origins of Scientific Co-authorship." *Scientometrics* 1 (1978): 65-84.
The first study of scientific collaboration in historical terms. The authors explore the historical origins of coauthorship and discover that the first professionalized scientific community was that of Napoleonic France. Here collaborative research took place before it did in England and Germany. In contrast to Germany and England, the state supported collaborative research in France. The existence of state-funded institutions such as the Ecole Polytechnique, the Ecole Normale Supérieure, the Musée d'Histoire Naturelle, and the Institut de France encouraged the teaching of science, and their members became part of the official elite under Napoleon. The French state supported system became a model

for its European counterparts during the nineteenth century. Statistical tables and bibliographical notes.

Crosland, Maurice P. *The Society of Arcueil: A View of French Science at the Time of Napoleon I.* Cambridge, Mass.: Harvard University Press, 1967.
A detailed and scholarly study of scientific activity in Paris between 1795 and 1825. The subtitle more accurately describes the subject of this monograph than does the title, as the reader does not encounter the society until Chapter 5. The introductory chapters discuss in some detail Napoleon's patronage of science and the general state of science itself. The author continues by discussing of the various scientific bodies, such as the First Class of the Institut and the Bureau des Longitudes under Napoleon. There is much information on the role played by Berthollet and Laplace in the society which was named for the Paris suburb where they lived. An indispensable work on its topic. Bibliographical references.

Goldstein, Jan Ellen. *Console and Classify: The French Psychiatric Profession in the Nineteenth Century.* New York: Cambridge University Press, 1987.
A detailed and thoughtful discussion of the genesis of French psychiatry. Places the growth of the psychiatric profession in the context of both the medical profession and the idea of professionalism as it developed in France. Key figures in the story are Philippe Pinel and Etienne-Jean Georget. The first section of the book is relevant to Napoleonic period. Discusses the law of 1803, which governed the practice of medicine for most of the nineteenth century. Illustrations, index, and bibliography.

Huard, Pierre. *Sciences, médecine, pharmacie, de la Révolution à l'Empire (1789-1815).* Paris: Dacosta, 1970.
A pioneering work in the history of French medicine, written by a professor of surgery and historian of medicine. The focus of the book, which is encyclopedic in scope, is medicine rather than science or pharmacy. Huard covers all aspects of medicine during this period: military, naval, civil medicine, and surgery. The introductory chapter surveys the scientific background. The medical institutions, and the reforms made by the revolutionaries and Napoleon, are discussed. Huard's experiences as a military doctor are reflected in the book. More than one hundred illustrations,

many in color, enhance this well-produced work. Charts, bibliography, and index of names.

Imbert, Jean. *Le Droit hospitalier de la Révolution et de l'Empire.* Paris: Recueil Sirey, 1954.
Written by a legal historian, this book summarizes the evolution of hospitals and social welfare policy during the revolutionary and Napoleonic era. Pages 147-441 concern the Napoleonic regime. The analysis includes not only France but also the incorporated territories of the Empire. The author proves that the administrative system of hospitals remains essentially the same today as under the Directory and the Empire. Map, bibliographical references in footnotes.

Lesch, John. *Science and Medicine in France: The Emergence of Experimental Physiology, 1790-1855.* Cambridge, Mass.: Harvard University Press, 1984.
A reappraisal of French physiology from the standpoint of several institutional and intellectual contexts. Argues that the fact that physiology arose as a discipline when it did in France was not a coincidence. The upheaval of French life from the Revolution through the Empire to the Restoration strongly marked the educational and professional institutions in which physiology was cultivated. Discusses the development of this profession during the first half of the nineteenth century. Its establishment as a distinct scientific field was one of the great achievements of the Napoleonic regime. Illustrations, index, and bibliography.

Ramsey, Matthew. *Professional and Popular Medicine in France, 1770-1830: The Social World of Medical Practice.* Cambridge, England: Cambridge University Press, 1987.
The medical reforms of both revolutionary and Napoleonic France are dealt with in Chapter 2 of Part I of this fascinating study of professional and popular medicine in France. Ramsey argues that the Napoleonic state reestablished the medical profession on firm ground; modern French medicine began with Napoleon. A detailed, excellently researched examination of the experience of the first generations who lived under the new medical regime, which started in 1803. Illustrations, index, and bibliography.

_____. "Public Health in France." *Clio Medica* 26 (1994): 45-118.

In his study of this topic during the nineteenth century, Ramsey argues that France was a pioneer in public health in that it helped to found the modern public hygiene movement and instituted public health as a scientific discipline. In the first twenty pages of the article, Ramsey outlines developments in this realm of medicine during the revolutionary and Napoleonic period. He stresses the complexity of the history of public health in France which he attributes to the instability of French political regimes. Based on a variety of printed primary and secondary sources. Bibliographical footnotes.

Weiner, Dora B. *The Citizen-Patient in Revolutionary and Imperial Paris*. Baltimore: Johns Hopkins University Press, 1993.
A masterful synthesis of political and medical history. One achievement of the revolutionary and Napoleonic eras was an increased focus on medical problems, with nuns playing a key role. Specializations emerged in geriatrics, psychiatry, neonatology, and pediatrics; smaller hospitals, outpatient facilities, and nursing homes developed. Contains a well-informed section on psychiatry focusing on Pinel and Pussin. Unlike most scholars in this field, the author deals with the role of women both as nurses and as midwives. The best work on its topic since that of Lanzac de Laborie (see Chapter 8). Illustrations, index, and bibliographical references.

_____. "The French Revolution, Napoleon and the Nursing Profession." *Bulletin of the History of Medicine* 46 (1972): 274-305.
An examination of the destruction and reconstitution of the nursing profession. Weiner begins with a survey of the structure of the orders and the role of nurses during the Old Regime, then proceeds with a discussion of the dramatic changes that occurred between 1789 and 1815. The profession was rationalized and modernized by Chaptal, Napoleon's minister of interior, beginning in 1800. An informative and interesting study of a neglected topic, based primarily on printed primary sources. Appendices and extensive bibliographical footnotes.

Chapter 5

THE NAPOLEONIC LEGEND

Barni, Jules. *Napoléon et son historien M. Thiers.* Geneva: Chez les Principaux Librairies, 1865.
This is a direct attack on Thiers and his famous history. The author rejects Thiers' mostly uncritically positive interpretation of Napoleon. Barni argues that Napoleon was a despot who destroyed liberty. The significance of this work is that it stimulated a new debate on Napoleon and his influence. Bibliographical footnotes.

Bonaparte, Louis. *Réponse à Sir Walter Scott sur son Histoire de Napoléon.* Paris: C. J. Trouvé, 1829.
A reply by Louis Bonaparte, former king of Holland and brother of Napoleon I, to Sir Walter Scott's polemical biography of Napoleon (cited below). Bonaparte clearly asserts that Scott's objective is not merely to denigrate the glory of Napoleon but also to humiliate the entire French nation and, in particular, France's immortal armies. These armies were always triumphant; they had not been defeated but compromised by betrayal in 1814. In addition, the author contends that Scott intended to associate Napoleon with all the excesses and horrors of the French Revolution, which were exaggerated by Scott. Scott presented Napoleon as a foreigner in France. Bonaparte "rectifies" several "factual errors" of Scott about Napoleonic battles. Lastly, a volume-by-volume critique is provided. Extremely useful for the legend as an attempt to restore Napoleon's former glory. This work also demonstrates the tremendous impact of Scott's work in France.

Deschamps, Jules. *Sur la légende de Napoléon.* Paris: Honoré Champion, 1931.

A scholarly and critical discussion of the legend, especially in the nineteenth century. Contests the assumptions of Gonnard (cited below), who argued that the legend originated with the Saint Helena writings. Deschamps contends that from the first Italian campaign, Napoleon started to organize his legend, which Deschamps defines as the ensemble of effects in the realm of sentimentality produced by the history of Napoleon not only in France but throughout the whole world. Divided by theme and nation, this work is generally acclaimed to be the best study in comparative literature of the Napoleonic legend. Three appendices, "Popular Napoleonic Legend in England," "From Napoleon to Lamartine," and "Return of the ashes as seen by Alphonse Karr"; bibliographical footnotes, index, and bibliography.

Descotes, Maurice. *La Légende de Napoléon et les écrivains français du XIXe siècle*. Paris: Lettres Modernes, 1967.

The author's stated purpose is to dissociate the historical figure of Napoleon from the legend. Descotes begins by tracing the origins of the Napoleonic legend, which he argues are in the writings of Saint Helena. He continues by examining the role of Napoleon in the works of Madame de Staël, Constant, Lamartine, Vigny, Stendhal, Hugo, Balzac, and Chateaubriand. For each of these writers, Napoleon was either a god or a monster. The section on Madame de Staël, who saw Napoleon as an ogre, is particularly good, as Descotes attempts to disprove or refine some of the stereotypes of their relationship. An intricate analysis. Bibliography.

Galarneau, Claude. "La Légende napoléonienne au Québec." *Recherches Sociographiques* 23 (1982): 163-174.

Galarneau addresses the response to the Napoleonic era in the French-speaking region of Canada that came under British control in 1763. The initial reaction to revolutionary events in France was positive, but the tide turned when war broke out between Britain and France in 1793. The English authorities conducted a propaganda war with the aim of discrediting Napoleon. The divided loyalties of the French-speaking people, their resistance to military service, and their growing admiration for Napoleon, as evidenced in popular songs and in children's names, are investigated. The Napoleonic legend followed a pattern in Quebec similar to that in France and other European countries, beginning as a popular phenomenon. However, it was also present among the more educated classes, appearing prominent journals such as *Le Canadien* and *La Minerve*, and in the theater.

Geyl, Pieter. *Napoleon: For and Against*. London: Jonathan Cape, 1949.
A crucial work in Napoleonic historiography. In chronological order, the author analyzes French schools of thought and individual French historians and writers' views on Napoleon from the early nineteenth century to 1940. Authors and schools are divided into categories of "for" or "against" Napoleon. An invaluable guide to Napoleonic historiography and the legend itself. Maps, indexes, footnotes, and an appendix composed of a chronological table.

Goldsmith, Lewis. *The Secret History of the Cabinet of Napoleon*. London: Richardson, 1811.
Lewis was a contemporary of Napoleon who lived in France for a time during the Consulate and worked for Talleyrand. His work, written after Napoleon's departure from France in 1809, greatly contributed to the dissemination of the "black" legend of Napoleon. He left the country under the threat of arrest. Jacques Godechot contends that Lewis' study is credible because of his knowledge of the "secrets" of French politics at the time. The book enjoyed a huge success in England.

Gonnard, Philippe. *Origines de la légende napoléonienne, l'oeuvre historique de Napoléon à Sainte-Hélène*. Paris: Calmann-Lévy, 1906.
A vast and difficult subject, which Gonnard has discussed in an interesting and competent manner. Although he does not consider the authenticity of some of the literature of Saint Helena, he does establish an important distinction between the memoirs and the memorials, thereby sketching an exact portrait of the memorialists, such as Las Cases, O'Meara, and Montholon. Gonnard believes that Gourgaud was the true biographer of Napoleon. The Napoleonic legend, he asserts, originated at Saint Helena, where Napoleon and his memorialists put forth the thesis that he was the son of the Revolution, that he was the defender of the principles of 1789, and that he upheld the principle of nationalities. This controversial thesis has since been disputed by scholars such as Deschamps and Tulard. Bibliography.

Guérard, Albert Léon. *Reflections on the Napoleonic Legend.* New York: Charles Scribner's Sons, 1924.

Guérard is an American writer of French descent who is sympathetic to Napoleon. In Part I, he examines Napoleon as soldier, administrator, and popular leader, claiming that much of Napoleon's success was attributable to his ability to sell himself to the French people. Part II studies the origins, manifestations, and development of the legend, especially in the Romantic era. Guérard sees Napoleon as a great general, but not a genius, who came to power by circumstances and by outmaneuvering the competition; he brought defeat and misery to France. A valuable introduction to early nineteenth century historiography. Index and bibliographical references.

Hazlitt, William. *The Life of Napoleon Buonaparte.* 4 vols. London: Hunt and Clarke, 1828-1830.

Hazlitt's biography was intended to counterbalance the effect of Scott's anti-Napoleonic account. Unlike Scott, Hazlitt believed that Napoleon was the most outstanding figure of his day, a liberator who freed France and the nations he conquered. Hazlitt was a supporter of the French Revolution, and that was what attracted him to Napoleon. Although he disagreed with Scott's interpretation, he nevertheless borrowed extensively from the latter's nine-volume biography. In addition, Hazlitt depended on sources favorable to Napoleon, such as the Saint Helena literature. This biography was Hazlitt's last major work, and it is renowned for its literary excellence. It contributed to the cult of the Emperor.

Horward, Donald D., and James Friguglietti (commentary). "Napoleon and Sir Walter Scott: A Study in Propaganda." *Proceedings of the 9th Annual Meeting of the Western Society for French History.* Lawrence, Kans.: Western Society for French History, 1982, 133-147.

A study of Scott's works on Napoleon and the evolution of his attitude toward the Emperor. Argues that Scott was part of the "against" camp and stresses that he was a propagandist paid by the British government. Examines various works by Scott including poems, culminating in an analysis of Scott's famous *Life of Napoleon.* An insightful but short article, of interest to scholars looking at the Napoleonic myth. Forty-seven notes.

_____. "Napoleon, His Legend and Sir Walter Scott." *Southern Humanities Review* 16 (1982): 1-13.

Horward begins by stressing the impact of the Saint Helena writings on nineteenth century European writers. One of these was Sir Walter Scott, who, as the author clearly demonstrates, created the black legend of Napoleon. Surveys Scott's attitudes toward Napoleon and his exploits in Europe. Some attention is paid to the sources Scott used for his book. Horward shows the significance of the publication of Scott's *Life of Napoleon* in 1827 for the Napoleonic legend. Based primarily on the literature of the Napoleonic legend, such as the works of Las Cases and O'Meara, and Scott's *Journal* and his *Life*. Thirty-two notes.

Kennett, Lee. "Le Culte de Napoléon aux Etats-Unis jusqu'à la Guerre de Sécession." *Revue de l'Institut Napoléon* 122 (janvier 1972): 145-156.

A survey on the Napoleonic legend in the United States from the time of Napoleon to 1861. The author states that Americans have always had a strong interest in Napoleon, and this attraction started at the time of Napoleon's career. Kennett examines the literature on Napoleon published in the United States, beginning with the first biography, written by George Bourne in 1906. In addition to books, Kennett mentions plays and music about Napoleon written and performed in America. Based on printed primary material and secondary sources. Forty-four notes.

Lucas-Dubreton, Jean. *Le Culte de Napoléon, 1814-1848*. Paris: Albin Michel, 1960.

A well-documented study of the formation of the Napoleonic cult during the first half of the nineteenth century. Like the historian Louis Madelin, Lucas-Dubreton sees the Napoleonic legend as beginning with the tales of Waterloo. The *Memorial* did not invent it, but established it. Useful as a guide for regional research on the cult. Bibliographical references.

Napoléon, Joseph-Charles-Paul Bonaparte. *Napoléon et ses détracteurs*. Paris: Calmann-Lévy, 1887.

Translated and edited by Raphael Ledros de Beaufort as *Napoleon and His Detractors*. London: W. H. Allen, 1888.

Written by Prince Napoleon, son of Jérôme, with the purpose of countering those who had produced works against his uncle, Napoleon Bonaparte. Prince Napoleon was one of the great champions of the Napoleonic legend which depicted the Emperor as a son of the French Revolution and a man of the people. This volume is composed of chapters refuting works by Taine, Metternich, Bourrienne, Madame de Rémusat, LAbbé Pradt, and Miot de Mélito. Taine relied on works by Metternich to write his *Histoire de la France contemporaine*, which Prince Napoleon thought to be of questionable accuracy. Also included is a discussion of the official correspondence and a section on the princes opinions of his uncle.

Rosebury, Archibald Philip Primrose, 5th earl. *Napoleon, the Last Phase*. New York: Harper, 1900.
A brilliant analysis of Napoleon in exile. With its publication in 1900 began the interest of English historians in the problem of Napoleon Bonaparte. Although the book is mostly concerned with the final years of the Emperor's life, it also critically analyzes the different "voices of Saint Helena," the works of Las Cases, Montholon, Antommarchi, O'Meara, and Gourgaud's journal. The first critical analysis of the legend makers of Saint Helena. Index.

Scott, Sir Walter. *The Life of Napoleon Buonaparte, Emperor of the French*. 9 vols. Edinburgh: Ballantyre & Co., 1827. New York: Leavitt and Allen, 1858.
Scott wrote his biography of Napoleon to prevent bankruptcy. Although this popular man of letters insisted his work was objective, it is one of the best-known anti-Napoleonic works ever written. For Scott, Napoleon was a bloody villain. As a work of history, his biography fails considerably, in that it contains numerous factual errors. If it had been written by anyone other than Sir Walter Scott, it might never have been noticed. It caused considerable outcry from Bonapartists at the time. General Gourgaud, at one point, challenged Scott to a duel, but it never materialized. The chief importance of the history is that it articulated the basic anti-Napoleonic argument for the next 150 years; hence it remains important as a source of historiography. For an informative contemporary review of Scott, researchers would do well to read John Stuart Mill's "The Life of Napoleon Buonaparte, Emperor of the French. With a Preliminary View of the French Revolution." *Westminster Review*, IX (April 1828): 251-313. Mill's review has been reprinted in the *Collected Works of John Stuart Mill*, Vol. 20, *Essays on French History and*

Historians, edited by John Robson (Toronto: University of Toronto Press, 1985).

Tulard, Jean. *L'Anti-Napoléon: La Légende noire de l'empereur.* Paris: R. Julliard, 1964.
In this work, using the writings of emigrants and ultras, Tulard demonstrates the origins of the black legend of Napoleon: the ogre who devoured Europe with his armies, a new Attila the Hun. Tulard studies the attempts made by contemporaries, including Constant, Madame de Staël, and Gentz, to create the legend of Napoleon as a monster. Provides biographical notes on the creators of the black legend.

_____. *Le Mythe de Napoléon.* Paris: A. Colin, 1971.
The image of Napoleon has undergone many transformations throughout history. In this work, Tulard examines these changes from the time of his fall from power to the 1960s. Focusing on the works of famous literary figures, both French and foreign writers, including German and French Romantics in the 1830s and 1840s, and Marx and Proudhon in mid-century, Tulard describes the evolving "myth of Napoleon." An excellent guide to the origins and development of the Napoleonic myth. Bibliography, filmography, and discography.

Wren, Keith. "Victor Hugo and the Napoleonic Myth." *European Studies Review*. 10 (1980): 429-458.
Victor Hugo was one of the nineteenth century's greatest proponents of the Napoleonic myth. This article discusses the impact of Napoleon on Hugo's literary output, particularly his poetry. Wren analyzes how Hugo's attitude to Napoleon changed over a fifty-year period, redressing a gap in the study of the interaction of history and literature during this period. Based on contemporary works and secondary sources. Twenty-three notes.

Chapter 6

MILITARY HISTORIES

Alexander, D. W. *Rod of Iron: French Counter-insurgency Policy in Aragon during the Peninsular War.* Wilmington, 1985.
An excellent work examining a neglected topic: the French occupation in Aragon. The author successfully demonstrates that the goals of the French commanders Suchet and Reille were to obtain enough revenue to meet the expenses of the garrison, to suppress Spanish resistance, and lastly, to ease the annexation of the left bank of the Ebro by Napoleon. Spanish resistance, both conventional and guerrilla, is investigated in the light of Suchet's attempts to conciliate the province by using the Church and the local nobility as well as by other methods, such as retaliation, threat, and amnesties. A welcome addition to studies of the Peninsular War. Maps, index, and bibliography.

Alexander, Robert S. *Bonapartism and Revolutionary Tradition in France: The Fédérés of 1815.* Cambridge, England: Cambridge University Press, 1991.
The *fédérés* were a large paramilitary political group that championed Napoleon's cause during the Hundred Days. Although they were active during the Revolution, they had been idle until they were revitalized in 1814 to protect France against foreign and domestic enemies. They were opposed to the restoration of the Bourbon monarchy. This extensive book, based on the author's doctoral dissertation, covers these paramilitary groups in the cities of Dijon, Rennes, and Paris, examining the part they played during the Hundred Days and the second restoration of Louis XVIII. It is the only work on this topic. Index and bibliographical references.

Bartel, Paul. *Napoléon à l'île d'Elbe.* Paris: Perrin, 1947.

A well-regarded and scholarly survey. Bartel has consulted archival material in London and Paris, but a lack of notes makes it difficult to determine from where he derived his knowledge. He paints a vivid portrait of a restless, ambitious, and frustrated Napoleon negligently supervised by Sir Neil Campbell, the British officer whose journal is a major source for the monograph. Subjects under discussion include Napoleon's surrender at Fontainebleau, his voyage to Elba, and the various reforms he introduced on the island. Worth consulting. Maps, illustrations, and bibliographical references.

Becke, Archibald Frank. *Napoleon and Waterloo: The Emperor's Campaign with the Armée du Nord, 1815; A Strategical and Tactical Study.* 2 vols. London: Kegan Paul, 1914, rev. ed., 1939. Reprint of 1914 edition. Freeport, N.Y.: Books for Libraries Press, 1971.
A scholarly, lengthy, chronological, and clearly written narrative by a British officer. The first volume ends with 17 June 1815. It contains many documents and a great deal of information in charts and maps. Overly pro-British, it is nevertheless valuable for its details. Offers a good analysis of Napoleon's masterly conception of an advance with "two wings and a reserve." Becke has, however, been criticized for being too easy on the Emperor and too harsh on his subordinates; his discussion of Wellington is more balanced. Portraits and bibliography.

Bertaud, Jean-Paul. "Napoleon's Officers." *Past and Present* 112 (1986): 91-111.
Using the letters and speeches of Napoleon in addition to numerous laws and decrees, Bertaud investigates the nonmilitary role Napoleon assigned to his officers. He argues that, through a combination of Old Regime and French Revolutionary components, the officer corps was supposed to transform society. The officers originated from different social backgrounds and were able to attain a higher status than civilians. They conveyed to the French people the idea of honor that was taught by Napoleon in the camps. They composed the chief power base of Napoleon's dictatorship. Two tables and one appendix.

Best, Geoffrey. *War and Society in Revolutionary Europe 1770-1870.* Oxford, England: The Clarendon Press, 1982.

A stimulating survey of the impact of war on European society during this period. Best states that a new style of warfare was accomplished by Napoleon and attempts to answer at what cost to society this was achieved. Chapter 9, "Napoleon and the French," is particularly useful to readers interested in Napoleon as a leader, outlining the reasons for his military successes. Sections dealing with the relationship between Napoleon and the French people are very thoughtful and insightful. An intelligent, lively, and innovative work on the social aspects of war. Index and bibliographical references.

Blond, Georges. *La Grande Armée, 1804-1815*. 2 vols. Paris: Robert Laffont, 1979.

This work is more than simply a military history of the Empire. What makes it original is the way it provides a description of the army that formed the bulwark of the Napoleonic state. Through the quasi-yearly campaigns, Blond depicts a continually changing army. The horrors of war—its dirtiness and atrocities—comprise the focus of this passionate account. The author clearly demonstrates which sacrifices made the Empire great. Maps, index, and bibliography.

Cate, Curtis. *The War of the Two Emperors: The Duel between Napoleon and Alexander, Russia 1812*. New York: Random House, 1985.

Surprisingly, there is a lack of good histories of the Russian campaign by English-speaking scholars. This work is a welcome contribution. Cate focuses on the leaders and, in doing so, deals with figures such as Field Marshal Kutuzov more realistically than Tolstoy did in *War and Peace*. Although a well-written survey drawn from primary sources, it is rather one-sided, leaning to the French (perhaps because of a majority of French sources) and weak on the Russian domestic scene, which is crucial to an understanding of their contribution to the war. Nevertheless, Cate's book serves as a useful, and rare, introduction to the Russian campaign. Index and bibliography.

Chandler, David G. *The Campaigns of Napoleon*. New York: Macmillan, 1966.

A detailed description of Napoleon's campaigns and battles, including a thorough examination the Emperor's concepts of tactics and strategy by an expert from the Royal Military Academy, based primarily on the printed *Correspondance* and secondary sources. The years between 1800 and 1815 are addressed on pages 253-1,095. Stressing Napoleon's personal role, battles in which Napoleon did not participate are not included. Of great value are the chapters depicting the evolution of the French army. Chandler relates Napoleon's practice of warfare to that of his predecessors before and during the French Revolution. This is generally considered the best narrative in English on Napoleon's military career. Maps, illustrations charts, indexes, and bibliography. Appendix composed of a glossary of military terms.

Chardigny, Louis. *Les Maréchaux de Napoléon*. Paris: Flammarion, 1946. Reprint. Paris: Tallandier, 1977.
A general history of the marshalate, composed of brief biographies of the marshals. Chardigny considers why Napoleon was induced to revive the French marshalate and how he chose the men whom he honored with this dignity. He argues that it is impossible to discuss Napoleon without also discussing these men, who formed an intimate entourage during all of his campaigns. What was Napoleon's opinion of his closest companions? How did he treat them? What kind of men were they? What were their wives like? These are a few of the interesting questions under consideration in this intelligent survey of Napoleon's marshals. Bibliography.

Connelly, Owen. *Blundering to Glory: Napoleon's Military Campaigns*. Wilmington, Del.: Scholarly Resources, 1987.
A thoughtful, well-written, and original reassessment of Napoleon as a military commander. Connelly argues that although Napoleon was a military genius, he did not have an overall design for his campaigns, and his success came from his innate abilities, his generals, and the blunders of his enemies. He often won battles by sheer luck. Generally recognized as the most credible interpretation of Napoleon's multifaceted military makeup, the study covers Napoleon from his youth to the Waterloo debacle. Although the author is critical of Bonaparte, he concludes, like most historians, that "Napoleon was probably the greatest commander of all time." Where Connelly differs from many of his predecessors is in his assertion that Napoleon's "genius lay in scrambling and not in carrying out a preconceived plan." A good use of maps compliments the excellent narrative. Index, illustrations, and bibliography.

Corbett, Sir Julian Stafford. *The Campaign of Trafalgar*. London: Longmans, Green, 1910. New ed., 2 vols. London: Longman, 1919.

A commendable narration of the campaign, stressing the services of the men who assisted Nelson. Corbett reconsiders the campaign, stating that it was not simply a defense against invasion but an offensive closely tied to the development of the Third Coalition. In this balanced account, Nelson's role is not overrated, and the strategists Barham and Cornwallis are given their well-deserved credit for the victory. Corbett is critical of Napoleon in viewing his attempt to control the Channel as impracticable and desperate. Much of his book is based on Desbrière's documentary evidence (see below). Index and bibliography.

Delmas, Jean. *Histoire militaire de la France. Vol. 2, De 1715 à 1871*. Paris: Presses Universitaires de France, 1992.

The title of this work is not entirely accurate, as it is more concerned with noncombat matters than with military campaigns or warfare in general. Chapters 12 and 13 deal with all matters of detail related to Napoleon's soldiers: conscription, the organization of the army, military schools, and the attitude of the army toward the regime. Other sections are concerned with the wars of the Empire from Ulm and Austerlitz to Waterloo. Finally, the last chapter, on the Napoleonic era, concerns the Navy during both the Revolution and Empire. These chapters provide excellent summaries of the topics under consideration. With the exception of authors Richard Cobb and Samuel Scott, English works on the subject are neglected. The essays are based almost entirely on French secondary sources. Index and bibliography.

Desbrière, Edouard. *La Campagne maritime de 1805: Trafalgar*. Paris: R. Chapelot, 1907. Edited and translated by Constance Eastwick as *The Naval Campaign of 1805*. Oxford, England: The Clarendon Press, 1933.

An extremely well-researched work and therefore the classic on this battle. Desbrière gives a thorough account of the French side of the battle based upon the logs of French and Spanish ships and reports and journals of the officers. Desbrière's work reveals the defects in Napoleon's battle plans and the almost insurmountable difficulties that faced the Spanish and French fleets. Particularly useful for researchers are the rare documents, the footnotes, and the appendices. In addition, extensive tables provide the names of ships, their armaments, and commanding officers.

Dodge, T. A. *Napoleon: A History of the Art of War.* 4 vols. Boston: Houghton Mifflin, 1904-1907. Reprint. New York: AMS Press, 1970.
In its time, it was the best military history of Napoleon. Although outdated, it remains a serviceable study of warfare during the Napoleonic era. Volumes 2-4 deal with the years from 1800 to 1815. Dodge's work is based on the premise that the "great captain is the product of exceptional intellect, exceptional force of character and exceptional opportunity." On the whole, the author is complimentary to Napoleon. Contains many particulars on campaigns and battles. Illustrations and maps.

Dupont, Marcel. *Napoléon en campagne.* Vol. 2, *De Marengo à Essling.* Paris: Hachette, 1952.
Dupont is a expert on Napoleon, his family, and the campaigns. This second volume in a series on his campaigns attempts to accurately portray his manner of living and working. The author studies Napoleon's triumphant period, 1800-1809, covering battles in Italy, Germany, Austria, and Spain. Not only does this book tell the story of Napoleon's victories; it also demonstrates the merits of his opponents and the often imperfect state of Napoleon's own armies.

Elting, John R. *Swords around a Throne: Napoleon's Grande Armée.* New York: Free Press, 1988.
More than thirty years of research went into this book, in which Elting considers almost every possible subject pertaining to the Grand Army: its origins, development, organization, personnel, training, weaponry, food, pay, tactics, and strategy. This wealth of information should be used as a research tool rather than a source of knowledge about the political or institutional importance of the Grand Army for the era. Illustrations, maps, index, and bibliography.

Emsley, Clive. *British Society and the French Wars, 1793-1815.* London: Macmillan, 1979.
Emsley examines in chronological sequence the impact of the French wars on British society and government. He argues that over the period under consideration, the impact of the Napoleonic

wars was more pervasive than that of the Industrial Revolution. Topics covered include the methods and problems of recruitment, the growth of wartime taxation, and the economic effects of the wars in stimulating some sectors and depressing others. An excellent study of the Napoleonic wars viewed from the English perspective. Index and bibliography.

Epstein, Robert M. *Napoleon's Last Victory and the Emergence of Modern War.* Lawrence: University Press of Kansas, 1994.
In this study of Napoleon's last victorious campaign, Epstein is interested in restoring military history to its roots: the management of warfare. The social and economic consequences of warfare are not under consideration here. He attempts to place the Franco-Austrian War in the context of the emergence of modern warfare. Through his analysis of the battles that composed Franco-Austrian War of 1809, he proves that this campaign marked a major turning point in the evolution of warfare. For the first time, enormous armies composed of conscripts and formed into army corps operated under a broad strategic plan across many theaters. Modern warfare had begun. Maps, index, and bibliographical references.

Esdaile, Charles J. *The Spanish Army in the Peninsular War.* Manchester: Manchester University Press, 1988.
A very important study of the role of the Spanish army during the Napoleonic wars between 1808 and 1814. Previous works about this subject have focused either on the British forces or on the Spanish guerrillas. Instead, Esdaile concentrates on the regular Spanish army. He opens with an account of the army at the time of the Old Regime, which was an army whose upper echelons were dominated by the nobility. He continues by chronicling the changes and developments during the revolutionary and Napoleonic years, particularly during the 1808 to 1814 period. Maps, index, and bibliography.

_____. *The Wars of Napoleon.* London: Longman, 1995.
In a new series entitled Modern Wars in Perspective, this work intends to bring military history into the center of academic literature. Esdaile makes his position clear in the preface, where he explains the need for yet another book on Napoleonic warfare. He states that the Napoleonic bibliography is uneven in that there are far too many books on the famous marshals and the great battles and not enough on the impact of Napoleon's wars on

European society. His analytical study sets out to discover the purpose, consequences, and significance of these wars. Particularly useful is the author's focus on the social, economic, and political aspects of the wars set in an international context. Smaller states such as Sweden and Sicily, often neglected, are given coverage in this intelligent and innovative book. Based primarily on printed secondary sources. Index, maps, detailed chronology, and bibliographical essay.

Forrest, Alan. *Conscripts and Deserters: The Army and French Society during the Revolution and Empire.* Oxford, England: Oxford University Press, 1989.

An exemplary piece of historical scholarship based on the archives of fourteen French departments, the best study on the topic. The author studies the response of villages to the military conscription under the French Revolution and Napoleon. In this account of the struggle between a French state determined to obtain the necessary recruits for war and a rural population which did everything to resist this pressure, Forrest demonstrates that both conscripts and village people often became rebels not for ideological opposition, but merely because they opposed a central government whose conscription disrupted their lives. Maps and bibliographical references.

Foucart, Paul Jean. *Campagne de Prusse (1806) d'après les archives de la guerre.* 2 vols. Paris: Berger-Levrault, 1887-1890.

An essential work on the topic. Chronicles the capitulation of Erfurt, the changes in the army of the line, communication systems, and the various battles. Contains a large collection of correspondence, including Marshall Soult's letters, arranged chronologically. Foucart also included many other documents, notes, charts, and lists.

Gates, David. *The Spanish Ulcer: A History of the Peninsular War.* New York: W. W. Norton, 1986.

One of the rare accounts in English that includes details on the campaigns of the Spanish armies. The first 469 pages are a general chronological survey of the war based on primary sources, both printed and archival. The rest of the book consists of appendices that provide detailed lists of various army units. Gates interprets the war as France's Vietnam. He argues that the French forces were the cause of France's downfall. An introduction to the topic;

for an in-depth study, see Charles Oman's multivolume work (cited below). Illustrations, maps, index, and bibliography.

Glover, Michael. *The Peninsular War, 1807-1814: A Concise Military History.* Newton Abbot: David & Charles, 1974.
Glover is one of Britain's best military historians, and this is one of the most competent single-volume studies on the subject. Glover sketches the political environment in Europe and provides information on the character, equipment, and tactics of Napoleon's opposing armies. He covers the campaigns of Moore, Wellington, and Napoleon. All aspects of the war between England and France in the Peninsula are presented. Readers should keep in mind that Glover draws his information largely from British sources and thus presents a rather one-sided view, favorable to the British. Illustrations and bibliography.

Glover, Richard. "The French Fleet, 1807-1814: Britain's Problem and Madison's Opportunity." *Journal of Modern History* 39 (1967): 233-252.
A fresh look at Napoleon's development of the French navy from 1807 to 1814. Glover suggests that Napoleon's navy was more of a threat than previously believed. Even Napoleon's loss at Trafalgar did not destroy his power to launch naval warfare. From 1807 onward, Napoleon put much effort into building ships, frigates, and new harbors throughout the ports of his empire. His entire naval effort was channeled into one goal: the destruction of Great Britain. Seventy-nine bibliographical footnotes.

Hamilton-Williams, David. *Waterloo: New Perspectives, the Great Battle Reappraised.* London: Arms and Armour Press, 1993.
The main objective of Hamilton-Williams' study is to reappraise the battle of Waterloo, on the basis of new evidence. Generally accepted as one of the best accounts of the political and military aspects of the battle, this is an unbiased account. In his preface, the author states that too many histories of Waterloo have been written from a national perspective, heading to a serious distortion of the facts. Hamilton-Williams spent six years researching the book, and his materials come from British state papers from the Foreign Office, Cabinet, and Treasury; contemporary politicians' correspondence; and the archives of Germany, France, and the Netherlands. Given the vast amount of material collected, the author was unable to include everything in one book. The present

volume concerns the campaign of 1815. Hamilton-Williams is currently preparing a second volume, "The Fall of Napoleon: The Final Betrayal," which is on the topic of the campaigns of 1813 and 1814. Finally, a third book, "Joachim Murat: The Last Campaign, 1815," concerning the Neapolitan campaign, leading to the judicial murder of Napoleon's brother-in-law, will complete the series. Illustrations, maps, plans, index, and bibliographical references.

Harford, Lee Shartle, Jr. "The Bavarian Army under Napoleon, 1805-1813." Ph.D. dissertation. Tallahassee: Florida State University, 1988.
A study of the role and achievements of the Bavarian army under Napoleon from 1805 to 1813. Harford's thesis is that Napoleon's interests were similar to those of Bavaria, and therefore they formed a military alliance. He demonstrates the crucial role of the Bavarian army in the War of the Fifth Coalition in 1809 in defeating the Austrians, and later its role in destroying Napoleon's armies in 1814. Of concern to military historians and others interested in the details of one contemporary army and its impact. Bibliography.

Horward, Donald D. *Napoleon and Iberia: The Twin Sieges of Ciudad Rodrigo and Almeida, 1810.* Tallahassee: University of Florida Press, 1984.
Narrated from the French perspective and based on materials from the Portuguese, Spanish, British, and French archives, and in particular the papers of Massena, Horward's is an outstanding scholarly account. A specialist in the campaigns of Spain and Portugal, he has depicted the sieges of Ciudad Rodrigo and Almeida by the French in 1810 in meticulous detail, besginning with an examination of the conditions of war in the Iberian peninsula and continuing to the French capture of Almeida. Illustrations, index, and bibliography.

Houssaye, Henry. *1814*. Paris: Perrin, 1888. Translated by R. S. McClintock as *Napoleon and the Campaign of 1814*. London: Rees, 1914.
_____. *1815: La Première Restauration: Le Retour de l'île d'Elbe. Les Cent Jours.* Paris: Perrin, 1893.
_____. *1815: Waterloo.* Paris: Perrin, 1898. Translated by A. Euan-Smith as *1815: Waterloo.* London: A & C Black, 1900.

_____. *1815: La Seconde Abdication. La Terreur blanche.* Paris; Perrin, 1905.

_____. *Le Retour de Napoléon.* Paris: Flamarrion, 1933. Translated by T. C. Macaulay as *The Return of Napoleon.* London: Longmans, Green, 1934.

Henry Houssaye wrote several tomes of Napoleonic military history in the 1880s. At the time, they achieved great success in both scholarly and literary terms. For detail and extensiveness, they remain unsurpassed. Each volume follows the same pattern of a dense, chronological narrative of the events beginning in February 1814. Although his work is scholarly and based on primary sources such as contemporary memoirs and newspapers, readers should be cautioned that Houssaye had a tendency to quote Napoleon's words inaccurately and to attribute to him things he never said—presumably a result of his admiration of Napoleon. In addition, Houssaye denounced all those he considered to be opponents of Napoleon, including royalists and foreigners. In spite of these shortcomings, and if read with caution, Houssaye's narratives are still of value for their detail. *Le Retour de Napoleon* is composed of sections from his *1815* series. Bibliographical footnotes.

Johnson, David. *Napoleon's Cavalry and Its Leaders.* London: B.T. Batsford, 1978.

Written by a British soldier and writer, this work summarizes the battlefield record of Napoleon's cavalry between 1796 and 1815. It covers the often difficult relationship between Napoleon and his major cavalry commanders. Based on printed sources, the method is biographical. Included are sketches of many commanders, such as Bessières, Ney, Kellerman, Murat, and Sebastiani. Eight leaves of plates, index, and bibliography.

Jomini, Antoine Henri de. *Vie politique et militaire de Napoléon racontée par lui-même, au tribunal de César, Alexandre et de Frédéric.* 4 vols. Paris: Angelin, 1827. Another edition. 2 vols. Brussels: Petit, 1841. In English. *Life of Napoleon.* Translated by Henry Wager Halleck. 4 vols. and atlas. New York: van Nostrand, 1864.

Jomini was a leading military theoretician during the nineteenth century. He served as an officer in the French army from 1804 to 1813, and later in the Russian army. In his writing, he stressed strategy as the key to success. His history of Napoleon was one of the most influential military sources of the century. Although his *Vie* has been criticized as more a work of theory than of tactics, and some factual details have been queried, it continues to be a crucial guide to the military history of the period.

Lachouque, Henry. *The Anatomy of Glory: Napoleon and His Guard.* Translated by Anne S. K. Brown. Providence, R.I.: Brown University Press, 1962.
Lachouque's is an outstanding contribution to the history of the Napoleonic wars, which will be of interest to collectors and students. Written in a lively narrative, it describes the birth, life, and death of the Imperial Guard. The account is constructed around quotations from the letters and reports of the participants. The illustrations are of excellent quality and number 173, with 90 in color, many never published before. Most are of uniforms, but there is also a good selection of battle scenes and personal portraits. The book also contains 14 maps and plates of the general's great battles. Lachouque does not, however, contribute anything new to our knowledge of Napoleonic warfare. His is an examination of the past through the eyes of a soldier rather than those of an historian. The work is also useful for its account of the Napoleonic legend.

_____. *The Last Days of Napoleon's Empire: From Waterloo to St. Helena.* Translated by Lovett F. Edwards. London: Allen and Unwin, 1966.
A well-written account of the fifty days from Waterloo to Napoleon's departure for Saint Helena, providing a good analysis of the weaknesses of the regime at this moment in its history. These included Napoleon's tactical errors, the serious defects in the Imperial Army (particularly the soldiers' lack of discipline), and the general weaknesses that followed the defeat at Waterloo. Fouché's intrigues also are examined in great detail. This thorough study provides an excellent elucidation of the numerous problems after Waterloo. Bibliography.

_____. *Napoleon's Battles: A History of His Campaigns.* Translated by Roy Monkom. London: Unwin, 1966.
A general study of Napoleon's campaigns, taken from the conquest of Italy in 1796-1797 to the Battle of Waterloo. The author writes with authority, and the work provides a valuable introduction, but readers should keep in mind that the author does have a romantic

allegiance to Napoleon and his armies. Maps, index, and illustrations.

Langsam, W. C. *The Napoleonic Wars and German Nationalism in Austria*. New York: Columbia University Press, 1930. Reprint. New York: AMS Press, 1930.

A study of the components leading to the rise of nationalism in Austria during the Napoleonic years. Factors considered include the French ideas of liberty and equality as well as Napoleon's arrogance. The government's efforts to stimulate this nascent nationalism through the use of the press and Count Stadion's policies are examined. In addition, the wars of the period, which in many ways were responsible for the development of nationalism, are discussed. A comprehensive work based on a Ph.D. dissertation which draws heavily on archival sources. Bibliography.

Le Gallo, Emile. *Les Cents Jours: Essai sur l'histoire intérieure de la France depuis le retour de l'île d'Elbe jusqu'à la nouvelle de Waterloo*. Paris: Alcan, 1924.

A published French doctoral thesis completed in 1923. It is scholarly, detailed, and chronological. Almost entirely based on original sources and much more objective than Houssaye's work, Le Gallo concentrates on the internal history of France rather than on Napoleon the man, describing how liberals composed with Napoleon and how royalists maneuvered against him. Bibliographical footnotes.

Lynn, J. A. "Toward an Army of Honor: The Moral Evolution of the French Army, 1789-1815." *French Historical Studies* 16 (Spring 1989): 152-182.

An investigation of the development of the French army between 1789 and 1815. Lynn's thesis is that the French army changed in aspects more fundamental than tactics or command. The moral and motivational principles of the army were transformed from revolutionary virtue to Napoleonic honor. The article includes a response by Owen Connelly who disagrees with Lynn's use of Montesquieu as an authority on military virtue and honor. Lynn, in turn, replies to Connelly's objections. A lively and insightful discussion of the evolution of the French army.

Mackenzie, Norman, Ian. *The Escape from Elba: The Fall and Flight of Napoleon 1814-1815*. Oxford, England: Oxford University Press, 1982.
A detailed and largely objective narrative from March 1814 to March 1815. Despite its title, it deals little with the fall and flight of Napoleon. The fall is dispensed with in the first chapter, and the flight is not discussed until Chapter 18. In the intervening two hundred pages, one finds a chronicle of the ten months Napoleon spent on this island. Still the best work in English on its theme. Illustrations, maps, index, and bibliography.

Mackesy, Piers. *The War in the Mediterranean, 1803-1810*. London: Longmans, Green, 1957. Reprint. Westport, Conn.: Greenwood Press, 1961.
A study of naval operations in the Mediterranean and land operations in Sicily and southern Italy. Covers a previously neglected aspect of the war in the Mediterranean against Napoleon. A balanced view which does not revere Nelson. Mackesy states that naval control of the Mediterranean was not guaranteed by the British victory at Trafalgar. Illustrations, maps, and bibliography.

Mahan, Alfred Thayer. *The Influence of Seapower upon the French Revolution and Empire. 1793-1812*. 2 vols. London: Sampson Low, 1892-1893.
Mahan wrote with a specific purpose, which was to persuade the generation of the 1890s of the importance of strong navies. With this in mind, the author, a captain in the United States Navy, produced an influential history of the Napoleonic struggle with England, the standard authority on this subject for years. He interpreted the French war with England as one of commerce, and it was Britain's control of the seas that made France unsuccessful.

Maine, René. *Trafalgar: Napoleon's Naval Waterloo*. Translated by Rita Eldon and B. W. Robinson. New York: Scribner, 1957.
A well-written survey. Depicts an interesting picture of the French fleets under the Consulate and Empire. Demonstrates that crews were usually unprepared and ill-trained. Presents a sympathetic view of French commanders and clearly shows Napoleon's anger at finding his fleets less tractable than the armies. Illustrations.

Manceron, Claude. *Austerlitz: The Story of a Battle*. Translated by George Unwin. New York: W. W. Norton, 1966.
An account of the important victory at Austerlitz in 1805 by a novelist and an amateur historian. Places the battle in its European setting, with most of the book dealing with battle details. Strategic minutiae are explained for nonmilitary experts. A balanced account. Illustrations, maps, index, and bibliography. Appendix composed of a revolutionary calendar.

Marshall-Cornwall, James H. *Napoleon as Military Commander*. Princeton, N.J.: Van Nostrand, 1967.
Considered a classic introduction to the subject, this is an analysis of Napoleon's campaign written by a British general and based largely on Napoleon's *Correspondance*. To compress Napoleon's battles into three hundred pages is a considerable achievement, but in doing so something must suffer. In this case, it is analysis. A very factual approach; battles tend to be oversimplified. Illustrations, maps, and bibliography.

Matthews, Joseph J. "Napoleon's Military Bulletins." *Journal of Modern History* 22 (1950): 137-144.
A study of Napoleon's military bulletins from the perspective of propaganda. Matthews asserts that their content, the methods of their distribution, and their reception reveal Napoleon to be an expert at psychological warfare. He defines the term "bulletin" in the Napoleonic context, which meant a newsletter recounting a battle, written by the Emperor himself. Matthews questions the conventional wisdom that the bulletins are useful only for gaining insights into the Emperor's character. Indeed, as Matthews shows, they demonstrate his skills as a propagandist. A concise and thoughtful introduction to this topic. Forty-two bibliographical notes.

Moody, Walton Smith. "The Introduction of Military Conscription in Napoleonic Europe, 1798-1812." Ph.D. dissertation. Durham, N.C.: Duke University, 1971.
A study of the Napoleonic impact on conscription from the Jourdan law of 1798 to the Russian campaign of 1812. Based on a variety of primary sources, including the correspondence of Napoleon and his officers, as well as memoirs, decrees, and other legislation concerned with conscription. The author deals with all aspects of

conscription and the problem of desertion under Napoleon in all parts of the Empire. Maps and bibliography.

Morvan, Jean. *Le Soldat impérial (1800-1815)*. Paris: Plon, 1904.
A survey of the workings of the Imperial Army, discussing topics such as how it was drafted, clothed, paid, fed, drilled, and armed. Morvan's aim is to demonstrate, from the statistics about military budgets, reports on arsenals, and conscription lists, the slow evolution of the Emperor's megalomania and his deliberate blindness to the limits of the possible. What appears on the surface to be a book of boring statistical data emerges as a fascinating account of Napoleon's personality, chronicling the transformation of one of the greatest generals of all time into a dreamer who believed he could accomplish the unthinkable and who refused to take any form of advice. An excellent study in the decline of the Emperor's judgment and personality.

Napier, Sir William Francis Patrick. *History of the War in the Peninsula and in the South of France from the Year 1807 to the Year 1814*. 6 vols. London: Boone, 1828-1840.
A monumental work of literature written by a British officer who served in some of the important campaigns of the Peninsular War. Napier amassed a great amount of information about the war, especially from some of the leading participants, including Wellington. Included are conversations with Wellington. This work has been praised for its literary merit but criticized for its factual inaccuracies and for its one-sidedness. Nevertheless, it is a military classic that has influenced all succeeding works on the topic. Plates and maps.

O'Brien, Patrick Karl. "The Impact of the Revolutionary and Napoleonic Wars, 1793-1815, on the Long-Run Growth of the British Economy." *Review: Journal of the Fernand Braudel Center for the Study of Economies, Historical Systems, and Civilizations* 12, no. 3 (Summer 1989): 335-395.
A consideration of the relationship of the French revolutionary and Napoleonic wars from 1793 to 1815, and the rise of the British economy. Heavily statistically oriented, the article centers on the following topics: changes in Britain's wealth, losses in manpower, effects of warfare upon agriculture, industry, foreign commerce, capital formation, and consumption. O'Brien suggests

that the economy as a whole did not suffer as a result of the conflict. Tables and bibliography.

Oman, Sir Charles. *A History of the Peninsular War*. 7 vols. Oxford: The Clarendon Press, 1902-1930. Reprint. London: Greenhill Press, 1995.
Based on material from the archives of England, France, Spain, and Portugal, as well as family papers, this is one of the finest English-language military histories. At the time of its publication, it was called a masterpiece by contemporary reviewers. Oman spent more than a dozen years collecting the material for this multivolume set, which took nearly thirty years to complete. A very detailed, masterful study which corrects previous errors in the work of William Napier. Moreover, it is a balanced study: the author admires Napoleon the soldier but detests Napoleon the politician. Remains the standard work on the Peninsular War. Index.

Palmer, Alan Warwick. *Alexander I: Tsar of War and Peace*. London: Weidenfeld and Nicolson, 1974.
Although technically a biography of the Russian tsar, this work contains several chapters useful to students of the Napoleonic era. An excellent source of information for the Russian interpretation of the events, such as the execution of the duke d'Enghien, the Battle of Austerlitz, the Treaty of Tilsit, the Continental System, Napoleon's invasion of Russia, and the allied invasion of France. Given the paucity of works in English on Russia during this period, Palmer's study provides a very useful contribution. Maps, genealogical table, plates, index, and bibliography.

Parker, Harold T. *Three Napoleonic Battles*. Durham, N.C.: Duke University Press, 1983.
A comparison of three renowned Napoleonic battles, Friedland (1807), Essling (1809), and Waterloo (1815). Parker explains the reasons for the decline in Napoleon's strategies and tactics, arguing that what links the three battles is Napoleon's temperament and the increasing inflexibility that characterized his later military career. Parker is best in clearing up minor discrepancies between eyewitness reports about events on the battlefield. Much emphasis is on tactical details. Maps, index, footnotes, and bibliography.

Peruta, Franco Della. "War and Society in Napoleonic Italy: The Armies of the Kingdom of Italy at Home and Abroad," in *Society and Politics in the Age of Risorgimento*, edited by John A. Davis and Paul Ginsbourg. Cambridge, England: Cambridge University Press, 1991, 26-48.
A sociological analysis of the Italian Napoleonic army. The article opens with a discussion of army personnel, including the numbers of officers and their living conditions. Examines the roles of soldiers in Russia and Spain, the main theaters of war, as well as their impact in the Kingdom of Naples, Switzerland, Dalmatia, the Illyrian provinces, and Germany. Maps, index, and bibliography. Provides a useful introduction to this author's major ideas and summarizes his full-length study *Escercito e societa nell'Italia napoleonica: Dalla Cisalpina al Regno d'Italia* (Milan: F. Angeli, 1988).

Petre, Francis Loraine. *Napoleon's Campaign in Poland, 1806-7: A Military History of Napoleon the First*. London: Low, Marston, 1901.

_____. *Napoleon's Conquest of Prussia-1806*. London: John Lane, The Bodley Head, 1907.

_____. *Napoleon and the Archduke Charles*. London: John Lane, The Bodley Head, 1909. Reissued. London: Arms and Armour Press, 1976.

_____. *Napoleon's Last Campaign in Germany, 1813*. London: John Lane, The Bodley Head, 1912.

_____. *Napoleon at Bay, 1814*. London: John Lane, The Bodley Head, 1914.

This five-volume series on the Napoleonic campaigns from 1801 to 1814 offer clearly written, thorough accounts of the battles dealing with the origins of the wars, the armies, their weaponry, their strategies, and their leaders. Because of their factual accuracy and in the absence of a better work, they continue to remain the standard texts in English. Maps, illustrations, indexes, and bibliographies in most volumes. Selections from the five volumes have been reprinted by E. Albert and A. Nofi in *Napoleon at war: Selected Writings of F. Loraine Petre* (New York: Hippocrene books, 1984), a good introduction to the five volumes.

Phipps, Ramsay Weston. *The Armies of the First French Republic and the Rise of Napoleon's Marshalls*. 5 vols. Reprint. Westport, Conn.: Greenwood Press, 1980.

A standard history of the war, this vast and detailed scholarly work is generally considered one of the best English-language military histories of the period. An exhaustive list of authorities are consulted, and almost every page is documented, but the work is written in the style of the valiant gentleman whose life was spent as a "soldier of the Queen," and in contributing to the greatness of the British Empire. Argues that one cannot understand the Consulate and Empire without first studying the Revolution. Map.

Pivka, Otto von. *Armies of the Napoleonic Era*. Newton Abbott: David and Charles, 1979.

A very detailed description of the composition, uniforms, equipment, and tactics of the armies of the Napoleonic era, this is one of the best works on the subject. Provides an immense amount of information not available elsewhere in English. Although Pivka concentrates on the armies of the major powers, those of smaller states are also given attention. Part I covers weapons, equipment, tactics, and national sections. Part II deals with all armies of the epoch and weapon effectiveness. Illustrations and bibliography.

_____. *Navies of the Napoleonic Era*. Newton Abbott: David and Charles, 1980.

Pivka's book on the navies follows a plan similar plan to that of his previous work on the armies (cited above). He has written a concise, readable account of the navies, the ships, and their achievements from 1792 to 1815. The navies and their battles are considered within the political, social, and economic context. Part I, "Ships and Men," deals with interesting details about the construction of ships, life at sea, and the tactics of European navies, including the British, on a national basis. Part II is military history covering the battles, while Part III, "The National Navies," considers them by country and includes Turkey and the United States in addition to the European countries. Maps, illustrations, bibliography, and appendices.

Read, Jan. *War in the Peninsula*. London: Faber & Faber, 1977.

A study of the war as a whole, not simply the campaigns and battles. Read emphasizes the sacrifices made by the guerrillas and the popular resistance of the Spanish people. The war is interpreted as part of a long-term movement of independence. An unconventional and interesting approach to the war. Illustrations, maps, index, and bibliography.

Riehn Richard K. *Napoleon's Russian Campaign.* New York: McGraw-Hill, 1990.
The most recent treatment of this well-trodden subject. The story is retold accurately, based largely on a new source, Major Freiherr von der Osten Sacken und der Rhein's account, *Der Felzug von 1812* (Berlin, 1901). Riehn's reasons for the French failure are usually convincing, but he tends to underestimate the strategic effects of Napoleon's army in Spain. The work was criticized for sanitizing human suffering in the war. A number of long appendices offer statistical details. Illustrations, maps, portraits, and bibliographical references.

Rogers, Hugh Cuthbert Basset. *Napoleon's Armies.* London: Allen, 1974.
A short and general summary of the French army, written by an officer in the British army. Much detail about the arrangement, function, and equipment of each branch, and about the medical, engineering, signal, and administrative services of the French army as it evolved from Valmy to Waterloo. Rogers' explanation of how Napoleon's army functioned in the field and how it was able to defeat the opposition is inferior to Chandler's in *The Campaigns of Napoleon* (cited above). Illustrations and bibliography.

Ropes, John Codman. *The Campaign of Waterloo: A Military History.* New York: Charles Scribners Sons, 1892.
A detailed, well-documented, and chronological narrative, principally a defense of Napoleon's plans and critical of his subordinates. A master of the copious contemporary literature on the battle, Ropes presents a balanced assessment, analyzing the role of the generals and showing that Napoleon had greatly deteriorated from his earlier campaigns. A valuable treatment in English. Map, index, thirty-two documents, and bibliographical references.

Rothenberg, Gunther, E. *The Art of War in the Age of Napoleon.* London: B. T. Batsford, 1977.
An examination of European wars during the Napoleonic period, rather than simply those dealing with France and Britain. The study starts with a discussion of armies and warfare during the

closing years of the Old Regime. It continues with a survey of each of the revolutionary and Napoleonic wars. Considered to be an commendable survey. As a former soldier, it is not surprising that Rothenberg focused on the realities of warfare rather than military theory, or the impact of warfare on society. Arms, equipment, and tactics provide the primary subjects. Illustrations, maps, plans, index, and bibliography. Appendices composed of statistics on the major battles and sieges.

_____. *Napoleon's Great Adversaries: The Archduke Charles and the Austrian Army, 1792-1814*. London: B. T. Batsford, 1982.
An investigation of the Austrian army and its commander, Archduke Charles, during the revolutionary and Napoleonic eras. A sequel to his previous work, *The Art of War in the Age of Napoleon*, it provides useful information on the state of the Habsburg army and the campaigns between 1792 and 1815. Providing a good deal of detail on the tactics, weapons, uniforms, training, daily life, social origins of the soldiers, and structure of the army, this work fills a gap in our knowledge. Illustrations, maps, index, and bibliography.

_____. "The Origins, Causes and Extension of the Wars of the French Revolution and Napoleon." *Journal of Interdisciplinary History* (Spring 1988): 771-793.
This article seeks to determine whether a general theory on the causes and origins of warfare can be applied to the French revolutionary and Napoleonic wars. Rothenberg argues that the question of the origins of both wars has been the subject of wide debate among historians. Concerning the Napoleonic wars, he posits that Napoleon was the author of his own wars through his expansionist policies; no external or internal forces were responsible for them. Rothenberg concludes that a general theory of causation cannot explain the outbreak of either war. An insightful review of the debates.

Sarramon, Jean. *La Bataille de Vitoria: La Fin de l'aventure napoléonienne en Espagne*. Paris: J.C. Bailly, 1985.
The first study in French of this battle of 21 June 1813, which marked the end of Napoleon's power in Spain. Based on years of work in the French and Spanish archives, Sarramon demonstrates that Wellington's victory was due to superiority in numbers as well as the strategic mistakes of Jourdan, the French military

commander. Discusses the numerous consequences of this battle for the Empire. Illustrations, maps, index, and bibliography.

Saunders, Edith. *The Hundred Days*. London: Longman, 1964.
Saunders concentrates on the Waterloo campaign in ten of the seventeen chapters in this skillfully written narrative account, intended for the layperson. She examines the reasons for the defeat, holding Napoleon principally responsible, although the campaign began brilliantly. However, on those four successive mornings in June, his offensive was delayed. The marshals, according to Saunders, were not without their faults either. She bases much of her factual information on Houssaye, which makes her book a good alternative for those who do not want the density of his study. Good illustrations and maps accompany the volume. Index, appendices, and bibliography.

Schom, Alan. *One Hundred Days: Napoleon's Road to Waterloo*. New York: Atheneum, 1992.
Not simply another narrative detailing the battle itself, Schom's account provides a fine discussion of the political events before and after the battle, including the reaction of the Bourbon monarchy to the return of Napoleon, Napoleon's journey to Paris, the formation of the Grand Army, the French public's response to Napoleon's return, the battle itself, and Napoleon's defeat by the allies. The story is told from a biographical position, and the major actors apart from Napoleon are the Minister of Police, Fouché, the slippery foreign minister Talleyrand, and Marshals Soult and Ney. A significant contribution to our knowledge of the historical circumstances surrounding the Hundred Days. Illustrations, index, and bibliographical references.

_____. *Trafalgar: Countdown to Battle, 1803-1805*. New York: Atheneum, 1990.
Schom's study concentrates on the background to the battle rather than the events of the battle itself. He argues in his Preface that the battle of Trafalgar was the completion of a much longer campaign which had actually started in June, 1803, over two years previously. Other historians who have written on the battle such as Corbett, have overlooked this important fact. His book is therefore really the story of the French preparations for the invasion of Great Britain. This is a well researched work, based on many previously neglected army and navy documents in the

French Archives Nationales and the Royal Navy documents in the British Public Record Office. It makes a contribution to our knowledge of the battle plans from the French side. Illustrations, index, and bibliographical references.

Sherwig, John M. *Guineas and Gunpowder: British Foreign Aid in the Wars with France, 1793-1815*. Cambridge, Mass.: Harvard University Press, 1969.
An original and interesting diplomatic and military history of an important but ignored facet of the French revolutionary and Napoleonic wars. Sherwig provides a thorough account of Britain's financial assistance to her continental allies, which exceeded £65 million, almost half of which was spent between 1810 and 1815. In this analysis of Britain's use of finance to defeat the French, Sherwig demonstrates that the British had a distinct policy which only began to develop in 1804. Fundamental for insight into the structure and financing of the anti-French coalitions. Illustrations, maps, and bibliography.

Tarasulo, Yitzhak Yankel. "The Napoleonic Invasion of 1812 and the Political and Social Crisis in Russia." Ph.D. dissertation. New Haven, Conn.: Yale University, 1984.
An interesting examination of the effects of Napoleon's invasion of Russia on the indigenous peasant population and its relationship with the ruling nobility. Primarily analyzes the reasons why Napoleon did not abolish serfdom as he had done in other parts of Europe; the reaction of the Russian ruling class to Napoleon's ideological menace; the participation of the peasants in the War of 1812; and finally, peasant insurrections. Tarasulo's study is concerned with the extent to which peasant (i.e., popular) uprisings were related to the Napoleonic invasion. He argues that peasant rebellions were more common in regions where Napoleon's occupation was of the longest duration. The Russian army and bands of noblemen expended much energy in putting down these rebellions. Provides a slant on the war not provided in published works on this topic. Bibliography

Tarlé, E. *Napoleon's Invasion of Russia, 1812*. Oxford, England: Oxford University Press, 1942. Reissued. New York: Octagon Books, 1971.
The complete history of the resistance to the invasion of 1812 by the most notable Russian historian of Napoleon. A fusion of

Russian works combined with research by the author, including previously unavailable correspondence. The author's portrayal of the characters involved is brilliant, vividly depicting the resistance of the Russian people and the heroism of the troops, but at the same time criticizing the higher echelons of the military for its lack of coordination and the intrigues between the generals sometimes fostered by the tsar himself. Index.

Thomazi, Auguste Antoine. *Les Marins de Napoleon*. Paris: J. Tallandier, 1978.
Written in 1951 by a French naval officer, this is the first full account of the Napoleonic navy and its men. It is also the first full length study to expose the maritime goals and ideas of Napoleon. Among the topics discussed are the recruitment of sailors and officers, naval schools, and major naval battles. Not only does Thomazi cover the entire period, from Napoleon's youth to his departure for Saint Helena; he also provides a useful index containing short biographies of the important figures in the Napoleonic navy. Indexes, illustrations, and bibliography.

Tone, John Lawrence. *The Fatal Knot: The Guerrilla War in Navarre and the Defeat of Napoleon in Spain*. Chapel Hill: University of North Carolina Press, 1994.
A study of the resistance of the Spanish guerrillas in Navarre to Napoleon's attempt to integrate Spain into the Empire. Tone centers his work on Navarre because it was the region that produced the most effective guerrilla army in the Iberian peninsula. He argues not only that the guerrillas were successful in warfare but also that they came to control the local inhabitants, which was the ultimate objective of guerrilla warfare. Since this important topic was previously neglected by historians, Tone makes a useful contribution. Index and bibliographical references.

Tranié, J., and J. C. Carmigniani. *Napoleon's War in Spain: The French Peninsular Campaigns, 1807-1814*. Translated by Janet S. Mallender and John R. Clements. London: Arms and Armour Press, 1982, 1994.
Based on the notes and papers belonging to the late Commandant Henry Lachouque, whose works were geared to the mass market, this volume is devoted to the history of the Peninsular War. It has a strongly French bias, and more attention is given to the French successes than the allied operations. Nevertheless, the

details of the French struggle are described well. The authors stress the major factors contributing to the French failure in the peninsula, such as the ineffectiveness of the French marshals, the hostility of the Spanish people toward the French, and Wellington's superior ability. A major contribution, given the lack of monographs devoted to this subject. Illustrations, maps, index, and bibliography.

Woloch, Isser. *The French Veteran from the Revolution to the Restoration*. Chapel Hill: University of North Carolina Press, 1979.

The bulk of this book is concerned with the disabled veterans from the revolutionary and Napoleonic wars who were housed in the Hôtel des Invalides. There is a brief section on the Hôtel during the Old Regime and a conclusion dealing with the fate of the injured men during the Restoration. Changes in the government's attitude and policies toward injured soldiers are studied, and the lives of the army veterans are discussed, with reference to with many case histories. Illustrations, maps, index, and bibliography.

_____. "Napoleonic Conscription: State Power and Civil Society." *Past and Present*, 111 (1986): 111-129.

On the basis of contemporary documents of laws and reports contained in the French Archives Nationales, Woloch argues that conscription overshadowed every problem of administration in Napoleonic France. Given its imperial ambitions, the regime depended on it for survival. Woloch maintains that conscription was efficient and effective until 1810, explaining how men were recruited and discussing draft evasion. Napoleon continued to have faith in his men even after 1813, when public opinion was opposed to conscription. A good source of information on this topic. Appendix, "Return by the Prefect of the Department of Hautes-Alpes on the Levée of 1806." Sixty-eight bibliographical notes.

Young, Norwood. *Napoleon in Exile at Elba*. Philadelphia: John C. Winston, 1914.

Young is concerned with events from the entry of the allies into Paris on 31 March 1814 to Napoleon's return from Elba a year later. He contends that despite all signs that the end of the war was near—the allies were about to enter Paris—Napoleon refused to accept the reality of the situation, continuing to believe that he would emerge triumphant. It is from this perspective that Napoleon is considered during his stay at Elba. The work is entirely free from rhetoric and polemic and is carefully documented. Thorough and detailed. Illustrations.

Yorck von Wartenburg, Hans Ludwig Daniel Maximilien (Graf). *Napoleon als Feldherr.* 2 vols. Berlin: Mittler, 1885-1886. Translated by Walter James as *Napoleon as a General.* 2 vols. London: Kegan, Paul, Trench, Trübner, 1902.
Written by an officer of the Prussian general staff, this major work examines Napoleon as a general and is based on Napoleon's official *Correspondance.* He distinguishes Napoleon as the foremost general of all times, brilliant in warfare. Considered an excellent specialized study that influenced the work of Dodge. Index.

Chapter 7

WOMEN DURING THE CONSULATE EMPIRE

Albistur, Maïté, and Daniel Armogathe. *Histoire du féminisme français du moyen âge à nos jours*. 2 vols. Paris: Editions des Femmes, 1977.
Chapter 2, "La Période napoléonienne, les rigueurs du code civil," in Volume 2, provides an excellent introduction to the position of women under Napoleon. Summarizing and analyzing the passages of the Civil Code relevant to women, the authors assess Napoleon's personal input. Other subjects include the attempt by some women to combat their inferior position, Madame de Staël's works and her personal opposition to Napoleon, and the journal *L'Athénée des Dames*. Bibliography in Volume 2.

Burton, June K. "Human Rights Issues Affecting Women in Napoleonic Legal Medicine Textbooks." *History of European Ideas*. 8 (1987): 427-434.
A brief study of the legal codes pertaining to women under Napoleon. Focuses on issues such as rape and infanticide and the laws related to them. Discusses how the Penal Code of 1810 restored the death penalty for infanticide and imposed life sentences on abortionists and women who had abortions, except in those cases in which the abortion was necessary to save the mother's life. Based on printed treatises of legal medicine from Napoleonic France. Fifty-two notes.

Burton, June K., and Jeanne A. Ojala (commentary). "The Contents of Humanistic Manuals of Home Economics during the Napoleonic Era." *Consortium on Revolutionary Europe, 1750-1850: Proceedings* 12 (1983): 681-696.

An examination of the several instruction manuals for French women which were published during the Napoleonic era. These texts reveal the way in which people during the period regarded women and their role in society. Burton challenges the traditional notion that women were viewed as inferior to men. Topics covered include household economics, care of farm animals, marriage, sex, and child-rearing. Based on primary sources.

Cère, Emile. *Madame Sans-Gêne et les femmes soldats, 1792-1815*. Paris: E. Plon, Nourrit et Cie, 1894.
A biographical compendium of various women who fought in the revolutionary and Napoleonic wars. The best-known of these women was Thérèse Figueur, more commonly known as Madame Sans-Gêne. Also included in this collection are chapters on Virginie Ghesquière, the heroine of the Spanish wars, Marie Schellinck, and Angélique Brulon. Napoleon admitted women to the Legion of Honor for their service in the wars. Since this is a relatively neglected topic, Cère's biographical portraits serve as a useful source of information.

Conner, Susan P., and Sally T. Gershman (commentary). "Les Femmes Militaires: Women in the French Army 1792-1815." *Consortium on Revolutionary Europe, 1750-1850: Proceedings* 12 (1982): 290-302.
Based on material from the Archives Nationales, documents from the Bibliothèque Nationale of France, and dossiers in the Service Historique de l'Armée, this article examines women soldiers after the French Revolution of 1789. Provides useful information on the origins and role of these women, who served as fighters rather than the more traditional support personnel. The attitude of the male soldiers toward these women is also discussed. Includes a list of female soldiers on pages 316-317. The only study in English on this subject.

Conner, Susan, and Jeanne A. Ojala (commentary). "The Merveilleuse and the Coquette: Women during the Directory and the First Empire." *Consortium on Revolutionary Europe, 1750-1850: Proceedings* 10 (1980): 49-57.
During the years of the Directory and the First Empire, women lost many of the liberties they had acquired earlier, during the French Revolution. This change is demonstrated in an examination of the life of Laure Junot, duchesse d'Abrantes, who had a

prominent salon in Paris. When she began to interfere in politics, she and her husband fell out of Napoleon's favor. His treatment of the couple illustrates his attitude that a woman's place was in the home. Based on records in the French Archives Nationales and published primary sources. Forty-three notes.

Durieux, Joseph. "Napoléon et les jeunes filles de la Légion d'Honneur." *Revue des études napoléoniennes* 38 (1934): 26-52. Napoleon created schools for the female relations of his Legionnaires. These were l'Institut des Maisons Impériales Napoléon, established in 1809, and the Maisons d'Orphelines, which dated from 1810. This pioneering article discusses the nature of these schools, their personnel (both in terms of students and directors), their philosophy, and their curricula. Their goal was to turn little girls into virtuous women. An interesting and informative paper on a neglected subject. Based on contemporary printed and secondary sources. Seventeen notes.

Garver, Karen. "Madame Campan, Madame Guizot, and the Education of Women in Napoleonic France." *Proceedings of the Annual Meeting of the Western Society for French History* 7 (1979): 58-66.
A useful contribution to a neglected topic: the education of women during the Napoleonic era. Focuses on the ideas on this subject through the works of two prominent women, Jeanne-Louise-Henriette Genêt de Campan and Pauline de Meulan Guizot. Argues that the popularity of their writings demonstrates that the upper classes in France were concerned about educating their daughters. The curriculum and methods of implementing their program are also discussed. A brief but insightful introduction to this topic, based on printed primary and secondary works. Twenty-nine notes.

Harsin, Jill. *Policing Prostitution in Nineteenth Century Paris.* Princeton, N.J.: Princeton University Press, 1985.
A useful and well-documented survey, the only study of this subject in English. Part I is a detailed examination of the establishment of the regulatory system of prostitution under Napoleon. Part II examines the effects of the system on prostitutes, who, because of laws passed under Napoleon, were constantly subject to police control and harassment. Although the system owed much to the Old Regime, Harsin demonstrates that the

nineteenth century system originated under the Empire. The aim was to combat venereal disease. Index and bibliography.

Knibiehler, Y. "La Nature féminine au temps du Code Civil." *Annales, economies, sociétés, civilisations* 31 (1976): 824-845.
An attempt to analyze the stereotype of "femininity" at the beginning of the nineteenth century, a stereotype that would dominate French society until the end of World War I. Knibiehler believes the French Revolution and Napoleonic Empire marked a relative regression in the condition of women: new rights were created only for men. Women were not granted the right to vote, and the Civil Code deprived married women of rights considered "natural" only a few years previously. Knibiehler explains this regression as an outgrowth of the influence of medical science and the theories propounded by men such as Moreau, de la Sarthe, and Virey, who stressed woman's physical weaknesses. Based on printed contemporary sources and secondary works. Twenty-seven notes.

Montfort, Catherine R. "From Public to Private Sphere: The Case of Mme de Sévigné and Mme de Stäel." In *Literate Women and the French Revolution of 1789*, edited by Catherine R. Montfort. Birmingham, Ala.: Summa Publications, 1994, 111-126.
A useful introductory article on the importance of the works of the leading female intellectual during the Napoleonic years. The author recounts the significance of her books for Napoleon, who interpreted them as a threat to his regime. These included *Delphine* (1802), which supported divorce and defended Protestantism; *Corinne* (1807), a defense of the self-determination of nations and a work that praised England; and *De l'Allemagne* (1810), written in praise of the German people. Napoleon ordered the latter work seized and destroyed. Illustrations and bibliographical references.

Rogers, Rebecca. *Les Desmoiselles de la Légion d'Honneur: Les Maisons d'éducation de la Légion d'Honneur au XIXe siècle.* Paris: Plon, 1992.
A solid study of the schools founded by Napoleon in 1807 for the daughters of members of the Legion of Honor. The author centers her work on the three schools of Saint-Denis, Ecouen, and Les Loges for NCOS that survived into the nineteenth century. She discusses the purposes, programs, successes, and personnel

of the schools, using surviving diaries of students and other primary material. Although all three schools had a similar goal in producing model wives who would help guarantee the stability of the state in transmitting its values to future generations, the differences between the three establishments are brought out. Illustrations, map, and bibliographical references.

Van de Walle, Etienne. *The Female Population of France in the Nineteenth Century: A Reconstruction of 82 Departments.* Princeton, N.J.: Princeton University Press, 1974.
A statistical base for an analysis of the decline of fertility in France. The study forms part of the European Fertility Project, conducted under the auspices of the Office of Population Research at Princeton University. It is a vast collection of data concerning the nuptiality, fertility, mortality, and migration of the female population from the beginning of the nineteenth century to the early twentieth century. Van de Walle bases his investigation on information published by the French government beginning with the first census of 1801, discussing the qualities of the data and citing many of the intended falsifications of statistical data. A fundamental source for the study of the female population of France. Index, statistical tables, maps, and bibliography.

Woloch, Isser. "War-Widows Pensions: Social Policy in Revolutionary and Napoleonic France." *Societas* 6 (Autumn, 1976): 235-254.
An examination of the changes in government policy to war widows pensions from their introduction during the French Revolution to the reforms inaugurated by Napoleon under the Consulate and the Empire. Woloch contrasts the policy of the revolutionaries: from egalitarian and extensive during the early years to more arbitrary toward the end. Under Napoleon, the system was much less egalitarian and much more limited. His data demonstrate that at a time when casualties were increasing, the number of pensions granted declined. This interesting and enlightening article is based on documents in the Archives Nationales, the Archives de la Guerre, the Maclure Collection at the University of Pennsylvania, and other printed primary and secondary sources. Four tables and forty-seven notes.

Chapter 8

SOCIETY UNDER NAPOLEON

Bergeron, Louis. *France under Napoleon*. Translated by R. R. Palmer. Princeton, N.J.: Princeton University Press, 1981.
A translation of Bergeron's social history of France under Napoleon, *L'Episode napoléon: Aspects intérieurs*, published in 1972 as Volume 4 of the Seuil series Nouvelle Histoire de la France Contemporaine. It was universally hailed as a welcome addition to the literature which had previously focused on Napoleon the man rather than on life in Napoleonic France. Bergeron is a distinguished historian identified with the Annales school and, as such, is more concerned to examine the underlying structures of French society than to describe events and personalities. As a study in the "new social history," this work concentrates on the development of Napoleonic notables and the evolution of the economy. Chapters on aspects of Napoleonic society concerned with bankers, businessmen, and manufacturers which have been neglected by Anglo-Saxon historians of the period are particularly welcome. There is much quantitative information treating personal incomes, the tax system, and population trends. Probably the best introductory work on the domestic history of Napoleonic France. Index, bibliographical references in footnotes, and appendix containing a chronology. Palmer shortened the footnotes and omitted the bibliography in the English edition.

_____. *La Statistique en France de l'époque napoléonienne*. Bruxelles: Centre Guillaume Jacquemyns, 1981.
This volume presents the proceedings of a one-day conference held in Paris in February 1980 on the use of statistics during the Napoleonic years. The most outstanding paper in the collection is Stuart Woolf's paper on the origins of statistics from 1789 to

1848. As a collection, this is one of the few printed sources dealing with the uses and dangers of the massive statistical data of the period. Bibliographical references.

Bergeron, Louis, and Guy Chaussinand-Nogaret. *Les "Masses de granit": Cent mille notables du Premier Empire*. Paris: Editions de l'Ecole des Hautes Etudes en Sciences Sociales, 1979.
A study of the *grands notables*, or the people who directed and administered France from 1800 to 1814. An important work, this monograph contains a wealth of information on the imperial nobility. In the first section, the demographic aspects of the nobility are discussed: locations, ages, marriages, professions, mobility, and personal fortunes. The second part provides tables and graphs of regional data. Maps, footnotes, and appendices of numerous graphs and charts.

Bertaud, Jean-Paul. *Le Consulat et l'Empire*. Paris: Armand Colin, 1989.
This expert in the revolutionary and Napoleonic eras has succeeded in writing a clear and concise work. In the space of 160 pages, he describes the "structures" of society and the mechanism of power in Napoleon's France. Much space is devoted to the economy and to the methods and machinery of government. Other topics under consideration include demography, and a sociological analysis of civil and military personnel. Bertaud's thesis is that, with the growing militarization of the regime, the Consulate and Empire were less a conclusion of the Revolution, already over in 1799, than an introduction to the nineteenth century. A vital contribution to the literature. Illustrations and bibliography.

Biver, Marie-Louise, comtesse. *Le Paris de Napoléon*. Paris: Plon, 1965.
The Paris created by Napoleon was rich in monuments and public buildings; in many respects, he was the primary creator of modern-day Paris. The Louvre owes more to Napoleon than to any of his royal predecessors. As Biver clearly demonstrates, however, Napoleon was not simply concerned with monuments. Before Baron Haussmann's modernization of the city in the mid-nineteenth century, Bonaparte improved its amenities—for example, ensuring an adequate water supply. This is a lavishly illustrated work based extensively on the archives of the Empire. Illustrations and bibliography.

Cabanis, André. *La Presse sous le Consulat et l'Empire, 1799-1814.* Paris: Société des Etudes Robespierristes, 1975.

Based on a Ph.D. dissertation, this thorough work studies the effects of Napoleonic censorship in Paris and the provinces. Cabanis demonstrates that Napoleon's suspicion of the press took him to extraordinary lengths: the press was used to support the regime by the falsification of reports and addresses to the Emperor and the insertion of deceptive military information. This will be the standard work for some time to come. Illustrations, maps, bibliography, footnotes, and appendices of charts, graphs, and tables.

Célestin, Nicole. "Les Notaires de Paris sous le Consulat et l'Empire." *Revue de l'Institut Napoléon* 109 (1968): 165-170.

A resume of the author's thesis at Section VI of the Ecole Pratique des Hautes Etudes in Paris. It examines lower-middle-class men who became notaries, rising to a position of prominence under Napoleon during the Consulate and Empire. The article was considered groundbreaking at the time and was published at the request of Jean Tulard, who hailed it as "an important and new contribution to the economic and social history of Imperial Paris." Based on material from the Archives Nationales of France. Sixty-four notes.

_____. "Le Notariat parisien sous l'Empire." *Revue d'histoire moderne et contemporaine* 17, no. 3 (1970): 694-708.

An exploration of the notary profession, its connections, origins, and marital arrangements. The author studies the upward mobility of the men forming this profession, from lower-middle-class to middle-class landowning status during the Empire. Like Célestin's earlier study on the same subject, it is well-documented piece of work, based on unprinted sources in the French Archives Nationales.

Ellis, Geoffrey. "Rhine and Loire: Napoleonic Elites and Social Order." In *Beyond the Terror: Essays in French Regional and Social History 1794-1815*, edited by Gywnne Lewis and Colin Lucas. London, England: Cambridge University Press, 1983.

An excellent analysis of notables under Napoleon in these two regions. Based on primary material from two contrasting regional angles, the departments of the Bas-Rhin and the Loire Inférieure, the study clearly demonstrates that the elites came from the social class of lawyers and civil servants. They came increasingly to represent landed wealth as they successfully integrated themselves into the social hierarchy by traditional methods. Includes a bibliographical guide to the major secondary works on the subject, and an index.

Godechot, Jacques. *The Counter-Revolution: Doctrine and Action, 1789-1804*. Translated by Salvator Attanasio. New York: Fertig, 1971.
Based on lectures and not intended to be definitive, this work contains a useful chapter surveying the counterrevolutionary movement during the Empire. After 1800, the movement changed from regional opposition to one of plots against Napoleon. The Cadoudal, Pichegru, and Moreau conspiracies are all examined. Index, bibliography, and footnotes.

_____. *Les Institutions de la France sous la Révolution et l'Empire*. Histoire des Institutions, Collection Dirigée par Louis Halphen. Paris: Presses Universitaires de France, 1951.
The first volume in a series on the history of institutions, this is an exquisite history of institutions during the revolutionary and Napoleonic periods. Written by an expert in the field, the book focuses on nonpolitical institutions, but political institutions are not neglected. Topics covered during the years 1800 to 1815 consist of education, poor relief, finance, business, and the family. The author interprets the Napoleonic empire as a police state whose institutions were based on the ideas of the men of 1789 and were the work of an enlightened despot. Maps, index, bibliography, and footnotes.

Guerrini, Maurice. *Napoleon and Paris: Thirty Years of History*. Translated and edited by Margery Weiner. London: Cassell, 1970.
A worthwhile compliment to the biographies, this interesting essay in social history considers Napoleon's life and works in Paris. Contains a wealth of detail on the city's relationship to Napoleon and numerous descriptions of the public works projects completed under the Consulate and the Empire, including the sewers, roads, and buildings. Maps, index, bibliography, and six appendices.

Holtman, Robert B. *The Napoleonic Revolution*. Baton Rouge: Louisiana State University Press, 1967, reprint 1978.

The aim of this work is to show how and why Napoleon maintained and sometimes developed the heritage of the French Revolution. In ten brief chapters, Holtman surveys the institutional changes and the domestic innovations that characterized Napoleon's rule. This book is particularly useful to anyone with an interest in Napoleon's reforms in education, law, and religion. Succinct and clearly written, it has the merit of being the best short survey in English of Napoleon's reforms. Maps, index, bibliography, and footnotes.

Kilbourne, Lawrence J. "The Notables of the Loire under the First Empire." Ph.D. dissertation. Waltham, Mass.: Brandeis University, 1982.

A local case study of this topic. The opening chapters set the problem in its historiographical context and describe the geographical and economic characteristics of the region. Also included is a survey of the French Revolution in this department. The substance of the thesis is a detailed and mainly statistical study of the notables during the Empire, based on administration records, notarial documents, and death declarations. Kilbourne also wrote the volume on the Loire in Louis Bergeron and Guy Chaussinand-Nogaret's Grands Notables series. Bibliography.

Lanzac de Laborie, Léon. *Paris sous Napoléon.* 8 vols. Vol. 1, *Consulat provisoire et Consulat à temps.* Vol. 2, *Administration grands travaux.* Vol. 3, *La Cour et la ville, la vie et la mort.* Vol. 4, *La Religion.* Vol. 5, *Assistance et bienfaisance approvisionement.* Vol. 6, *Le Monde des affaires et du travail.* Vol. 7, *Le Théâtre-Français.* Vol. 8, *Spectacles et musées.* Paris: Plon, 1905-1913.

A classic series of works on all aspects of life in Paris under Napoleon. All volumes are based on primary sources and are well documented. Volume 1 summarizes the changes in the city at the beginning of the century. Religion is covered in both Volumes 1 and 4. Volume 1 concentrates on the period of the Consulate to the promulgation of the Concordat, while Volume 4 provides an explanation of the Concordat in Paris from 1802 to 1814. Also discussed are the policies toward Protestants, Jews, and Freemasons. Volume 2 deals with the administration of great monuments and palaces as well as municipal finances, streets, and shops. Public festivals and ceremonies, which comprised the major activities of the public space, are the subjects of concern for Volume 3. Topics covered include the numerous public celebrations after Napoleonic victories, festivals at court, the salons, balls, and even funerals. The justice system, including the roles of the courts and lawyers, is also discussed. Hospitals, charitable societies, and questions of provisioning are handled in Volume 5. Volume 6 covers commerce, industry, and the stock exchange. Finally, the last two volumes discuss theaters and museums. Remains the most complete work on the subject. A detailed table of contents, which serves as an index, and bibliographical references are found in each volume.

Poisson, Georges. *Napoléon et Paris*. Paris: Berger-Levrault, 1964.
A study of Napoleonic architecture, beginning with a chapter on the Consulate. All aspects of architectural style are covered, from markets to the Arc de Triomphe. Poisson specifically considers monuments forgotten by other historians of the same discipline: the opening of the rue de Rivoli from the Concorde to the Louvre, the two arcs of triumph, the Vendôme column, the Madeleine church, and the Paris Stock Exchange. The author's specialty is the twelve fountains built by Napoleon. He examines the completion of the courtyard of the Louvre and draws the reader's attention to the close connection between the architecture of the Old Regime and that of the Napoleonic era. A work similar to that of Biver except that Poisson has more to say about political history. Illustrations and bibliography.

Revue d'histoire moderne et contemporaine: La France à l'époque napoléonienne. Paris: Armand Colin, 1970.
A special edition of the journal containing the papers and discussions from the October 1969 conference at the Sorbonne in honor of the Two hundredth anniversary of the birth of Napoleon. The papers, all by French experts such as Tulard, Bergeron, Woronoff, and Godechot, are grouped under four general headings: demography, economy, society, and institutions. Under the first heading are papers about marriages and births, age structure, population movements, losses because of wars, and general problems concerning demographic studies at the time. Bergeron draws participants' attention to gaps in research and knowledge on economic matters, and Tulard confronts social problems disputed by historians. The issue also offers general papers on Napoleonic institutions, the Church, and universities. A useful volume not only showing the state of Napoleonic studies at the time but also containing much useful information. A selection of

these papers is published in the *Annales historiques de la Révolution française*, vol. 42 (janvier-mars 1970).

Soboul, Albert. *La Civilisation et la Révolution française*. Vol. 3, *La France napoléonienne*. Paris: Arthaud, 1970.
A French Marxist historian's account of the Napoleonic regime by an historian better known for his works on the French Revolution, particularly his book on the *sans-culottes*, than for his Napoleonic scholarship. The reforms of Napoleon are interpreted in the light of his Marxist ideology: the Civil Code was an attempt by the bourgeoisie to impose their "rules of the game" on the rest of French society. The French Revolution brought the bourgeoisie to power, the Civil Code consolidated this power, and Napoleon exercised it with despotism. One of the merits of the book is the attention devoted to the French peasantry. Other subjects under discussion are festivals, the Continental Blockade, notables, the Legion of Honor, and French industry. Although not everyone will agree with his Marxist interpretation, Soboul's work remains essential for the study of civilian society from 1800 to 1815. Maps, illustrations, bibliography, and index.

Tulard, Jean. *Napoléon et la noblesse d'Empire: Avec la liste complète des membres (1808-1815)*. Paris: Tallandier, 1979, 1986.
Ostensibly this work examines the nature of the nobility under the Napoleonic empire, but there is much more to it than a study of Napoleon's nobles. It deals with the nature of the society created by Napoleon, which Tulard argues was ordered and hierarchical, reversing the French Revolution's philosophy of advancement by merit. Only those who had profited from the Revolution's sale of national lands or those who were already wealthy had the chance to do well under Napoleon. Ennoblement under Napoleon was reserved for the Old Regime's nobility, holders of public office, and high-ranking officers. Finally, the author asserts that the Napoleonic regime rapidly and irreversibly turned to caesarism, and that in the final analysis, Bonaparte's system rested on the notables, not on the people. Illustrations, index, bibliography, and footnotes.

_____. *Nouvelle Histoire de Paris: Le Consulat et l'Empire, 1800-1815*. Paris: Hachette, 1970.
The first volume in a series concerning the history of Paris, this is an indispensable tool for those interested in the political, social,

and economic history of the city under Napoleon. Chapters in Part I deal with all aspects of life in the capital, such as population changes brought about by the revolutionary and Napoleonic wars, religious attitudes of Parisians, and the opinions of Parisians toward artistic and intellectual questions. Part II studies the various problems confronting the capital, mainly of a social and economic nature. Finally, Part III examines the fluctuations in the regime's popularity. Illustrations, maps, indexes, bibliography, footnotes, and appendices consisting of tables of the population of Paris, the social and economic structures, great works, and private construction.

_____. *La Vie quotidienne des français sous Napoléon.* Paris: Hachette, 1978.
The subject of this book is the daily life of the French people during the Napoleonic years. It is excellent for its details on the downside of life, strategies for coping with the war, corruption, the weakness of the administration, and the general decline in morality. Tulard debunks the myth of the Empire as always under the glory of the Austerlitz sun. He also makes evident the power of Napoleonic propaganda, which captivated the ordinary French people. Other themes explored include antimilitarism, brigandage, and the daily routine of farmers. Bibliographical notes.

Villes et territoire pendant la période napoléonienne. Acts du colloque organisé par l'Ecole Française de Rome et l'Assessorato alla Cultura de la Ville de Rome avec la participation de la Maison des Sciences de l'Homme. (Paris), Rome, 3, 4, et 5 mai 1985. Rome: Ecole Française de Rome, 1987.
The Napoleonic period represented a rupture at the European level from the point of view of relationships between municipal authorities and cities. The inherent question at this meeting was to discover how far this rupture was related to the establishment, during the period of the Empire, of a more systematic consideration of urban and territorial phenomena. Papers concerning bridges and roadways give an insight to the role played by engineers in urban settings. Many essays deal with concepts of urbanism and "urban projects," meaning the technical and cultural development which transformed cities. Other papers discuss population and the general structuring of territory during this period. The salient argument is that the Napoleonic period saw the map rewritten to suit the needs of the military. A new science was developed that attempted to explain economic and demographic realities.

Chapter 9

NAPOLEONIC COLONIES AND EMPIRE

Annales historiques de la Révolution française, no. 36 (1964): 349-386.
A special edition devoted to revolutionary and Napoleonic Poland. The three papers concerning the Napoleonic period are perceptive studies written by major Polish specialists, all of whom who have published extensively in Polish. These essays make their work more accessible, as they are written in French. Barbara Grochulska, in "Sur la structure économique du Duché de Varsovie (1807-1813)," analyzes the economic effects of the Continental Blockade on the Duchy of Warsaw. Wladyslw Sobocinski also studies the duchy, but from the point of view of international relations, focusing on its relationship to the Empire. Finally, Monika Senkowska examines the Polish lands Napoleon gave to his soldiers. She argues that the existence of these soldiers created numerous social and economic problems. All essays are based on extensive primary research in the Polish archives and libraries, including the Central Archives in Warsaw and the Czartoryski Library in Cracow, as well as numerous secondary Polish works.

Askenazy, S. *Napoléon et la Pologne*. Translated by Henri Grégoire, 3 vols. Paris: Maurice Lamertin, 1925.
The author dedicated many years to producing this key work on Poland. The three volumes cover the entire Napoleonic period, starting with the division of Poland at the end of the eighteenth century, the revolutionary impact, and the creation of Polish legions. Askenazy begins with a narration of how Napoleon came into contact with the Poles and continues with an account of how the Polish nation spilled its blood with the French during this

period and never ceased to consider France the world's great educator. Notes are mostly bibliographical.

Berdahl, Robert M. *The Politics of the Prussian Nobility: The Development of a Conservative Ideology, 1770-1848*. Princeton, N.J.: Princeton University Press, 1988.
A study of the Prussian nobility during the first half of the nineteenth century. Berdahl's principal statement is that the Prussian nobles justified their control over the peasantry through the exercise of a paternalistic ideology that conflicted with changing social affiliations during this period. Although there is much more to this book than the Napoleonic period, it elucidates a good deal about it. Includes an important study of the reforms undertaken by the Prussian bureaucracy in response to the Napoleonic victories, such as the elimination of feudal constraints on peasant lands, and a liberalization of trade. Index and bibliographical references.

Berding, H. *Napoleonische Herrschafts-und Gesellschaftspolitik im königreich Westfalen 1807-1813*. Göttingen, Germany: Vandenhoeck and Ruprecht, 1973.
A brief but informative study of the social consequences of Napoleon's practice of rewarding his subordinates with Crown domains in the German satellite state of Westphalia. No other conquered territory was subject to such extensive expropriation. Berding shows how Napoleon's policies, including his war demands, took precedence over revolutionary principles. He demonstrates that Napoleon's reward policies make the concept of Westphalia as a model state untrue. Bibliography.

_____. "Le Royaume de Westphalie, état-modèle." *Francia* 10 (1982): 345-358.
A shorter version of his book, this article studies the kingdom of Westphalia which was created by Napoleon in 1807, and ruled by his brother Joseph until 1813. Napoleon's intention was to create a barrier against Prussia. Westphalia was established as model state with a centralized government, a unified tax system, the abolition of noble privileges, and equality before the law. Berding demonstrates that, as a model state, Westphalia failed because of the military demands of the Napoleonic Empire and the economic consequences of the Continental Blockade. The

article is useful for those who cannot read Berding in German. Twenty-one notes.

Besson, Maurice, and Robert Chauvelot. *Napoléon colonial.* Paris: Société d'Éditions Géographiques, Maritimes et coloniales, 1939.
The first full-length monograph devoted to the role of Napoleon's colonial policies in his foreign policy. Besson and Chauvelot set out to discover Napoleon's faculty for colonial affairs. They attempt to prove that Napoleon was indeed very adept at colonial matters and that he possessed a real colonial spirit, evidenced in his administration of Egypt, his hopes of expansion in America, his dream of ending colonial chaos in the French West Indies, and his longing for an eastern empire. Bibliography.

Bilan du monde en 1965. Rapports Conjoints. Comité International des Sciences Historiques. XIIe Congrès International des Sciences Historiques, Vienne, 29 août-5 septembre 1965. Paris: Editions du Centre National de la Recherche Scientifique, 1966.
Four papers in this collection form the proceedings of the Twelfth International Congress of Historical Sciences, which met on the 150th anniversary of the conclusion of the Napoleonic wars. Three of the four papers deal with the years from 1800 to 1815, covering various aspects of the Napoleonic Empire from social and political ideas (A. Z. Manfred) to the position of the British Empire at the end of the Napoleonic wars (G. S. Graham). Perhaps the most significant paper in the collection is that of the Russian scholar Professor A. L. Narotchnitzki, who addresses the historical importance of the Continental Blockade. Partially historiographical, the paper discusses the scholarship on this topic from an international coterie of historians, including the works of the Russian scholars V. K. Iatsounski and A. V. Predtétchenski. Since these works are hard to obtain and are written in Russian, the article, written in French, is a useful contribution to the effects of the Continental System on Russia.

Blanning, T. C. W. *The French Revolution in Germany: Occupation and Resistance in the Rhineland 1792-1802.* Oxford, England: The Clarendon Press, 1983.
A study of German society under French occupation and the methods and motives of German resistance to it. It attempts to discover what the occupation of the Rhineland meant for the German people. Blanning focuses on the region north of Alsace-

Lorraine, but he also deals with Belgium, Holland, and Italy. Based on local chronicles, diaries, pamphlets, and newspapers as well as documents from major archives, this is the best work on the subject. Although the book is primarily concerned with the revolutionary period, ending in 1802, it provides excellent background reading for the study of the period immediately preceding annexation. Index and bibliography.

Bond, Gordon C. "Louis Bonaparte and the Collapse of the Kingdom of Holland." *Consortium on Revolutionary Europe, 1750-1850: Proceedings* 4 (1974): 141-153.
An examination of the Netherlands under Louis Bonaparte. Bond stresses Bonaparte's personal role in the kingdom and in its demise. The author maintains that the kingdom was never conceived as a permanent creation, and the dissension between Napoleon and Louis accelerated its breakdown. Reasons for the downfall of the kingdom include Louis Bonaparte's refusal to follow his brother's orders in an effort to become a popular king and his inability to defend Holland against military onslaughts. Based on printed and manuscript sources. Fifty-four notes.

Bourgin, G., and Jacques Godechot. *L'Italie et Napoléon (1796-1814)*. Paris: Recueil, 1936.
This brief volume is in the Cahiers de la Révolution Française series. The first essay by Bourgin is a rather benevolent account of the behavior of the French army in Italy between 1795 and 1796. Much more impartial is Godechot's analysis of Napoleon's policies after 1805. He clearly establishes the wide gap between democratic promise and dictatorial behavior displayed by Napoleon. Bibliography.

Broers, Michael. "Revolution as Vendetta: Napoleonic Piedmont 1801-1814." *Historical Journal* 33 (1990): 787-809.
A rigorous, well-documented study of the internal politics of Piedmont. Establishes the failure of French attempts at ending the violence and obliterating hatreds among the local notables. In this interesting and stimulating article, the bitter struggle for provincial power is chronicled. Broers asserts that the local nobles were reluctant to accept official posts during the early years of the Consulate. The impact of the French judicial system, which established new courts and judges, is also analyzed. 110 notes.

Bruun, Geoffrey. *Europe and the French Imperium, 1799-1814.* New York: Harper and Brothers, 1938.
Although dated, this continues to be a reliable survey of the period written by an expert in the field. The title is somewhat misleading, as it is mainly concerned with developments inside France and other European nations are dealt with only in terms of their reactions to the French. It is an attempt to get beyond the traditional confines of political and military history without entirely neglecting them. These topics are discussed alongside developments in the economic, financial, social, religious, cultural, and artistic spheres. Albeit not a biography, the book does examine the personality of the Emperor. Designed for students and general readers, clearly written and relatively unbiased. Index, valuable historiographical essay, and good bibliography last updated in 1963.

Bush, Robert D. "French Colonial Administration in Louisiana, 1800-1804." *Consortium on Revolutionary Europe, 1750-1850. Proceedings* 9 (1979): 164-174.
An examination of the work of the Napoleonic prefect Pierre Clément Laussat, who officially administered the colony for twenty days, from 30 November to 20 December 1802. Bush maintains that although Laussat's tenure in Louisiana was brief, it illustrates Napoleon's ideas about the administration of colonies. Thirty-seven notes.

Cestaro, Antonio. "Messogiorno e classi sociali." *Sociologia* 17 (maggio-agosto 1983): 3-29.
A study of the impact of the Napoleonic government after 1806 on the social classes of southern Italy, focusing on the transition from the feudal system to capitalism. Cestaro emphasizes the change in attitude of the peasantry toward the new landlords. While the old landlords were tied to investment and usury incomes and exhibited a strongly conservative worldview, the new class benefited from the liquidation of ecclesiastical lands and adopted a more liberal attitude in post-unification politics. The article is based on primary materials consisting of agricultural records, emigration statistics, and early census reports.

Connelly, Owen. *Napoleon's Satellite Kingdoms.* New York: Collier Macmillan, 1965.

An excellent comparative study of the five Napoleonic kingdoms: Italy, Naples, Holland, Spain, and Westphalia. As a work of synthesis, it serves as a good general introduction to each of these kingdoms. Connelly summarizes the enlightened reforms introduced in these countries. The background to the establishment of each kingdom is discussed as is the relationship between Napoleon and the members of his family whom he placed on the thrones of Europe. Maps and bibliographical references.

Davico, R. *"Peuple" et notables (1750-1816): Essais sur l'Ancien Régime et la Révolution en Piédmont.* Paris: Bibliothèque Nationale, 1981.
An important detailed analysis of the impact of the French Revolution and Napoleon in Piedmont. This heavily documented work, by an expert in the field who wrote a French doctoral thesis (1967) on Piedmont under Napoleon, stresses economic and social aspects and examines subjects such as demography, price movements, agricultural production, industry, and metallurgy. The author highlights the social continuities in this region and demonstrates that, at least for this part of Italy, much had been done to abolish the feudal system before Napoleon. Index and bibliography.

Davies, Norman. *God's Playground: A History of Poland.* Vol. 2, *1795 to the Present.* New York: Columbia University Press, 1982.
A survey in English by a specialist in Polish history, based on a wide variety of primary and secondary sources. Chapter 12, "Varsovie: The Duchy of Warsaw," deals with Napoleon's management of Poland and the changes brought about by the introduction of the constitution of 1807. Given the lack of major published works in English, this synthesis provides a useful contribution to the literature. Index, maps, illustrations, and bibliographical references.

Diefendorf, Jeffrey. *Businessmen and Politics in the Rhineland 1789-1834.* Princeton, N.J.: Princeton University Press, 1980.
The published version of the author's doctoral dissertation, this study illustrates the political education of Rhenish businessmen by specific reference to three Left Bank cities, Aachen, Cologne, and Crefeld. Diefendorf describes four phases of political education from French occupation in 1792 to Prussian integration in 1832. Of these four, the most significant was the second phase, from 1797 to 1814, and in that phase, the Napoleonic period was

paramount. Diefendorf holds that the businessmen of this region sincerely supported the Napoleonic regime because it provided concrete economic and political improvements. An excellent English-language introduction to this topic. Maps and bibliographical references.

Driault, Edouard. *Napoléon en Italie (1800-1812)*. Paris: Félix Alcan, 1906.
A good, but not a definitive, political history of Napoleon's relations with Italy, based mostly on original sources from the French Archives Nationales and the unedited political correspondence found in the French Ministère des Affaires Etrangères archives. Unfortunately, the relevant archives in Italy were not consulted. Heavy reliance on Bonaparte's official correspondence. If used in conjunction with more recent works, this well-written and well-constructed study remains valuable; on its own, it is out of date.

Dunan, Marcel. *Napoléon et l'Allemagne: Le Système continental et les débuts du royaume de Bavière (1806-1810)*. Paris: Plon, 1942.
A major pioneering work that summarizes the Napoleonic hegemony in Bavaria. Dunan describes the leading reforms, including the establishment of a centralized modern administration, the abolition of previous judicial, economic, and local privileges, and the introduction of the Napoleonic Code. This study is the result of fruitful research in the archives of Paris, Munich, Stuttgart, and Vienna. Dunan clearly demonstrates the influence of France on the internal and external politics of Bavaria, as well as Bavaria's impact on other southern German states. Index of cited works and bibliography of principal manuscript sources.

_____, ed. *Napoléon et l'Europe*. Paris; Editions Brepols, 1961.
A collection of important articles resulting from the Commission Internationale pour l'Enseignement d'Histoire conference in 1960. The subject under consideration by experts in the field is the Napoleonic hegemony in Europe. Countries discussed include Italy (Max Tacel), Holland (E. ten Brink), Germany (Dunan), and Switzerland (L. E. Roulet). Many have an economic bias. For example, Tacel argues that the integration of Italy into the Napoleonic system had diverse implications for the economy; these economic ramifications are examined in some detail. Other

papers include a discussion of Napoleon and the Beaux-Arts (Ferdinand Boyer), and the Sorel thesis that French ascendancy defied the balance of power is revived by L. Halkin. Illustrations and selective bibliography.

Ellis, Geoffrey. *Napoleon's Continental Blockade: The Case of Alsace*. Oxford, England: Oxford University Press, 1981.
A detailed analysis of the economic consequences of the Continental Blockade in Alsace. Ellis posits that the blockade's goal was not to create a common European market but to make France the predominant economic power. Strasbourg and Mulhouse profited substantially from the blockade. Based on a wide variety of documents from regional, local, and national archives in Germany and France, Ellis's book is an important contribution to the economic history of the Napoleonic period. Index and bibliography.

Fehrenbach, Elisabeth. *Traditionale Gesellschaft und revolutionäres Recht. Die Einführung des Code Napoléon in den Rheinbundstaaten*. Göttingen: Vandenhoeck and Ruprecht, 1974.
The author is a specialist in the effects of the Napoleonic Code on the administrative and legal system of Germany during the first half of the nineteenth century. In this work, Fehrenbach examines both the circumstances leading to the introduction of the Napoleonic Code in the Confederation of the Rhine and its reception there. Fehrenbach claims that Napoleon was fully conscious of the limitations between the new system and his foreign policy and that the feudal system hampered attempts at reform. Index and bibliography.

Fisher, Herbert A. L. *Studies in Napoleonic Statesmanship: Germany*. Oxford, England: The Clarendon Press, 1903.
A study of the civil and administrative history of the Napoleonic system in Germany. Fisher devotes equal space to the two phases of Napoleon's political activities in Germany. The first half of the book deals with the conquests, secularization, and confiscation that occurred from 1799 to 1807. The economy and government established in Berg, Westphalia, and other German territories are covered in the second part, which ends with the Russian campaign. The Rhineland departments receive a chapter of their own. Remains one of the best studies in English on Napoleonic Germany. Maps.

Fugier, André. *Napoléon et l'Espagne, 1799-1808*. 2 vols. Paris: Félix Alcan, 1930.

Written by a specialist in the history of the First Empire and a professor at the University of Lyons, this discussion of the origins of the Spanish "ulcer" attempts to address the questions concerning Napoleon's obsession with Spain. Contains much information on state of the Spanish navy. Argues that Tilsit led Napoleon to treat the Spanish Bourbons with increasing arrogance. Fugier consulted the French, Spanish, British, and Portuguese archives. The unprinted archives documents are from the Archives du Ministère des Affaires Etrangères, the Archives Nationales, the Archives du Ministère de la Guerre, and the Archives de la Marine and the Bibliothèque Nationale in Paris. In Madrid, Fugier made use of the Archivo Histórico Nacional, the Archivo de Simancas, the Archivo de la Real Casa y Patrimonio and the archives of the Biblioteca Nacional. He consulted the Arquivo Histórico do Ministério dos Negócios Estrangeiros in Lisbon and the Foreign Office records at the Public Record Office in London. The bibliography is extensive, covering pages xii-xliv at the beginning of Volume 1.

_____. *Napoléon et l'Italie*. Paris: Janin, 1947.

This clear and dense synthesis, written from printed French and Italian documents, It covers the years from 1800 to 1815 and discusses Bonaparte's influence in Italy. Very useful for internal aspects such as the constitution, the Italian Concordat, and religious questions. Fugier contends that Italy was always foremost in Napoleon's mind. Although dated, this work remains useful. Bibliography.

Geoffroy de Grandmaison, Charles Alexandre. *L'Espagne et Napoléon*. 2d ed. 3 vols. Paris: Plon Nourrit, 1908-1931.

A scholarly, detailed, and well-written survey of France's association with Spain from 1804 to 1814, based almost entirely on original sources. Grandmaison is particularly good on guerrilla warfare, the Spanish princes at Valençay, and Joseph Bonaparte as king of Spain and general of the imperial forces. A chapter on the prisoners of war on both sides is insightful. The only shortcoming lies in his treatment of the Spanish people; the French bias in his account does not allow him to give the reader much insight into the Spaniards' religious fervor and nationalism. The essential history on this topic. Index and bibliographical references.

Gray, Marion W. *Prussia in Transition: Society and Politics under the Stein Reform Monarchy of 1808.* Transactions of the American Philosophical Society, no. 76. Philadelphia: American Philosophical Society, 1986.

One of the few English studies of Prussia during the Napoleonic period. It summarizes the organizational changes implemented by the government as well as the first steps toward dealing with the nearly overwhelming financial challenge faced by the state resulting from the Peace of Tilsit. Gray examines the many proposals for the introduction of representative institutions in Prussia at the rural, municipal, provincial, and national levels. Depicts the nature of pre-reform Prussian society. Index and bibliography.

Handelsman, Marcel. *Napoléon et la Pologne, 1806-1807.* Paris: Alcan, 1909.

The purpose of Handelsman's work is to sketch the relations between Napoleon and Poland. The work is not concerned with military endeavors. Handelsman describes Napoleon's Polish policy, which he shows was characterized by indecisiveness. He argues that Napoleon used Poland as a pawn in the diplomatic game with Russia and Prussia. The work concludes with a discussion of the Grand Duchy of Warsaw, created in 1807. The documents, composed of diplomatic briefs and correspondence and which occupy almost half the book, are not annotated and are French translations. They come from the French Archives Nationales, the archives of the French Ministère des Affaires Etrangères, and various Polish archives. A well-balanced account. Index and bibliography.

"L'Italie jacobine et napoléonienne." *Annales historiques de la Révolution française* 49, no. 230 (octobre-décembre 1977): 501-676.

A special issue devoted to articles by Italian scholars on aspects of revolutionary and Napoleonic Italy, based on papers presented at the colloquium in Rome from 25 to 27 March 1974 and organized by L'Institut d'Histoire de la Révolution Française de l'Université de Paris, with the collaboration of the Ecole Française of Rome. Articles concerning the Napoleonic years include the following: "Démocrates et masses populaires à Bologne (1796-1802)" (M. Leonardi), "Le Choix des préfets dans la République et le royaume d'Italie," (L. Antonielli); "Les collèges électoraux de la République italienne et du royaume d'Italie" (C. Capra),

"Quelques Aspects de la vie économique italienne à l'époque napoléonienne" (P. Villani), "Mines et usines en Piédmont au début du XIXe siècle" (R. Davico), "La Législation du travail en Lombardie à l'époque napoléonienne" (A. L. Forti-Messina), and "L'Etat des pauvres et mendiants (Département de l'Arno, 1812)" (S. J. Woolf). These papers are an excellent example of the new history of Napoleon in that the primary concern is not the man himself, but rather the transformations that occurred in the political, economic, and social spheres from 1800 to 1815.

Johnston, R. M. *The Napoleonic Empire in Southern Italy and the Rise of Secret Societies.* 2 vols. New York: Da Capo Press, 1973.
At the time of its original publication in 1904, Johnston's work was a major contribution to the subject. It is a detailed study of Naples under Joseph and Murat which continues to the Restoration and looks at the growth of secret societies. Johnston stresses the importance of the Naples in the Empire. Although dated, it contains a wealth of information. Maps, appendices, and a short bibliography at the end of each chapter.

Klang, Daniel Michael. "Bavaria and the Age of Napoleon." Ph.D. dissertation. Princeton, N.J.: Princeton University, 1963.
Klang focuses on the impact of Napoleon on the electorate and kingdom of Bavaria from 1799 to 1814. He holds that Napoleon was the son of the French Revolution, and attempts to prove this through a thorough examination of the changes implemented in Bavaria. The first half of the thesis is concerned with Napoleon's reorganization of Bavaria to the Franco-Austrian war of 1809, while the second section focuses on the German war of liberation of 1813 and 1814. The thesis also considers the opposition of the ultra-Montanist Catholics to Napoleonic reforms. Bibliography.

Kossmann, E. H. *The Low Countries, 1780-1940.* Oxford, England: The Clarendon Press, 1978.
Although only one chapter, "The Great Revolution, 1792-1815," concerns the Napoleonic period, this general history provides a useful summary of French occupation of the Netherlands and Belgium. The author demonstrates that although both the Dutch and the Belgians were under the same French influence, they responded very differently. The Dutch resisted French domination, while the Belgians were much more acquiescent. Consequently, the two nations turned away from each other and developed quite

differently. Indexes, maps, a useful chronological appendix, and an extensive bibliography.

Lokke, Carl Ludwig. *France and the Colonial Question: A Study of Contemporary French Opinion 1763-1801*. New York: Columbia University Press, 1932.
A study of the changes in contemporary French opinion concerning colonial policies from the end of the Seven Years' War in 1763 to Napoleon's occupation of Egypt and its evacuation in 1801. In this well-researched and balanced work, drawn from his Ph.D. dissertation, the author argues that there was a renewal of interest in the West Indies during the Consulate. Bibliography.

Lovett, Gabriel H. *Napoleon and the Birth of Modern Spain*. Vol. 1, *The Challenge to the Old Order*. Vol. 2, *The Struggle Without and Within*. New York: New York University Press, 1965.
This is the best English-language scholarly account of the history of Spain under Napoleon. Although the military aspects are dominant, political developments are also addressed. The author emphasizes the themes of the origin of Spanish nationalism and the conflict between the two opposing forces of liberalism and conservative reaction. Much attention is also devoted to the writings of liberal leaders and thinkers. Bibliography.

Lovie, J. and A. Palluel-Guillard. *L'Episode napoléonien: Aspects extérieurs*. Paris: Seuil, 1972.
This volume appeared in the same series as Bergeron's *Aspects intérieurs* (cited in Chapter 7) but has not been translated into English. It is much more traditional than Bergeron's study of the internal aspects of the Empire. The authors describe Napoleon's campaigns, and there is a good chapter concerning the "instruments" of Napoleon's policies: the army and diplomatic corps. In spite of Napoleon's profound influence in Europe, a mere twelve pages are dedicated to this subject. Maps, index, and bibliographical references.

Mansuy, Abel. *Jérôme Napoléon et la Pologne en 1812*. Paris: Félix Alcan, 1931.
The real significance of this work is its contribution to our understanidng of the Polish situation and the background to the Russian campaign. A well-noted and scholarly study based on many original sources, it was originally written as a thesis at the

Université de Strasbourg. Jérôme Napoleon arrived in Poland on 10 April 1812 and remained there until June of the same year. This work discusses his impact on Poland and is therefore indispensable for the background of the Russian campaign. Illustrations, maps, index, and bibliographical references.

Nipperdey, Thomas. *Deutsche Geschichte 1800-1866: Bürgerwelt und Starken Staat.* München: C. H. Beck, 1983.
A major history on the development of modern Germany. Nipperdey claims that modern Germany began with Napoleon in the form of military imperialism. He cites four features of what he considers to compose modernization—a demographic revolution, urbanization, industrialization, and capitalism—to have started under Napoleonic rule. In addition, he examines two long-term effects of Napoleonic domination: that political change was possible only from above, and that Napoleonic foreign policy had an impact, both negative and positive, on all aspects of German life. Much attention is devoted to the force and often anti-modern character of the German Romantic movement. Index and bibliography.

Occupants-Occupés, 1792-1815. Colloque de Bruxelles, 29 et 30 janvier 1968. In *Actes.* Brussels: Université Libre de Bruxelles, Institut de Sociologie, 1969.
The proceedings of a conference on the subject of the occupied territories under the French Revolution and Napoleon, which took place at the University of Brussels in 1968. The conference was chaired by Jacques Godechot and papers were presented on Spain (P. Vilar), Holland (C. H. E. de Wit), Italy (A. Saitta), Switzerland (J. Suralteau), and Belgium (R. Devleeshower). These papers seek to determine the nature and types of opposition to the French during the French Revolution and Empire. They endeavor to examine not only French policy but also local reactions to the occupation. A report on this important conference is contained in *Annales, economies et sociétés* 23 (5) (1968): 1111-1116.

Ostergard, Uffe. "Peasants and Danes: The Danish National Identity and Political Culture." *Comparative Studies in Society and History* 34 (January, 1992): 3-27.
An examination of the impact of the Napoleonic wars and German unification on the nature of the Danish nation-state. Ostergard focuses on the internal repercussions of the loss of Norway in 1814 and the Schleswig-Holstein war of 1864. As a result of these

wars, the essential function of Danish schools was to teach grammar, literature, and patriotism. Schools had the goal of embodying folk culture and transmitting it to the peasants. This cultural nationalism resulted from the defeat of the Danes in 1807, and again in 1814.

Outram, Dorinda. "Education and Politics in Piedmont, 1796-1814." *Historical Journal* 19 (1976): 611-633.
An examination of the political education of the men who emerged as prominent rulers in the government of Piedmont in 1820. These men had all accepted prominent positions in the Napoleonic government. Outram strives to answer two questions in this penetrating study: how the pre-revolutionary Italian ruling aristocracies reacted to Napoleon's rule in Italy, and how the Napoleonic experience affected their attitude toward the events of the succeeding decade. She examines the reactions of a group of Piedmontese nobles in the circle of Prospero Balbo, who collaborated with the French. Since education was closely related to politics in Piedmont, the author includes in this discussion an analysis of changes in education in this region. A valuable contribution to the literature. Based on unpublished documents and published secondary sources. Sixty-six notes.

_____. "Education and the State in Italian Departments Integrated into France between 1802 and 1814." Ph.D. dissertation. Cambridge, England: Cambridge University, 1975.
An examination of French education policy and administration in the Italian territories annexed between 1802 and 1809. Outram's thesis is that although educational institutions were managed by Italians, the government's intention was to indoctrinate the younger generation into the acceptance of French domination. In order to ensure success of this policy, conservative nobles rather than more radical professionals and intellectuals were appointed to run these institutions. An important contribution to a topic which remains neglected. Bibliography.

Pluchon, Pierre. *Histoire de la colonisation française*. vol. 1, *Le Premier Empire Colonial: Des Origines à la restauration*. Paris: Fayard, 1991.
A survey of French colonial history from its origins to 1815 by a specialist in the colonial history of the Old Regime. Pluchon asserts that the colonial adventure constituted a major achievement

and that it affected the country politically, intellectually, and psychologically. Pages 904-1002 deal with the Napoleonic years, surveying the major aspects of Napoleon's colonial policy. Pluchon states that neither the revolutionaries nor the Emperor renounced the policies of the Old Regime; from the start, their goal was to preserve their possessions. Indexes and bibliographical references.

Priestley, Herbert Ingram. *France Overseas through the Old Regime: A Study of European Expansion.* New York: Appleton-Century, 1939.
A brief survey of French colonial development which sketches the rise and fall of the first French Empire. Every stage of French overseas effort through to 1815 is a least mentioned in this detailed compendium. Material is organized by region: Canada, the West Indies, Guiana, Louisiana, and India. The concluding chapters concern the colonies under the revolutions and Napoleon. Index and bibliographical references.

Rath, Reuben John. *The Fall of the Napoleonic Kingdom of Italy.* New York: Columbia University Press, 1941.
An excellent study of Napoleon's domination of Italy, based on documents from the Italian and Austrian archives as well as published sources in German, French, Italian, and English. The two introductory chapters discuss the formation and organization of the Italian kingdom. Reuben then goes on to discuss the main subject of the monograph: the reasons for the overthrow of Napoleon and the growth of Italian nationalism. Maps, bibliographical footnotes, and bibliography.

Reddaway, W. F., et al., eds. *The Cambridge History of Poland.* Vol. 2, *From Augustus II to Pilsudski (1697-1935).* Cambridge, England: Cambridge University Press, 1941.
Written by Polish, British, and North American scholars, all of whom are specialists in the field. Three chapters cover the Napoleonic era and its impact on Poland. Marcel Handelsman discusses the Duchy of Warsaw; John Holland Rose covers Napoleon and Poland; and Maryan Kukiel examines the Polish military contribution to the Napoleonic wars. All three provide a good introduction to the subject for the English speaking student. Index and maps.

Saintoyant, Jules François. *La Colonisation française pendant la période napoléonienne (1789-1815)*. Paris: La Renaissance du Livre, 1931.
A detailed topical study of French colonialism based on extensive archival research. It begins with a summary of recent events, then continues with a examination of the policies of the colonial administration, and finally discusses events in the colonies. Saintoyant provides a summary of Napoleon's colonial policies. Critical of Napoleon, he argues that Napoleon reestablished the Old Regime in the colonies by restoring authority and order. Considered a good survey of the topic.

Schama, Simon. *Patriots and Liberators: Revolution in the Netherlands, 1780-1813*. London: Collins, 1977.
Generally considered to be the definitive work on the political history of the Dutch Republic and Kingdom during the French revolutionary and Napoleonic era. It is based on thorough research in the Algemeen Rijksarchief (in the Hague) and various provincial archives: Gemeente Archief, Amsterdam, Gemeente Archief, Utrecht, and Rijksarchief. He also made use of the Archives Nationales of France and the Archives of the Ministère des Affaires Etrangères in Paris. Schama believes 1780-1813 was a crucial period in the development of the modern Dutch state. The second part of the book, approximately half of it, deals with the revolutionary and Napoleonic period to 1805. Part III is devoted to the remainder of the Napoleonic years. Maps, index, and bibliography.

Sheehan, James. *German History 1770-1866*. Oxford, England: Clarendon Press, 1989.
The best synthesis of the period by a German specialist. Part II, "Germans and the French Revolution, 1789-1815," covers the Napoleonic years. In this straightforward, informative narrative of military and political history, Sheehan contends that no major technological advances occurred during these years and that the greatness of the Emperor stemmed from his facility to seize upon opportunities and settle problems posed by the sheer scale of warfare. On the political side, he examines the consequences of the abolition of the Holy Roman Empire, which had been the institutional framework of German lands for hundreds of years. What impact did its replacement with the Rhenish Confederation in 1806 have for German politics? Sheehan argues that Napoleon's

reorganization of these lands brought lasting changes as well as the consequences of the Napoleonic hegemony for Prussia, Austria, and smaller German states. As it is based primarily on recent German sources, Sheehan's chapters are particularly important for those who would not otherwise have access to this information. Index and bibliographical references.

Simon, Walter M. *The Failure of the Prussian Reform Movement 1807-1819.* Ithaca, N.Y.: Cornell University Press, 1955.
In this study of French occupation of Prussia, (except for one province), based on a Yale University doctoral dissertation, the author attempts to explain why the reforms, particularly agricultural and constitutional, did not meet the expectations of their framers. Simon explains that the main cause of the failure was the inability of German liberals and nationalists to come to a working alliance. He also attributes the collapse of the European balance of power to the Napoleonic hegemony. Index and bibliography.

Stanley, John Dudley. "The Adaptation of the Napoleonic Political Structures in the Duchy of Warsaw." *Canadian Slavonic Papers/Revue canadienne des slavistes* 31 (1989): 128-145.
Based on documents from the library of the Polish Academy of Sciences, this paper examines the impact of the Napoleonic Code on the Grand Duchy of Warsaw. Stanley states that the result of the code, and other reforms introduced by Napoleon, was the political modernization of Poland. This process, already under way with the Polish Enlightenment, created a peculiar political, legal, and cultural tradition that would last into the twentieth century.

_____. "A Political and Social History of the Duchy of Warsaw 1807-1813." Ph.D. dissertation. Toronto: University of Toronto, 1979.
A valuable study in English of the Duchy of Warsaw created by Napoleon. Focuses on the administrative, legal, and social structures put into place by the Emperor. Stanley argues that these aspects of the duchy outlived the duchy, and served Poland into the next century. Topics covered include the origins of the duchy, the constitution, the implementation of the Napoleonic Code and judicial system, and the treatment of the Jewish population. Based on manuscript sources in the Warsaw archives and the Cracow

library, as well as other printed primary and secondary sources. The most comprehensive study on this topic. Bibliography.

Thiry, Jean. *La Chute de Napoléon Ier.* Vol. 1, *La Campagne de France.* Vol. 2, *La Première Abdication.* Paris: Berger-Levrault, 1938-1939, 2d ed. 1948.
Written by a specialist in the fall of the Empire, these two volumes cover the period from January to the end of April 1814. Both are detailed and scholarly, based on original sources. Thiry made use of both foreign and departmental archives, printed primary sources such as Napoleon's correspondence, and memoirs. The authority on this subject. Bibliography.

_____. *La Seconde Abdication de Napoléon Ier.* Paris: Berger-Levrault, 1945.
A study of four weeks in the life of the Emperor, between his surrender of the British and his departure for Saint Helena. After sketching the French campaign of 1814 and the Hundred Days, the author narrates the dramatic period that followed. Thiry demonstrates the lassitude of Napoleon, and of the nation, the attitude of the Chamber of Commerce, the presence of foreign powers, and royalist influences. The exciting incidents of this brief period are related with sobriety and precision. A solid and studious book. Bibliography.

Tulard, Jean. *Le Grand Empire, 1804-15.* Paris: Albin Michel, 1982.
A study of the Napoleonic Empire from 1804 to 1814 by the leading French historian of Napoleon. Tulard begins by examining agents of French preponderance, and the heritage of the "Grande Nation," which leads to a description of the Empire at its height in 1808. In this chapter, Tulard examines each country composing the Empire: the France of 122 departments, vassal kingdoms, and dependent states. The second part is devoted to the functioning of the Empire in its economic, political, and religious dimensions. Finally, the third section deals with the collapse of the Empire. The research is well-documented in notes and has an excellent bibliography. Index.

Villani, Pasquale. *Italia napoleonica.* Naples: Guida, 1978.
Villani's book on Napoleonic Italy is mainly concerned with the Kingdom of Naples. This work reviews his major opinions published in earlier works, *Mezzogiorno tra riforme et rivoluzione*

(1962), covering the later eighteenth to the mid-nineteenth century, and *La vendita dei beni dello Stato nel regno di Napoli (1806-1815)*, published in 1964. The newer work covers Italy as a whole and concludes that traditional landlords were able to adjust to French control and endure, particularly in the sale of state lands. The old feudal estates persisted, as the major purchasers were lords themselves. Villani has published two articles in French for those without the Italian. These include his study of the Kingdom of Naples under Napoleon, "Le royaume de Naples pendant la domination française (1806-1815)," *Annales historiques de la Révolution Française* 44 (1972): 68-81; and his article on the Italian economy under Napoleon, "Quelques aspects de la vie économique italienne à l'époque napoléonienne," *Annales historiques de la Révolution française* 49 (1977): 587-617. Bibliographical references and index.

Wehler, Hans-Ulrich. *Deutsche Gesellschaftsgeschichte, I: 1700-1815*. München: C. H. Beck, 1987.
In this well-received and influential history of the modernization of Germany, the author holds that modernization predated the revolutionary and Napoleonic eras and that the incursions from France disrupted the balance of power, and hastened the development of a German national consciousness. The effects of the revolutionary and Napoleonic years were complex. Both had a negative impact in political, social, and economic spheres throughout the German lands, with the exception of Saxony and the Rhineland, which experienced a growth in cotton manufacturing. The only modernizing aspect that the years 1789-1815 brought to Germany was the growth of a "modern German nationalism." Indexes and bibliography.

Woolf, Stuart. "French Civilization and Ethnicity in the Napoleonic Empire." *Past and Present* 124 (1989): 96-120.
The French Revolution confirmed France's position as the carrier of Western civilization. This ideology had been developed long before the Revolution but was strengthened during the Napoleonic years by the reforms that France inflicted on its conquered lands. During this period, the French nation imposed its values on the peoples it ruled through a rational, uniform system of administration. French cultural imperialism was complicated by the problem of ethnicity. Three peoples are examined to demonstrate how the French endeavored to deal with these complications: Tuscans,

Dalmatian Slavs, and Jews. The revolutionary and Napoleonic age served to transform the ideas of French superiority and its civilizing mission from the intellectual to the practical sphere.

_____. *A History of Italy 1700-1860: The Social Constraints of Political Change*. London: Methuen, 1979.
A survey of the major developments in Italy from 1700 to 1860. It has the merit of using many sources in Italian not readily available to the English-language reader. On Napoleon, Woolf provides one chapter that serves as an excellent introduction to the Napoleonic impact on Italy. Covers the reaction of Italian administrators and rulers to Napoleonic changes, including the introduction of constitutions in these states. The kingdom of Naples is singled out for special attention. Index and bibliography.

_____. *Napoleon's Integration of Europe*. London: Routledge, 1991.
Drawing from sources in five languages previously unavailable to the English-language reader, Woolf investigates the impact of the Napoleonic hegemony from the position of the bureaucrats and soldiers of the Empire. His main subject is the extent to which the institutions of continental Europe were modernized during these years. The first overall study of the Napoleonic administrative system that existed in France, Italy, Belgium, Holland, Switzerland, Poland, Spain, and the German states. Indexes and bibliographical references.

Zaghi, Carlo. *Potere chiesa e società: Studi e ricerche sull'Italia giacobina e napoleonica*. Naples: Istituto Universitario Orientale, 1984.
An erudite study of Jacobin and Napoleonic Italy. Fully documented and chronologically structured, it begins with the 1780s and continues to Napoleon's creation of the Kingdom of Italy. Years of research went into this history, considered to be an important contribution to Italian historiography. Index and bibliographical references.

_____. *L'Italia di Napoleone dalla Cisalpina al Regno*. Turin: Unione Tipografico-Editrice Torinese, 1986.
A magisterial examination of northern Italy from 1796 to 1814, including a perceptive and detailed study of Napoleon—his policies, goals, and character. The author argues that Italians first

acquired a sense of national identification under Napoleon and that Napoleon opened the way for the Risorgimento. He also argues that the abolition of privileges and servitude did little to modify a system of land tenure based on land ownership and the exploitation of tenants and sharecroppers. Zaghi discusses not only political and military changes but also economic and social consequences, which emerge as the most important. Considered the best in contemporary Italian scholarship on this subject. Index and bibliographical references.

Chapter 10

RELIGION

General

Chlovy, Gérard, and Yves-Marie Hilaire. *Histoire religieuse de la France contemporaine, 1800/1880*. Toulouse: E. Privat, 1985.
A fully documented survey which has been generally well received. Written by five specialists of the French academic community in Roman Catholicism, Judaism, and Protestantism, it attempts to update Adrien Dansette's work of the same title. Unlike the latter, the current study examines religious cults outside the dominant tradition of Catholicism, making the monograph particularly valuable. It belongs to the new religious history focusing on religious mentalities and practices. Regional and sexual differences in practice are addressed. Index and bibliographical references.

Protestantism

Encrevé, André. *Les Protestants en France de 1800 à nos jours: Histoire d'une réintegration*. Paris: Stock, 1985.
In spite of its title, all but fifty pages of this study deal with the nineteenth century. A specialist of nineteenth century French Protestantism, Encrevé is well equipped to write a general history of this subject. The monograph is organized chronologically, and the Napoleonic era is covered in the chapter concerning Protestants of the Romantic age from 1800 to 1850. A good summary of the changes made to Protestantism under Napoleon, such as the Organic Articles, and the granting to the Protestant churches of

an official statute. Doctrinal trends and the offenses they engendered are also well depicted. Bibliography.

Poland, Burdette, C. *French Protestantism and the French Revolution: A Study in Church and State, Thought and Religion, 1685-1815.* Princeton, N.J.: Princeton University Press, 1957.
The title is rather misleading, as this is primarily a study of the French Huguenots during the revolutionary and Napoleonic eras. It is disappointing that other Protestant sects, such as the Lutherans, are neglected. Poland is more concerned with the behavior of the Protestants than with their doctrine. However, his survey remains the best English book on the topic. Based on a doctoral dissertation of the same name (Princeton University, 1954). Bibliography.

Robert, Daniel. *Les Églises réformées de France (1800-1830).* Paris: Presses Universitaires de France, 1961.
A classic work built on a doctoral thesis on the same topic. A very well-researched study using public and private documents of the Reformed Church in France during the early nineteenth century. Robert depicts in great detail the situation of Protestants and the organization of their churches from the end of the Old Regime to 1830. Argues that the Organic Articles gave new impetus to Protestantism. Indexes and bibliography.

Catholicism

Bindel, Victor. *Le Vatican à Paris, 1809-1814: Un Rêve de Napoléon.* Paris: Editions Alsatia, 1942.
A concise work summarizing the religious policies between 1809 and 1814, including the Council of 1811, Savona, and the Concordat of Fontainebleau. It focuses on the transfer of Pope Pius VII and his cardinals to Paris. Bindel attempts to demonstrate that the installation of the pontifical court in Paris was an essential element in the European empire that Napoleon dreamed of creating. For the author, this event was pivotal for the type of holy empire, in the tradition of the Middle Ages, that Napoleon envisaged, an empire consisting of two parts divided between God (and the Pope) and himself, the Emperor. The result was Catholicism as the state religion. Bibliographical note.

Boulay de Meurthe, Alfred. *Histoire de la négociation du Concordat de 1801*. Tours: A. Mame et Fils, 1920.

Based entirely upon a collection of documents published by the author, who is an expert in the history of Catholicism during the Napoleonic era, this is an extended, detailed, chronological description of the negotiations for the Concordat. Boulay de Meurthe discusses the background to the Concordat, beginning with the state of religion at 18 Brumaire, and chronicles Napoleon's attitude toward the Catholic religion. He also discusses the various obstacles and resistance to the Concordat from Rome. Considered by experts to be the leading work on this subject.

_____. *Histoire du rétablissement du culte en France (1802-1805)*. Tours: A. Mame et Fils, 1925.

A leading survey that narrates the decline of relations between Napoleon and the Pope from the Concordat to 1805. The author stresses the difficulties in the application of the Concordat resulting from the personalities of Pius VII and the Emperor, complicated by the resistance in the Tribunate and Legislative Body. Also under examination is the organization of the Protestant cult, particularly the Lutherans and Calvinists, as well as the role assigned to religion in the Empire. There is much valuable information in this monograph.

Carven, John W. *Napoleon and the Lazarists*. The Hague: Martinus Nijhoff, 1974.

The only study on Napoleon's role in the reestablishment and subsequent dissolution of the Congregation of the Mission of Vincent St. Paul, known as the Lazarists in France. In the first part of his book, Carven examines the social and religious context of the reestablishment, which involves a close study of the Concordat, including sections on the negotiations, implementation, and reactions in Europe. Part II concerns the Lazarists until their dissolution by Napoleon in 1809. Reasons for their dissolution are also considered. Carven drew his research from the archives of the Congregation of the Mission in Paris. Index and bibliography.

Chadwick, Owen. *The Popes and European Revolution*. Oxford, England: The Clarendon Press, 1980.

A favorably regarded survey of the Roman Catholic Church during the eighteenth and nineteenth centuries. Pages 485-534 consider the Napoleonic period. It contains a good introductory section on the French Concordat from the Roman perspective. Other topics dealt with include the Italian Concordat, the Coronation of Napoleon, Spanish policy, and the secularization of Germany. Index and bibliography.

Dansette, Adrien. *Histoire religieuse de la France contemporaine.* Vol. 1, *De la Révolution à la Troisième République.* Paris: Flammarion, 1948. Translated by John Dingle as *Religious History of Modern France.* Vol. 1, *From the Revolution to the Third Republic.* New York: Herder & Herder, 1961.
An excellent survey from the Roman Catholic perspective. Dansette praises Napoleon for restoring Catholicism in France. Book 3 deals with the Napoleonic period. Topics include the success of the religious settlement and the failure to subjugate the church to the state. The translation is an abridged version of the French text first published in 1948.

Delacroix, Simon. *La Réorganisation de l'église de France après la Révolution (1801-1809).* Vol. 1, *Les Nominations d'évêques et la liquidation du passé.* Paris: Vitrail, 1962.
Delacroix taught at the Institut Catholique of Paris and is an expert in history of the Catholic church. Based on a doctoral thesis of the same title, this outstanding work approaches its subject from a Roman Catholic viewpoint, examining the background and events leading to the Concordat. Delacroix analyzes the document itself, as well as the Organic Articles and the newly appointed bishops. Thanks to the superb use of many documents from the French Archives Nationales, he has shed much light on the religious policy of the First Consul and the attitude of the Church in the face of many delicate problems. Extensive bibliographcial footnotes.

Deries, Léon. *Les Congrégations religieuses au temps de Napoléon.* Paris: Félix Alcan, 1931.
A history of religious orders under Napoleon based on original material. Deries demonstrates Napoleon's caution in changing revolutionary policy toward these religious groups. The Emperor preserved intact the entirety of the repressive legislation while conferring by special degrees exemptions as he saw fit. Toleration was not extended to any "contemplative" order, but only to those who were useful to public service. Included in the discussion are

female orders which, the author informs us, Napoleon found less repressive. Bibliography.

Destrem, Jean. *Les Déportations du Consulat et de l'Empire.* Paris: Jeanmarie, 1885.

A major work on the deportations of priests during this period. The first 302 pages provide a description substantiated by many documents. The remainder of the book is a biographical dictionary with short biographies on those deported. The leading work on this subject. Biographical index of refuges.

Godel, Jean. "L'Eglise selon Napoléon." *Revue d'histoire moderne et contemporaine* 17, no. 3 (1970): 837-845.

An examination of Napoleon's relations with the Roman Catholic church. Godel studies the problems related to the annexation of the Papal States and the captivity of Pope Pius VII. He provides a description of the Concordat of 1801 and the disputes between the clergy and the government of the Empire in 1805. The eventual supremacy of Ultramontanism over Gallicanism is featured. Demonstrates Napoleon's failure in manipulating the Concordat to his benefit.

Hales, Edward Elton Young. *Napoleon and the Pope: The Story of Napoleon and Pius VII.* London: Eyre and Spottiswode, 1962.

Although brief, Hales's study is the major work in English on the subject and the standard text on the division in church-state relations. Hales is an expert on the papacy during this period. A detailed, detached chronology of the relationship between the two men, written from the Roman Catholic perspective, it favors the Pope as the moral superior of the two.

Haussonville, Gabriel Paul Othenin de Cleron, comte de. *L'Église romaine et le Premier Empire, 1800-14.* 5 vols. Paris: Michel Lévy Frères, 1868-1869.

An extensive study on this topic containing the complete history of the relationship between the First Empire and the Roman church. Pope Pius VII is portrayed as the victim of Napoleon, and the author is no admirer of the Concordat. Provides a day-by-day chronicle of the written negotiations and contains a large collection of documents. Still a fundamental source on this topic.

Langlois, Claude. *Le Catholicisme au féminin, les congrégations à supérieure générale au XIXe siècle*. Paris: Cerf, 1984.

An important contribution to both women's history and the study of the Catholic church during nineteenth century France, this published version of a three-volume French *doctorat d'état* does not make for light reading. The first section is concerned with the development of female orders under Napoleon. Explains the phenomenon of the huge growth of female religious orders in the period immediately following the French Revolution. Illustrations and bibliography.

Latreille, André. *L'Eglise catholique et la Révolution*. Vol. 2, *L'Ère napoléonienne et la crise européene (1800-1816)*. Paris: Cerf, 1970.

First published in 1950, this highly respected scholarly synthesis of the Roman Catholic church under Napoleon examines not only France, but also Napoleon's impact in Italy and Germany. Covers the conflict in the priesthood in the Empire and ends with a description of the beginnings of the Catholic restoration, summarizing the history of the period. Shows that the religious politics of Napoleon could not be suitable to Pope Pius VII. Bibliography.

_____. *Napoléon et le Saint-Siège, 1801-1808: L'Ambassade du cardinal Fesch à Rome*. Paris: Félix Alcan, 1935.

Based on documentary sources, including the papers of Cardinal Fesch, housed in the archives of Lyons, Latreille examines the history of relations between the Pope and the Emperor while the Church of the Concordat was establishing itself in France and the Empire. The focus of the erudite study is diplomacy: the problems for Napoleon because of the Pope's Italian policy. The Pope had counted on several advantages from the Italian Concordat, but from 1804 he was disappointed, as many parts of it were ignored and legislation contrary to the interests of the Church were introduced. Bibliography.

Latreille, Camille. *L'Opposition religieuse au Concordat de 1792 à 1803*. Paris: Hachette, 1910.

An important monograph, well documented with original sources, this severe treatment of Napoleon's religious policy argues that he abolished the Gallican church in favor of the Papacy. In providing extracts of responses and objections to Napoleon's religious policy, Latreille successfully demonstrates that there was much internal opposition to this policy. He stresses the faithfulness of the clergy to Louis XVIII, their hatred of the Revolution, and their consequent rejection of anything settled by Bonaparte, who, in their eyes, was the incarnation of the Revolution. Bibliographical references.

Leflon, Jean. *La Crise révolutionnaire.* vol. 20, *Histoire de l'église depuis ses origines jusqu'à nos jours.* Published under the direction of Augustin Fliche and Victor Martin. Paris: Bloud & Gay, 1951. A synthesis embracing both the revolutionary and Napoleonic eras. The information contained in this volume is extensive. Leflon makes considerable use of primary sources both Italian and French. Book II covers the entire Napoleonic period. The tome is organized chronologically and thematically and examines the religious consequences of Brumaire, Napoleon's personal religious views, the Concordat, its application in France, and the new organization of dioceses. Under the Empire, the religious policies from the Coronation are pursued. Here, the consequences of Napoleon's policies for the Empire are discussed. Bibliography.

O'Dwyer, Margaret M. *The Papacy in the Age of Napoleon and the Restoration: Pius VII, 1800-1823.* Lanham, Md.: University Press of America, 1985.
This brief yet thorough account of the Papacy during the Napoleonic and Restoration years does not say anything new, but it is useful in that it focuses on the Papacy rather than the Catholic church. Two-thirds of the book concern the Napoleonic era, concentrating on political and diplomatic history. Useful for anyone interested in the relationship between the Pope and Napoleon. Index, chapter notes, and bibliography.

Phillips, C. S. *The Church in France 1789-1848: A Study in Revival.* New York: Russell & Russell, 1966.
First published in 1929, Phillips' book provides a useful summary of the major changes to the Roman Catholic church under the French Revolution and Napoleon. It looks at the decline of the Church during the Revolution and its revival, beginning with the Napoleonic years. The author believes that Napoleon healed the revolutionary schism between church and state. Topics covered include the Concordat of 1801, the resulting breach with the Papacy, the National Council, and the Concordat of Fontainebleau.

Religion

There are no notes, but a select bibliography. Three chapters, 5-7, deal with the Napoleonic era.

Walsh, Henry Horace. *The Concordat of 1801: A Study of the Problem of Nationalism in the Relations of Church and State*. New York: Columbia University Press, 1933. Reprint. New York: AMS Press, 1967.
A study of the influence of nationalism on the relations between church and state, the best work in English on the subject. The chapters consider the background of and negotiations for the Concordat, including a concise treatment of the Concordat itself. Chapters on Chateaubriand, de Maistre, and others emphasize their role in the restoration of Catholicism. A well-documented and meticulous narrative of the problem of church and state during the Napoleonic years. Bibliography.

Judaism

Anchel, Robert. *Napoléon et les Juifs: Essai sur les rapports de l'état français et du culte israélite de 1806 à 1815*. Paris: Presses Universitaires de France, 1928.
Despite its date, Anchel's work remains the definitive study of the state of life for the Jews between 1789 and 1815. The focus of the book is the background and nature of the decrees of 30 May 1806 and 17 March 1808, both dealing with Jewish moneylenders. Demonstrates that Jews were liberated under Napoleon; they gained equal citizenship but not perfect equality. Scholarly, lengthy, and heavily documented. Bibliography.

Katz, Jacob. *Out of the Ghetto: The Social Background of Jewish Emancipation 1770-1870*. Cambridge, Mass.: Harvard University Press, 1975.
Regarded as a major work on the social, political, and ideological reasons for the new consideration of the place of Jews during this period in Central and Western Europe. Napoleon's calling of a Jewish Sanhedrin is viewed as the climax of the transformation of the previous isolation of Jews from the rest of society. Katz considers reasons for the meeting of the Sanhedrin, Napoleon's motives for it, and its consequences. In addition, he considers the ramifications of Napoleon's 1808 decree, which attempted to integrate Alsatian Jews into the fabric of French life. An excellent

study of Jewish emancipation that provides useful insight into the Napoleonic years. Index and bibliographical references.

Kobler, Franz. *Napoleon and the Jews*. New York: Schocken Books, 1976.
Kobler's intention is to contribute to our knowledge about Napoleon and his relationship with the Jewish people. In the introduction to this pioneering work, Kobler states that, previous to 1940, Napoleon's *Proclamation to the Jews* of 1799 was unavailable, and it is this document that provides the basis of his study. Its purpose is to recount Napoleon's attempt to restore Israel. Kobler begins with Napoleon's earliest contacts with the Jews, through his studies, and concludes with the consequences of Napoleon's policies for the Jews of the emancipation era and the rise of Zionism. Notes, index, and bibliography.

Malino, Frances. *The Sephardic Jews of Bordeaux: Assimilation and Emancipation in Revolutionary and Napoleonic France*. University: University of Alabama Press, 1978.
The best account in English on the effect of Napoleon's policies on Jews in Bordeaux. Malino's documentary evidence from the Bordeaux archives sheds new light on revolutionary emancipation, the operation of the Imperial Council, and Napoleon's relations with his ministers. Demonstrates that during the Napoleonic era, through both intimidation and consultation, the Jews of Bordeaux sacrificed their identity to become Frenchmen. Index and bibliography.

Piétri, François. *Napoléon et les Israélites*. Paris: Berger-Levrault, 1964.
Piétri attempts to remove the stigma of anti-Semite from Napoleon by arguing that he was the first liberator of the Jewish people. Although the author does not offer anything new, and his arguments are not entirely convincing in the light of the facts, he does provide a well-written summary of the major events in Jewish-French history from the Revolution to the Restoration. Illustrations and chronology.

Schwarzfuchs, Simon. *Napoleon, the Jews and the Sanhedrin*. London: Routledge and Kegan Paul, 1979.
Written for a general audience, this scholarly monograph considers the Jewish experience under Napoleon. Harshly critical of Napo-

leon's discriminatory attitude, it nevertheless concludes that Jews benefited from his polices. Good description of the Assembly of Jewish Notables and the Sanhedrin. Focuses on the re-definition of Judaism to meet the challenges of the modern nation-state. Argues that the rabbis significantly influenced the decisions of the Assembly of Jewish Notables. Chapters 7 and 8 examine the consequences of the Sanhedrin for the Jews of the Empire. Index and bibliographical references.

Soboul, Albert, and Bernhard Blumenkranz. *Le Grand Sanhedrin de Napoléon*. Toulouse: E. Privat, 1979.

Historians Soboul and Blumenkranz have produced a number of articles on the theme of the two assemblies called by Napoleon to provide judicial and religious organization to the Jewish population inhabiting his states. They address Napoleon's attempt to assimilate these people, examining the Jews of different regions: Alsace, Bordeaux-Bayonne, and the Netherlands. At the back of the book, they have reproduced the rare *Collection des Procès-Verbaux du Grand Sanhédrin* by Diogène Talma. Index and bibliographical references.

Chapter 11

DIPLOMACY

Blumenthal, Henry. *France and the United States: Their Diplomatic Relations, 1789-1914*. Chapel Hill: University of North Carolina Press, 1970.
Although this survey of relations between France and America focuses on the period between 1870 and 1914, it is still valuable for its section on the Napoleonic period. This scholarly study is based on French and American archives, including both family papers and published documents. The overall theme is that the historical friendship between France and the United States is more myth than reality. The author holds that Napoleon's policy toward America was self-defeating. His arrogance in dealing with Americans demonstrated his ignorance, and he incited the wrath of the American people. In conducting such a policy, Napoleon failed to exploit the opportunities the United States had offered in the Embargo of 1807. Index and bibliography.

Bourgeois, E. *Manuel historique de politique étrangère*. Vol. 2, *Les Révolutions 1789-1830*. Paris: Belin Frères, 1898.
This volume is part of a four-volume set on foreign affairs published between 1892 and 1927. Approximately 350 pages cover the years from 1800 to 1815. The most instructive work on the oriental vision of Napoleon's ambition. The author's thesis is that Napoleon as an adventurer was lured increasingly by the East. Bourgeois views expansion as the major driving force in Napoleon's foreign policy, even after the Russian campaign of 1812. A dated but important and influential narrative survey, which remains a valuable work for its detail. Bibliography.

Butterfield, Herbert. *The Peace Tactics of Napoleon, 1806-1808.* New York: Octagon Books, 1972.
An admirable study of wartime diplomacy from the defeat of the Prussians at Jena to the Treaty of Tilsit. Well written and well researched, it begins with the efforts of the Prussians to secure a peace treaty and Napoleon's hesitation in granting one. It continues with the Austrian attempt at mediation between the opposing countries. The culmination is the section of the Treaty of Tilsit. A reprint of the 1929 edition with a new preface by Butterfield.

DeConde Alexander. *This Affair of Louisiana.* New York: Charles Scribner's Sons, 1976.
A well-written investigation of this topic which encompasses the background, negotiations, and immediate outcome of the Louisiana purchase. Although much of the book is well-known material to those acquainted with the subject, DeConde does provide some new insights into the purchase, such as minimizing the importance of the pressure exerted on Spain and France, by American frontiersmen, which made it simpler for the Americans to obtain the land. For DeConde, America acquired Louisiana not through luck, or European distress, but through "conscious expansionism of an imperial creed promoting action." He adds that France did not have the liberty to sell Louisiana and that both Jefferson and Napoleon were well aware of that fact. Not considered the definitive work on this subject, but a thoughtful scholarly synthesis which places the purchase in its historical context, and the first major study on this topic since World War II. Illustrations, notes, index, and an excellent bibliographical essay.

Deutsch, Harold C. *The Genesis of Napoleonic Imperialism.* Cambridge, Mass.: Harvard University Press, 1938.
Based on an extensive use of France's Archives du Ministère des Affaires Etrangères and Archives Nationales and Austria's Hous-, Hof-, und Staats-Archiv in Vienna as well as printed primary and secondary literature, this is an excellent summary of the foreign policy of Napoleon from the Treaty of Lunéville in 1801 to the overthrow of the Third Coalition after Austerlitz in December 1805. Deutsch contends that Napoleon did not deliberately seek warfare. It was circumstances and his opportunistic following of the events of the time that led to a renewal of war in 1803 and 1805. In this interesting study, Deutsch clearly demonstrates that

Napoleon was a flexible diplomat, who often changed his views with changing circumstances, and that he was usually the winner for this behavior. Bibliographical footnotes, index, and bibliography.

Driault, Edouard. *Napoléon et l'Europe*: Vol. 1, *La Politique extérieure du Premier Consul.* Vol. 2, *Austerlitz: La Fin du Saint-Empire (1804-1806).* Vol. 3, *Tilsit: France et Russie sous le Premier Empire: La Question de Pologne (1806-1809).* Vol. 4, *Le Grand Empire, 1800-1812.* Vol. 5, *La Chute de l'Empire: La Légende de Napoléon, 1812-1815.* Paris: Félix Alcan, 1910-1927. Written for the purpose of refuting Albert Sorel's theories on the Napoleonic empire, these works, constituting a summary of the Empire, focus on the significance of Napoleon to France and to the rest of Europe. Driault argues that the Napoleonic design for Europe was the improvement of life for the people of the Empire. His goal was peace for Europe and the liberty of the individual. At the same time, he contends that Napoleon was an opportunist and that his fundamental concepts were Roman: his ambition was to create a new Roman Empire. Sources are limited to French archives. Endures as an epic work in the history of international relations. Bibliography.

_____. *Politique orientale de Napoléon: Sébastiani et Gardane 1806-1808.* Paris: Alcan, 1904.
A lengthy, detailed scholarly study of Napoleon's Eastern policy, focusing on the Balkans and Turkey. Above all, Napoleon desired a separation of Russia from Constantinople and the Mediterranean. His goal was to keep the Russians out of the Balkans. Driault speculates that Napoleon was drawn to the East by a secret desire to halt the expansion of barbarian Russia. The missions of Gardane to Persia and Sébastiani to Constantinople are highlighted. Based on official correspondence and other documents from the French archives. An indispensable work on foreign policy. Bibliography and footnotes.

Fugier, André. *La Révolution française et l'Empire napoléonien.* Paris: Hachette, 1954.
This is the fourth volume in a series on international relations from the early Middle Ages to the present. In this volume, Fugier examines the entire range of influences and activities that governed relations between world powers from 1799 to 1815. Included are

the New World, Asia, and Africa, as well as the European countries. Fugier sees Napoleon as the inspiration for European integration and a common European market. He argues that the European continent submitted completely to the economic and political domination of France. In addition, he notes that the French Empire tended to retard the economic development of the countries of the Empire. Napoleon was the great organizer of a unified Europe, well ahead of his time, and this fact turned out to be a disaster because of Europe's technical backwardness, particularly in terms of its transportation systems. A comprehensive work that remains useful for its detail and interpretation. Maps and bibliography.

Giddens, Paul H. "Contemporary American Opinion of Napoleon." *Journal of American History* 26 (1932): 189-204.
A survey of the attitudes of a number of prominent American politicians toward Napoleon. Giddens stresses the fact that Americans were not impervious to Napoleon's reign. American trade and commerce, as well as the lives of Americans, were directly affected by the conflict in Europe. Through an examination of the correspondence of various American statesmen, the author attempts to discover contemporary U.S. public opinion toward Napoleon. Some of the viewpoints examined include those of James Monroe, minister to France, Rufus King, minister to England, William Vans Murray, minister to the Netherlands, and John Quincy Adams, minister to Prussia in 1800. Giddens demonstrates that American attitudes were widely divergent, and the sample of opinions he has chosen is in no way representative of the entire nation. They did, however, illustrate those of the Federalist party. Bibliographical endnotes.

Gulick, Edward Vose. *Europe's Classical Balance of Power: A Case of the Theory and Practice of One of the Great Concepts of European Statecraft.* Ithaca, N.Y.: Cornell University Press, 1955. Reprint. Westport, Conn.: Greenwood Press, 1982.
A study of the theory and practice of the balance of power. The first third of the book is devoted to the theory, which Gulick applies to the formation of the coalition against Napoleon, the two Treaties of Paris, the Congress of Vienna, and the Quadruple Alliance. Gulick argues that the balance of power theory had a profound influence on the statesmen of the period. Much attention is paid to the Congress of Vienna. A lucid explanation of the phenomenon. Bibliographical footnotes and bibliographical essay.

Kaplan, Lawrence S. "France and the War of 1812." *Journal of American History* 57 (1970): 36-47.
Kaplan maintains that although the United States was a co-belligerent with France against Great Britain during the war, relations between the two nations were unfriendly. Discusses Napoleon's negligent and contemptuous manner toward Americans and the American response. A useful introduction to this conflict. Forty-three notes.

_____. "Jefferson, the Napoleonic Wars and the Balance of Power." *William and Mary Quarterly*, 3d ser. 14 (1957): 198-217.
A reevaluation of Jefferson's foreign policy from 1805 to 1815. Examining Jefferson's attitude toward the great powers of France and the United States, Kaplan demonstrates that Jefferson entered the Napoleonic wars because he presupposed that a small neutral nation like the United States had much to benefit from the conflict between the large powers. Sixty notes.

Lévy, Arthur. *Napoléon et la paix*. Paris: Plon, Nourrit, 1902.
A survey of Napoleon as a peacemaker from 1796 to 1815, this is a far-reaching scholarly monograph with a explicit interpretation of Napoleon. Lévy holds that Napoleon was a man of peace who fought only when necessary, in self-defense. His continual attempts to make peace in the face of aggression by the English and ruling classes of Europe are described. This work has been partially translated in pages 36-42 of David H. Pinkney's *Napoleon: Historical Enigma* (Lexington, Mass.: D. C. Heath, 1969).

Lyon, Elijah Wilson. *Louisiana in French Diplomacy 1759-1804*. Norman: University of Oklahoma Press, 1934.
Based on the author's doctoral dissertation, "Bonaparte's Proposed Louisiana Expansion" (University of Chicago, 1932), this study is an examination of France's viewpoint of Louisiana from 1759 to 1804. Lyon competently scrutinizes the intricate diplomacy between France and Spain, drawing from the French and Spanish archives. The book opens with the reasons that France relinquished Louisiana to Spain in 1763. It continues by demonstrating that unremitting French interest in Louisiana, from its transferral to Spain to French efforts to regain it, ended Napoleon's American colonial dream. More than half the book (pp. 101-150) is concerned with the period after 1800, during which Napoleon attempted to construct a colonial empire in North America. Lyon shows how

yellow fever and trouble in Saint-Domingo spoiled Napoleon's intentions for America. Remains the standard English text on this subject. Footnotes and bibliography.

Mowat, Robert Balmain. *The Diplomacy of Napoleon.* New York: Russell and Russell, 1971.
A study of French diplomacy from the Revolution to 1815, focusing on the period after 1793. Mowat examines Napoleon's diplomatic aims, his methods, and France's relations with foreign powers. Insists that state building absorbed more of Napoleon's energies than warfare, and that his armies were merely the instrument of his diplomacy. Rich in details on diplomatic negotiations, but assumes previous knowledge about the campaigns. Bibliographical footnotes.

Nicolson, Harold George. *The Congress of Vienna: A Study in Allied Unity, 1812-1822.* London: Constable, 1946.
A well-organized and clearly written narrative of diplomacy from 1812 to 1822. Nicolson begins with the year 1812 and Napoleon's retreat from Moscow. He covers the return of Louis XVIII to Versailles and the banishment of Napoleon to Saint Helena. The work concludes with the demise of Metternich in 1859. Nicolson focuses on the Congress of Vienna, which is interpreted as having restored the balance of power and as a model for the World War II generation. The biographical profiles of the leaders are excellent. Remains the most readable description of the Congress of Vienna. Bibliography.

Parker, Harold T. "Why Did Napoleon Invade Russia? A Study in Motivation and the Interrelations of Personality and the Social Structure." *Journal of Military History* 54 (April 1990): 131-146.
An interesting interpretation of Napoleon's motivation, which has not been addressed with elsewhere in the literature. Based on a paper presented at a meeting of the Consortium on Revolutionary Europe in 1989, this article, through an analysis of Napoleon's personality and the structure of international politics at the time, attempts to explain why Napoleon refused to listen to his advisors, who told him not to invade Russia. Parker traces traits in Napoleon's personality to his childhood in Corsica and at Brienne, suggesting that in order to adequately solve this problem, the tzar's personality also needs analysis. Based on Napoleon's correspondence. Twenty notes.

Puryear, Vernon J. *Napoleon and the Dardanelles.* Berkeley: University of California Press, 1951.
The title does not adequately reflect the content of the book, which examines Napoleon's policies in the entire Near East from 1802 to 1815. The author centers on the years from 1806 to 1808. Much space is devoted to the commercial rivalries between France and Great Britain in Egypt, and the diplomatic intrigues in Istanbul. Finally, the general state of relations between France and Turkey is discussed. A meticulous piece of research based mainly on the archives of the French Ministère des Affaires Etrangères. Considered a superb work on the diplomatic history of the era. Bibliographical note.

Ragsdale, Hugh A. *Détente in the Napoleonic Era: Bonaparte and the Russians.* Lawrence: Regents Press of Kansas, 1980.
A well-noted scholarly study of Napoleon's Russian policies from 1799 to 1801. Making extensive use of documentary sources in several languages including French, Russian, Swedish, German, and English, Ragsdale argues that Napoleon's foreign policy was governed by his relations with Russia. The title and subtitle are misleading, as the book does not deal with "détente" and only three years, rather than the whole period, are covered. Generally considered a valuable study that fills an important gap in the diplomatic history of the period. Index and bibliography.

Schroeder, Paul W. "Napoleon's Foreign Policy: A Criminal Enterprise." *Journal of Military History* 54 (April 1990): 147-161.
Written as a reply to Harold Parker's paper on why Napoleon invaded Russia (delivered at the meeting of the Consortium on Revolutionary Europe in 1989, and cited above), accepts Professor Parker's explanations of Napoleon's psychological makeup, and takes the analysis one step further, asserting that Napoleon's political and psychological viewpoints are "criminal." Schroeder defines the terms of international politics to mean that Napoleon did not observe international treaties and keep promises, proving his argument by examining the origins of the Napoleonic wars. An interesting slant on both the diplomacy of the time and Napoleon's personality. Bibliographical note.

Shupp, Paul Frederick. *The European Powers and the Near Eastern Question, 1806-1807.* New York: Columbia University Press, 1931.

A well-documented study—based on the archives of France, Austria, and Great Britain, but not of Russia—of the complicated web of international relations between the four great powers of Russia, Austria, France, Great Britain, and the Near East. Although the Near Eastern problem played only a minor role in Napoleon's foreign policy, the author sees it as important to the background to the Treaty of Tilsit. The book opens with the Treaty of Pressburg of 1805 and closes with Tilsit. Although dated, it remains the most authoritative work on the topic. Bibliography.

Sorel, Albert. *L'Europe et la Révolution française.* 8 vols. Vol. 6, *La Trêve-Lunéville et Amiens 1800-1805.* Vol. 7, *Le Blocus continental: Le Grand Empire 1806-1812.* Vol. 8, *Le Coalition, les Traités de 1815: 1812-1815.* Paris: E. Plon, Nourrit, 1885-1904.
A study of international relations of France and Europe during the Consulate and Empire, this was the first detailed scholarly examination of foreign relations during the Napoleonic era. It is based almost entirely on original sources and is well-organized, written, and documented. Sorel argues that the after the French Revolution, Napoleon could not have concluded a peace that did not include France's "natural frontiers." Each volume contains a detailed table of contents located at the back of the book. In addition, there is a "Table" published separately which provides a table of contents for each of the volumes.

Spillman, Georges. *Napoléon et l'Islam.* Paris: Librairie Académique Perrin, 1969.
Spillman is not an historian, but a general familiar with the Muslim world from his years of service in Morocco. This monograph was published to commemorate the bicentenary of the Emperor's birth. It begins with an account of the Egyptian campaign and then treats the whole of the Consulate's policies vis-à-vis the Muslim world. Prominent was the mission of Sebastiani to Turkey and those of Romieu, Jaubert, and Gardane to Persia. Spillman then recounts the lives of some of the Emperor's agents in the East: A. Burel, Badia Castillo y Leblich, Jaubert, and Charles-Nicolas Fabvier. Based partly on the dossiers of the Service Historique of the army, as well as private papers, this is a useful summary of its subject.

Vandal, Albert. *Napoléon et Alexandre Ier: L'Alliance russe sous le Premier Empire.* 3 vols. Paris: E. Plon, Nourrit, 1891-1897.

A detailed narration of the relations between the two rulers. Vandal promotes the theory that Napoleon tried to form a strong alliance with Alexander by offering him hope of parts of the Ottoman Empire. Based on French and Russian sources, this highly influential study won the author the prestigious Prix Goncourt twice and resulted in his election to the French Academy in 1897. Detailed table of contents at the back of each volume. Volume 1 contains an appendix with the "Treaty of Tilsit" and other documents related to it. In Volume 2 there is a copy of the "Proposition faite à l'Empereur Alexandre par un groupe de seigneurs galiciens et varsoviens à l'effet de reconstituer la Pologne en l'unissant à la Russie" in the appendix. The original is in the Saint-Petersburg archives in Russian. Finally, Volume 3 contains an appendix which reproduces the "Correspondance inédite de Napoléon Ier avec le Général de Caulaincourt, duc de Vicence (1808-1809)."

Whitcomb, E. A. "The Duties and Functions of Napoleon's External Agents." *History* 57 (1972): 189-204.

The article begins by stating that diplomatic history of Napoleon is exhausted but that the study of diplomatic institutions is in its infancy. It focuses on the functions of Napoleon's diplomatic agents, who had thirteen roles rather than the four or five usually attributed to conventional agents. Discusses these tasks in some detail. Based on the materials in the archives of the Ministère des Affaires Etrangères in Paris and the published correspondence of Napoleon. An original contribution to the topic. Forty notes.

Chapter 12

CULTURE

Albert, Maurice. *Les Théâtres des boulevards, 1789-1848*. Genève: Slatkine Reprints, 1969.
   In this reprint of the original, published in 1902, three chapters (8-10) provide a wealth of information on Napoleon's impact on the theater during the period of the Consulate and Empire. Albert includes many documents concerning the administration of the theater and attempts to show how much Napoleon concerned himself with the people and life of the theater, as well as how Napoleon used the theater to enhance the glory of the Empire. For the study of popular theater, this work is indispensable.

Bainbridge, Simon John Julian. *Napoleon and English Romanticism*. Cambridge: Cambridge University Press, 1995.
   The major thrust of this recent and exhaustive thesis is that Napoleon was the overwhelming influence on the work of the English Romantic writers. English Romanticism developed the way it did because of the Romantic writers' obsession with Bonaparte. In tackling several predominant issues of the era—the French Revolution, the hero, and the relationship between the political and the poetical—the English Romantics' perception of their world emerged. The intellectual battles they fought with Napoleon shaped their work and their ideas concerning the "spirit of the age." The writers under consideration here are Wordsworth, Coleridge, Southey, Byron, and Hazlitt. Illustrations, bibliographical notes, bibliography, and index.

Balayé, Simone. *Madame de Staël: lumières et liberté*. Paris: Klincksieck, 1979.

Balayé, an expert on the topic, offers an important synthesis of her knowledge. Not a biography in the traditional sense, the work examines the intellectual development of Madame de Staël. Balayé argues that it was by her "persuasive eloquence" that Madame de Staël became dangerous in the eyes of Napoleon. The author provides an analysis of all Staël's major works, including *De l'Allemagne*. Bibliography.

Benoît, François. *L'Art français sous la Révolution et l'Empire: Les Doctrines, les idées, les genres*. Genève: Slatkine-Megariotis Reprints, 1975.

A reprint of a published French doctorial thesis of 1897. A well-documented and lavishly detailed study of theory, institutions, artists, architecture, painting, and sculpture. Benoît begins with a discussion of the social and political pedagogical usefulness of art, and its relationship with the state. He continues by examining classical theories of architecture and then moves to the context of France. All genres of the visual arts are explored. The leading work on the arts of this period. Indexes, illustrations, tables, and bibliography.

Boime, Albert. *A Social History of Modern Art*. Vol. 2, *Art in an Age of Bonapartism, 1800-1815*. Chicago: University of Chicago Press, 1991.

The second in a five-volume series that is intended to be the standard work on its subject. The word "Bonapartism" in the title implies that ideology is the emphasis here, however, Napoleon's personal impact on the art of the period is nevertheless given much attention. The artists of the Empire are discussed. An accomplished survey by an expert in the field of art history, set in the military, social, and political climate of Napoleonic Europe. Illustrations and bibliographical references.

Burton, June K. *Napoleon and Clio: Historical Writing, Teaching and Thinking during the French Empire*. Durham, N.C.: Carolina Academic Press, 1979.

An examination of how history was written and taught under Napoleon. Burton discusses Napoleon's views about history, the teaching of history, and his influence on historians under the Empire. The study is based upon documents and primary printed material including books published at all levels from primary school textbooks to works of scholarship. A useful bibliography list these contemporary texts. Fills a gap in the history of the literature and culture of the period.

Charpentier, John. *Napoléon et les hommes de lettres de son temps.* Paris: Mercure de France, 1935.
Based on a variety of printed and secondary material, this is an examination of the attitude of Napoleon toward contemporary literary figures such as Chateaubriand, Benjamin Constant, and, in particular, Madame de Staël. Charpentier stresses the emphasis Napoleon placed on the suppression of ideas contrary to his own, citing his intimidation of the Tribunes belonging to the second classification of the Institute and the suppression of newspapers. Bibliographical references.

Chatelain, Jean. *Dominique Vivant Denon et le Louvre de Napoléon.* Paris: Librairie Académique Perrin, 1973.
Chatelain is a director of the museums of France writing about the role of a director-general of museums under Napoleon. The Louvre of Napoleon was exceptionally rich in treasures taken from conquered nations. Denon was charged with the important task of decorating the Arc de Triomphe of the Carousel, the Vendôme column, and other monuments constructed for the glorification of Napoleon. Chatelain argues that, in running the museum, the Napoleonic administration was more efficacious than that of the present day.

Clubbe, John. "Byron and Napoleon 1814-1816." *Littera Pragensia: Studies in Literature and Culture* 3, no. 5 (1993): 42-57.
Byron considered Napoleon to be his alter ego. In this close textual study of Napoleon's impact on Byron, Clubbe concentrates on the years between 1814 and 1816, although he does glance back to Napoleon's impressions on Byron as a young schoolboy. Five Napoleonic poems reveal Byron's extraordinary involvement with every aspect of the Napoleonic myth. In addition to his study of the Napoleon poems, usually neglected by Byron scholars, Clubbe draws attention to the similarities in the character of the two men. A valuable contribution which sheds new light on this subject.

Darst, Diane Wassman. "Napoleon in Romantic Thought: A Study of Hazlitt, Stendhal and Scott." Ph.D. dissertation. New York: Columbia University, 1976.

A detailed study of the impact of Napoleon on three major Romantic writers: Hazlitt, Scott, and Stendhal. Darst contends that these artists were attracted to Napoleon for two basic reasons: first, because of the common characteristics of the age in which they lived, and second, as a result of their values and perceptions as Romantic writers. Useful study for the opinions of the three writers' perceptions of Napoleon and the in-depth examination of their writings. Bibliography.

Descotes, Maurice. *L'Obsession de Napoleon dans le "Cromwell" de Victor Hugo*. Paris: Lettres Modernes, 1967.
Asserts that Hugo modeled his Cromwell character after Napoleon. Through a painstaking analysis of the personality, position, and entourage of Cromwell and Napoleon as seen by Victor Hugo, Descotes reveals striking similarities in these two figures, particularly during key episodes, such as the Cadoudal conspiracy and the Coronation. The author stresses the Napoleonic obsession in Victor Hugo's writings.

Fischer, Doucet Devin. "'The Grand Napoleon of the realms of Rhyme': Byron and History." Ph.D. dissertation. New York: New York University, 1989.
Through Byron's poetry, letters, and journals, Fischer investigates the impact of contemporary history—the rise and fall of Napoleon, and the Napoleonic wars—on Byron's writings. He maintains that Byron's poetry was the vehicle through which he responded to literary and political occurrences. Bibliographical references

Foakes, F. A. "Coleridge, Napoleon and Nationalism." In *Literature and Nationalism*, edited by Vincent Newey and Ann Thompson. Liverpool: Liverpool University Press, 1991, 146-151.
An interesting chapter providing fascinating insights into Coleridge's changing views of Napoleon. In 1800, Coleridge considered Napoleon to have founded a popular and enlightened dictatorship. By 1809, Napoleon had become a Charlemagne, and by 1814, a Genghis Khan. Coleridge cast Napoleon as a tragic figure who deserted his men during the Russian campaign. In addition, Coleridge linked the Emperor to Macbeth, and later to Edmund in King Lear. Yet another example of the important impact Napoleon had on some of history's greatest writers. Bibliographical references.

Fregnac, Claude. *Les Styles français de Louis XIII à Napoléon III.* Paris: Hachette Réalités, 1975.
An illustrated history of interior design during the Napoleonic era. Three sections, each with a brief introduction, show Napoleonic furniture, interior decoration, and *objets d'art.* Useful for understanding the impact of Napoleon on interior design. Illustrations, some in color, and an index.

Guillemin, Henri. *Madame de Staël, Benjamin Constant et Napoléon.* Paris: Plon, 1959.
An erudite analysis of the works of three writers in relation to Napoleon. Using Madame de Staël's *Considérations sur la Révolution française* and other works, the author declares that she was initially quite positive in her attitude toward Napoleon. Her changing perspective followed public opinion. Also studies Benjamin Constant under the Empire at the time of his rupture with Madame de Staël. Constant is portrayed as contemptible and as an apprentice of Talleyrand.

Hautecoeur, Louis. *L'Art sous la révolution et l'Empire en France, 1789-1815: Sculpture, peinture, arts appliqués.* Paris: Guy LePrat, 1953.
A beautifully illustrated work with 207 illustrations and a brief text. Chapters are divided into topics such as architecture, interior decoration, sculpture, painting, engraving, the decorative arts, and clothing during the Napoleonic era.

―――――. *Histoire de l'architecture classique en France. Vol 5, Révolution et Empire, 1792-1815.* Paris: A. et J. Picard, 1953.
This volume is devoted to what the author calls the third period of the eighteenth century and surveys architecture during the revolutionary and Napoleonic years, beginning with a discussion of the Romantic era, including the principal architects under Louis XVI. Chapter 2 treats the period of the Revolution and the Empire, discussing Napoleon's impact on architecture. Chapter 3 deals with teaching doctrines, and Chapter 4 concerns the characteristics of the major architectural works.

Healey, F. G. *The Literary Culture of Napoleon.* Geneva: Droz, 1959.
A study of Napoleon's literary knowledge and ideas in the intellectual context of the period. In Part 1, Healey sketches the development of Napoleon's literary preferences from his school

days at Brienne to his return from Egypt in 1799. Part 2, which comprises the bulk of the book, is concerned with Napoleon's literary ideas and policies, including those affecting the theater, while he was consul, emperor, and in exile. A scholarly, well-noted monograph which reveals that Napoleon had an appreciation of literature and the arts, but that he attempted to control them. There are several accompanying appendices. Appendix A lists books from which Napoleon made notes between 1786 and 1791. Appendix B lists the tragedies and comedies which Napoleon saw performed. Appendix C reproduces the Emperor's views on Corneille's *Polyeucte*. Appendix D reproduces Napoleon's letter to Fouché, about Raynouard and *les Templiers*, dated December 31, 1806. Appendix E provides Napoleon's analysis of the causes of Werther's suicide. Index and bibliography.

Heisler, Marcel. *Stendhal et Napoléon*. Paris: A. G. Nizet, 1969.
None of the great Romantic writers was indifferent to Napoleon, and this is certainly true of Stendhal, who went through several stages of dislike and admiration of Napoleon. Stendhal's changing views on the Emperor are examined chronologically in this work. All of the writer's historical and literary works are placed under scrutiny. Heisler asserts that there was not an essay, novel, or historical work written by Stendhal that did not contain either direct references or allusions to Napoleon.

Heit, Siegfried Edmund. "Napoleon and the German Intellectuals." Ph.D. dissertation. Gainesville: Florida State University, 1975.
Heit holds that the old order in Germany was completely shattered by the French Revolution and Napoleon. The practical reforms introduced by Napoleon greatly altered the nature of social and political institutions. Liberalism became associated with the foreigner, while conservatism emerged as "high" German nationalism. Most of the German intelligentsia, including Herder and Schleiermacher, became associated with the nationalist movement as a reaction to Napoleonic hegemony. Modern Germany, he demonstrates, began with Napoleon. Bibliography.

Heit, Siegfried Edmund, and Otto W. Johnston (commentary). "German Romanticism: An Ideological Response to Napoleon." *Consortium on Revolutionary Europe, 1750-1850, Proceedings* 10 (1980): 187-197.

An examination of the reaction of German intellectuals to the Napoleonic domination of their lands. The author demonstrates that the Napoleonic hegemony was greatly responsible for the development of a German cultural nationalism expressed in the writings of Herder, Fichte, and Kleist all of whom wrote nationalistic tracts, poetry, and songs. A good introduction to this topic. Twenty-eight notes.

Hemmings, F. W. J. *Culture and Society in France 1789-1848.* Leicester: Leicester University Press, 1987.
Hemmings is an expert on culture in France from the French Revolution to the end of the nineteenth century. Although only one chapter of fifty pages deals with the Napoleonic era, it fills a gap on a relatively neglected topic. A wealth of information can be found here about literature, theater, music, architecture, furnishings, and painting under Napoleon, as well as a discussion of the "Style Empire" and Napoleon's patronage of the arts. Index, illustrations, and bibliography.

Herold, J. Christopher. *Mistress to an Age: A Life of Madame de Staël.* Indianapolis: Bobbs-Merrill, 1958.
A serviceable and readable biography for those who do not have the French to read Balayé. Investigates the political, intellectual, and personal development of this important literary figure, who led the liberal opposition to Napoleon. Useful for the development of this resistance to Napoleon. Although directed to the general reader, this work can still be read with profit by scholars. Illustrations, index, and bibliographical essay.

Horward, Donald, D. "Napoleon and Beethoven." *Consortium on Revolutionary Europe, 1750-1850: Proceedings* 10 (1980): 3-13.
An examination of the important impact of Napoleon on the life and works of Beethoven. The author states that although the two never met, and it is likely Napoleon was not aware of Beethoven's music, Napoleon's influence is unquestionable. Until 1804, Beethoven adored Napoleon; however, Beethoven's attitude Napoleon became emperor and intruded into German lands. Beethoven's output between 1804 and 1814 turned nationalistic and contained attacks against Napoleon. After 1814, Beethoven once again revered the Emperor. Based on printed primary works. Thirty-three notes.

Johnston, Otto W. *The Myth of a Nation: Literature and Politics in Prussia under Napoleon.* Columbia, S.C.: Camden House, 1989.
A study of the relationship between German literature and politics during the period from 1807 to 1813. Johnston attempts to establish that certain patterns may be found in many anti-Napoleonic works which received their motivation from the Prussian reform movement led by Baron vom und zum Stein. The program of Stein and his supporters consisted of national education. They held that language and the study of heroic figures of the German past were important national characteristics. The concluding chapter focuses on the rebirth of particularism in the German lands after Napoleon's defeat. Index and bibliographical references.

Knight, Frida. *Beethoven and the Age of Revolution.* London: Lawrence and Wishart, 1973.
A masterful study of Beethoven and his music in the changing social and political context of the French revolutionary and Napoleonic upheaval. Each chapter deals with a few years, in some cases a single year of the composer's life and his times. Chapters 4-8 cover the years from 1800 to 1815. Chapter 6, "Napoleonic Peace and War, 1807-1811," sketches Beethoven's music before war became imminent and how the war affected his work and attitude toward France after the occupation. Illustrations, index, bibliography, and an appendix of compositions mentioned in the text.

Lean, Edward Tangye. *The Napoleonists: A Study in Political Disaffection, 1760-1960.* London, England: Oxford University Press, 1970.
Lean spent more than twenty years researching the Napoleonic impact in English political life and has added considerably to our understanding of English attitudes about Napoleon. During the Napoleonic years there was a small but important group of Napoleonists in London. Lean's work explores the careers of the some of these supporters of the Emperor. All were Whigs, and they were led by Charles James Fox and Samuel Whitbread in the House of Commons, and by Lord Holland in the House of Lords. Many, such as Byron, Leigh Hunt, Godwin, and Hazlitt, were writers.

Lecomte, Louis Henry. *Napoléon et le monde dramatique: Étude nouvelle d'après des documents inédits.* Paris: H. Daragon, 1912.
A fundamental source for this subject, concerned with all aspects of the performing arts in this period. This volume is mainly an

extensive collection of documents including lists of theaters, performances, and actors. In addition, the rules and regulations that governed the theater, opera, music, and ballet are provided. The author convincingly demonstrates that Napoleon was a great patron of the arts.

Maras, Raymond J., and June K. Burton (commentary). "Napoleon and Levies on the Arts and Sciences." *Consortium on Revolutionary Europe 1750-1850: Proceedings* 17 (1987): 433-446.
An examination of the practice of looting the cultural treasures of conquered lands and of making levies on the arts and sciences components of treaties. This procedure started with the Directory during the French Revolution and was continued by Napoleon. Items such as works of art, military metals, snakes, and the valuables discovered in churches, museums, pawnshops, and libraries became a significant source of income for the imperial government. The major source for the confiscated treasures was Rome, with Milan ranking second. Based primarily on documents from the French Archives Nationales, contemporary newspapers such as *Le Moniteur*, and memoirs. Forty-four notes.

Martin, Andrew. "Three Representations of Napoleon." *French Studies* 43 (January 1989): 31-46.
An interesting and useful article which focuses on the importance of Napoleon for three writers: Chateaubriand, Stendhal, and Hugo. Martin begins with an examination of the some of the writings of Chateaubriand, including his *Mémoires d'outre tombe*, and argues that Chateaubriand saw himself as the Napoleon of literature, and viewed Napoleon as the literature of politics. The impact of Napoleon on Stendhal is examined by reference to his famous novel *The Scarlet and the Black*. Hugo, Martin argues, is the least historical and most literary of the three under examination. In offering the reader insight into the writers' attitudes toward Napoleon and his impact on their works, Martin stresses the difficulty in achieving a true historical representation of such a multifaceted character as Napoleon. Based on contemporary writings. Twenty-two notes.

Millar, Eileen Anne. *Napoleon in Italian Literature 1796-1821*. Rome: Edizioni di Storia e Letteratura, 1977.
A study of what was written in Italy between 1796 and 1821 as a commentary on Napoleon's actions and rule. This work sketches

the reactions of Italian men and women to Napoleon's career and charts changes in public opinion. It includes a list of works relating to Napoleon produced in Italy during the period, as well as interesting quotations of minor poets whose works are not easily accessible. The introduction by Mario Praz in Italian has little direct relevance, to the book's topic, since it is concerned with attitudes toward the fine arts. Illustrations, index, footnotes, and bibliography. Appendices of poetry by Italian poets Redaelli and Pasquino; a list of works relating to Napoleon written in Italy between 1791 and 1824.

The Myth of Napoleon. Yale French Studies. New Haven, Conn.: Eastern Press, 1960-1961.
The title of this special edition devoted to Napoleon might also be "Representations of Napoleon in Art and Literature." The eclectic collection is divided into two sections: "Lui" and "Toujours," with the former composed of short papers on various portraits of Napoleon, either visual or mythological, and the latter composed of essays on Napoleon's impact on writers such as Coleridge, Chateaubriand, Vigny, Dostoevsky, Tolstoy, Goethe, and Heine. Other papers discuss the July Monarchy and Napoleon. Edgar Munhall examines paintings of Napoleon by David, Gros, and Ingres; Henri Peyre studies the devil and saint images of Napoleon depicted in the works of writers such as Taine and Tocqueville. An extremely interesting and informative work. Bibliographical references.

Napoléon et la littérature: Europe, nos. 480-481 (avril-mai 1969).
A special volume of the journal *Europe* dedicated to Napoleon in celebration of the bicentenary of his birth. The aim of the collection is to examine Napoleonic thought and the way in which it was disseminated among the masses. Books, the press, theater, circus, songs, and prints are discussed in the collection. Contains articles on diverse subjects ranging from those who have written on the Napoleonic myth (such as Chateaubriand, Stendhal, Balzac, German writers, and philosophers) to Madame de Staël's personal relationship with the Emperor. Other articles deal with Napoleon and Marx and Engels, Tolstoy, and Dostoevsky.

Ribner, Jonathan P. *Broken Tablets: The Cult of Law in French Art*. Berkeley: University of California Press, 1993.

A study of the portrayal of the legislator and the law in nineteenth century France. Chapter 2, "Legislative Imagery under Napoleon, 1800-1815," deals with this subject during the Consulate and Empire. An original and thoughtful discussion of the artistic representation of the legalistic and legislative achievements of Napoleon, the greatest of which was the Code Napoléon, which Ribner states has a sacred character. He attempts to demonstrate the enduring "mythology" of Napoleon as a great lawgiver. Also under consideration are the importance of the Assembly of Jewish Notables, called to discuss Jewish law and the *Imperial Catechism*. Color plates, index, and bibliographical references.

Richardson, Joanna. "Stendhal and Napoleon." *History Today* 23 (January 1973): 3-9.
A short summary of Napoleon's impact on Stendhal which provides a useful introduction to the subject. Richardson claims that for the generation of writers of the 1800s, Napoleon played only an episodic part in that he represented a stage in the development of their ideas. This was not true for Stendhal whose works all bear the influence of Napoleon. The author follows Stendhal's evolving attitudes toward Napoleon in the writer's life and works.

Roberts, Warren. *Jacques-Louis David, Revolutionary Artist: Art, Politics and the French Revolution*. Chapel Hill: University of North Carolina Press, 1989.
Roberts' objective is to examine David's life and work in an historical context. His is the only book to accomplish this. Despite its title, it contains considerable detail on the Napoleonic years and attempts to explain the reasons for David's attraction to Napoleon. The book has the special feature of relating David's career to political events throughout the Revolution and the years of the Empire, with the result that art and political history are fused. Interesting details concerning David's relationship with Napoleon are highlighted. Illustrations, index, and bibliography.

Robinson, Robert E. *William Hazlitt's Life of Napoleon Buonaparte: Its Sources and Characteristics*. Paris: Minard, 1959.
Written by a literature professor, this is a serviceable, close textual analysis of Hazlitt's *Life*, published in 1830, and should be read in conjunction with the original source. Robinson's purpose is to scrutinize the source materials, precepts, preconceived notions, and prejudices that determined the type of biography Hazlitt wrote.

He includes lengthy excerpts from Hazlitt to prove his point that the biography is often plagiarized from other authors, such as Sir Walter Scott. The author concludes that Hazlitt's work deserves less credit than it has received from earlier critics. Robinson includes four appendices that reveal the limitations in Hazlitt's sources: Appendix A lists sections for which Hazlitt's sources could not be found; Appendix B lists sections based on the Antommarchi, Fain, Scott, and Southey; Appendix C documents Hazlitt's alterations; and Appendix D consists of Hazlitt's insertions, which demonstrate his philosophy of history. Bibliographical and explanatory footnotes; partially annotated bibliography.

Root, Christina Macfarlane. "Representations of Napoleon in English Romantic Literature." Ph.D. dissertation. New York: Columbia University, 1991.
An analysis of the impact of Napoleon on Samuel Taylor Coleridge, William Wordsworth, Lord Byron, and William Hazlitt. Root argues that Napoleon was the determining factor in the way in which these writers viewed themselves in terms of their writing. Each of the writers receives separate chapter in which Root analyzes how these literary figures reacted to Napoleon. Bibliographical references.

Rose, John Holland. "Wordsworth, Schiller, Fichte and the Idealist Revolt against Napoleon." In *Napoleonic Studies*. London: G. Bell, 1904, 1-40.
An intelligent investigation of the birth of the literary movement against Napoleonic domination in England, Russia, and Germany. In all three countries, Napoleon had a significant impact on contemporary literature. The initial positive attitude of Wordsworth and Coleridge toward the French Revolution is contrasted with their disapproval of Napoleon. Popular opinion was most markedly anti-Napoleon in Germany, where Napoleonic incursions had led to German nationalism among writers like Schiller and Fichte. A well-written and informative introduction to this topic by a leading scholar of Napoleon during the early years of the twentieth century.

Rosenberg, Martin. "Raphael's *Transfiguration* and Napoleon's Cultural Politics." *Eighteenth Century Studies* 19 (1985-1986): 180-205.
A fascinating examination of the reasons for the pivotal artistic and political role played by the Italian painter Raphael under

Napoleon. Napoleon considered Raphael the greatest Italian painter, embodying the culture of the Renaissance and the glory of Rome. He hoped to emulate this glory to Paris and, in order to achieve this end, had his agents in Italy confiscate many of Raphael's paintings, drawings, and tapestries. Raphael's works were kept in the Musée Napoléon in Paris. Based on printed primary and secondary sources. Sixty-two notes.

Rosenblum, Robert. "Painting under Napoleon 1800-1814." In *French Painting 1774-1830: The Age of Revolution*. Detroit, Mich.: Detroit Institute of Arts, 1975, 161-174.
Painting in all genres changed dramatically during the Napoleonic years. In this brief consideration of these changes, Rosenblum discusses Napoleonic history in paintings and portraiture, using examples from the more famous painters, such as David, Gros, and Ingres, as well as less well-known artists. The number of themes and subjects to be painted expanded greatly during these years. By the close of the Napoleonic era, French painting had become more complicated and eclectic than it had been in the past. Napoleonic history made possible circumstances for chronicling everything from traditional heroism to exotic peoples, architecture, and landscapes. Illustrations and bibliography.

Stendhal (Henri Beyle). *Oeuvres intimes de Stendhal. Préface, notes et index par Henri Martineau*. Paris: Gallimard, La Pléiade, 1955.
_____. *Napoleon*. Edited and ananotated by Louis Royer, with a preface by Albert Pingaud. Paris: Champion, 1929.
Stendhal's *Journal* and his *Vie de Henri Brulard* are contained in this collection. Both are particularly rich in details about the personnel of the First Empire, the theater, the German occupation, the campaign of 1809, provincial life, Italy in 1811, and a fragment of the Russian campaign. Written between 1817 and 1818, the *Vie de Napoléon* was a corrective to Madame de Staël's *Considérations*, considered as libel by Stendhal. This volume contains insights into Napoleon's government, personality, and administrative system. Twenty years later, Stendhal returned to the subject of Napoleon and wrote a second volume, *Mémoires sur Napoléon*. This work is Stendhal's glorification of Napoleon. Consequently, it is much less objective than the previous volume. In 1818, he had tempered his admiration with reserve. By 1837, however, his attitude had returned to one of complete adoration and hero worship.

AUTHOR INDEX

A

Ackerman, Evelyn Bernette 95
Ackernecht, Erwin Heinz 95
Albert, Maurice 185
Albistur, Maïté, and Daniel Armogathe 132
Alexander, D. W. 106
Alexander, Robert S. 106
Anchel, Robert 173
Anderson, Frank Maloy, ed. 35
Arnold, Eric A., Jr. 34, 72
Artz, Frederick B. 89
Askenazy, S. 145
Atteridge, A. Hilliard 60
Aucoc, Léon 72
Aulard, François-Alphonse 35, 53, 89

B

Bainbridge, Simon John Julian 185
Bainville, Jacques 60
Balayé, Simone 185
Ballot, Charles 80
Barker, Richard J. 81
Barnard, Howard C. 90
Barnett, Corelli 60
Barni, Jules 99
Bartel, Paul 106
Beaver, D., and R. Rosen 95
Beck, Thomas D. 73
Becke, Archibald Frank 107
Benoît, François 186
Berdahl, Robert M. 146
Berding, H. 146
Bergeron, Louis 81, 137
Bergeron, Louis, and Guy Chaussinand-Nogaret 48, 138
Bertaud, Jean-Paul 49, 107, 138
Besson, Maurice, and Robert Chauvelot 147
Best, Geoffrey 107

Beugnot, Jacques Claude, comte. 36
Bindel, Victor 167
Biver, Marie-Louise, comtesse 138
Blanning, T. C. W. 147
Blond, Georges 108
Blumenthal, Henry 176
Boime, Albert 186
Bonaparte, Joseph 36
Bonaparte, Louis 99
Bonaparte, Lucien 36
Bond, Gordon C. 148
Bossenga, Gail 82
Boulay de Meurthe, Alfred 168
Bourdon, Jean 37, 73
Bourgeois, E. 176
Bourgin, G., and Jacques Godechot 148
Bourguet, Marie-Noelle 73
Bourrienne, Louis-Antoine Fauvelet de 37
Bradley, Margaret 90
Broers, Michael 148
Bruun, Geoffrey 149
Burton, June K. 132, 186
Burton, June K., and Jeanne A. Ojala 132
Bury, J. P. T. 74
Bush, Robert D. 149
Butterfield, Herbert 61, 177

C

Cabanis, André 139
Caldwell, Ronald J 49
Cambacérès 37 - 38
Carven, John W. 168
Cate, Curtis 108
Caulaincourt, Armand-Louis-Augustin, marquis de 38
Célestin, Nicole 139
Cère, Emile 133

THE IMPACT OF NAPOLEON, 1800-1815

Cestaro, Antonio 149
Chabert, Alexandre 82
Chadwick, Owen 168
Chandler, David G. 49, 61, 108
Chaptal, Jean-Antoine 38
Chardigny, Louis 109
Charpentier, John 187
Chateaubriand, René 39
Chatelain, Jean 187
Chevalier, Jean-Claude 90
Chlovy, Gérard, and Yves-Marie Hilaire 166
Choderlos de Laclos, Etienne 39
Church, Clive 74
Clubbe, John 187
Collins, Irene 74
Connelly, Owen 50, 61, 109, 149
Conner, Susan P., and Sally T. Gershman 133
Conner, Susan, and Jeanne A. Ojala 133
Constant de Rebecque, Benjamin 40
Coppolani, Jean-Yves 75
Corbett, Sir Julian Stafford 110
Crawley, Charles W., ed. 53
Cronin, Vincent 61
Crosland, Maurice P. 96
Crouzet, François 82 - 83

D

Dansette, Adrien 169
Darst, Diane Wassman 187
Davico, R. 150
Davies, Norman 150
DeConde Alexander 177
Delacroix, Simon 169
Delmas, Jean 110
Deries, Léon 169
Desbrière, Edouard 110
Deschamps, Jules 99
Descotes, Maurice 100, 188
Destrem, Jean 170
Deutsch, Harold C. 177
Diefendorf, Jeffrey 150
Dodge, T. A. 111

Dooley, Edwin L., Jr. 90
Driault, Edouard 151, 178
Dufraisse, R. 83
Dunan, Marcel 151
Dupont, Marcel 111
Durand, Charles 75
Durieux, Joseph 134

E

Ellis, Geoffrey 139, 152
Elting, John R. 111
Emsley, Clive 50, 75, 111
Encrevé, André 166
Epstein, Robert M. 112
Esdaile, Charles J. 112

F

Fabre, Marc-André 62
Fehrenbach, Elisabeth 152
Fischer, Doucet Devin 188
Fisher, Herbert A. L. 62, 152
Foakes, F. A. 188
Forrest, Alan 113
Foucart, Paul Jean 113
Fourcy, A. 91
Fournier, August 62
Fregnac, Claude 189
Frijhoff, W., and D. Julia 91
Fugier, André 153, 178

G

Galarneau, Claude 100
Garver, Karen 134
Gates, David 113
Gaudin, M. M. C. 40
Geoffroy de Grandmaison, Charles Alexandre 153
Geyl, Pieter 101
Giddens, Paul H. 179
Girnius, Saulius Antanas 83
Glover, Michael 114
Glover, Richard 114
Gobert, Adrienne 76
Godechot, Jacques 54, 140
Godechot, Jacques, Beatrice F. Hyslop, and David L. Dowd 54

AUTHOR INDEX

Godel, Jean   170
Goldsmith, Lewis   101
Goldstein, Jan Ellen   96
Gonnard, Philippe   101
Gontard, Maurice   91 - 92
Gourgaud, Gaspard, baron   40
Grab, Alexander, and Charles F. Delzell   84
Gray, Marion W.   154
Guérard, Albert Léon   102
Guerrini, Maurice   140
Guillemin, Henri   189
Gulick, Edward Vose   179

H
Hales, Edward Elton Young   170
Hamilton-Williams, David   114
Handelsman, Marcel   154
Harford, Lee Shartle, Jr.   115
Harsin, Jill   134
Haussonville, Gabriel Paul Othenin de Cleron, comte de   170
Hautecoeur, Louis   189
Hauterive, E. d'   41, 76
Hazlitt, William   102
Healey, F. G.   189
Hecksher, E. F.   84
Heisler, Marcel   190
Heit, Siegfried Edmund   190
Heit, Siegfried Edmund, and Otto W. Johnston   190
Hemmings, F. W. J.   191
Henri-Robert, Jacques   50
Herold, J. Christopher   41, 191
Higby, Chester P., and Caroline B. Willis   84
Holtman, Robert B.   76, 140
Horward, Donald D.   51, 115
Horward, Donald D., and James Friguglietti   102 - 103
Horward, Donald, D.   191
Houssaye, Henry   115
Huard, Pierre   96
Hueckel, Glenn Russell   85

I
Imbert, Jean   97

J
Johnson, David   116
Johnston, Otto W.   192
Johnston, R. M.   155
Jomini, Antoine Henri de   116
Jones, R. Ben   63
Jouvenal, Bertrand de   85

K
Kaplan, Lawrence S.   180
Katz, Jacob   173
Kennett, Lee   103
Kilbourne, Lawrence J.   141
Kircheisen, Friedrich M.   51, 63
Klang, Daniel Michael   155
Knibiehler, Y.   135
Knight, Frida   192
Kobler, Franz   174
Kossmann, E. H.   155

L
Lachouque, Henry   117
Lanfrey, Pierre   55
Langlois, Claude   171
Langsam, W. C.   118
Lanzac de Laborie, Léon   141
Las Cases, Emmanuel, comte de   41
Latour, F.   85
Latreille, André   55, 171
Latreille, Camille   171
Le Gallo, Emile   118
Lean, Edward Tangye   192
Lecomte, Louis Henry   192
Lefebvre, Georges   63
Leflon, Jean   172
Léon, Antoine   92
Lesch, John   97
Lévy, Arthur   64, 180
Lockhart, John Gibson   64
Lokke, Carl Ludwig   156
Lovett, Gabriel H.   156
Lovie, J. and A. Palluel-Guillard   156
Lucas-Dubreton, Jean   55, 103

Ludwig, Emile 64
Lynn, J. A. 118
Lyon, Elijah Wilson 180
Lyons, Martyn 56

M

Mackenzie, Norman, Ian 119
Mackesy, Piers 119
Madelin, Louis 56
Mahan, Alfred Thayer 119
Maine, René 119
Malino, Frances 174
Manceron, Claude 120
Manfred, Albert 65
Mansel, Philip 76 - 77
Mansuy, Abel 156
Maras, Raymond J., and June K. Burton 193
Marbot, Baron de 42
Marchand Louis 42
Marion, Marcel 85
Markham, Felix Maurice 65
Marshall-Cornwall, James H. 120
Martin, Andrew 193
Martineau, Gilbert 66
Martinet, André 66
Masson, Frédéric 66
Matthews, Joseph J. 120
Melchior-Bonnet, Bernardine 66
Melvin, Frank Edgar 86
Menais, Georges Paul 86
Metternich, Clement-Wenceslas-Lothaire 42
Meyer, Jack Allen, ed. 51
Millar, Eileen Anne 193
Miot de Mélito, André-François, comte 42
Mistler, Jean, ed. 56
Mollien, F. N. 43
Montfort, Catherine R. 135
Moody, Walton Smith 120
Morvan, Jean 121
Mousnier, R., E. Labrousse, and M. Bouloiseau 57
Mowat, Robert Balmain 181
Murat, Inès 67

N

Napier, Sir William Francis Patrick 121
Napoleon I 43 - 45
Napoléon, Joseph-Charles-Paul Bonaparte 103
Nicolson, Harold George 181
Nipperdey, Thomas 157
Noailles, Marquis de 46

O

O'Brien, Patrick Karl 121
O'Dwyer, Margaret M. 172
Oman, Sir Charles 122
Ostergard, Uffe 157
Outram, Dorinda 158

P

Palmer, Alan Warwick 122
Palmer, Alan. 51
Palmer, R. R. 92 - 93
Parker, Harold T. 122, 181
Pasquier, E. D. 47
Pelet, Jean Jacques Germain 47
Périvier, Antonin 77
Peruta, Franco Della 123
Petre, Francis Loraine 123
Phillips, C. S. 172
Phipps, Ramsay Weston 123
Piétri, François 67, 77, 174
Pietromarchi, Antonello 67
Pivka, Otto von 124
Pluchon, Pierre 158
Poisson, Georges 142
Poland, Burdette, C. 167
Ponteil, Félix 77, 93
Priestley, Herbert Ingram 159
Puryear, Vernon J. 182

R

Ragsdale, Hugh A. 86, 182
Rambaud, Jacques 68
Ramon, Gabriel 86
Ramsey, Matthew 97
Rath, Reuben John 159
Read, Jan 124

AUTHOR INDEX

Reddaway, W. F., et al., eds. 159
Régnier, Jacques 78
Ribner, Jonathan P. 194
Richardson, Joanna 195
Riehn Richard K. 125
Rigotard, Jean 78
Robert, Daniel 167
Roberts, Warren 195
Robinson, Robert E. 195
Rocquain, Félix 68
Roederer, Pierre Louis 47
Rogers, Hugh Cuthbert Basset 125
Rogers, Rebecca 135
Root, Christina Macfarlane 196
Ropes, John Codman 68, 125
Rose, John Holland 69, 87, 196
Rosebury, Archibald Philip Primrose, 5th earl 104
Rosenberg, Martin 196
Rosenblum, Robert 197
Ross, Michael 69
Rothenberg, Gunther, E. 125 - 126
Ruppenthal, Roland 87

S

Saintoyant, Jules François 160
Sarramon, Jean 126
Saunders, Edith 127
Savant, Jean 78 - 79
Schama, Simon 160
Schmidt, Charles 93
Schom, Alan 127
Schroeder, Paul W. 182
Schwarzfuchs, Simon 174
Scott, Sir Walter 104
Seeley, John Robert 70
Sheehan, James 160
Sherwig, John M. 128
Shinn, Terry 94
Shupp, Paul Frederick 182
Simon, Walter M. 161
Soboul, Albert 57, 143
Soboul, Albert, and Bernhard Blumenkranz 175
Sorel, Albert 183

Spillman, Georges 183
Staël-Holstein, A. L. G. Necker, baronne de 48
Stanley, John Dudley 161
Stendhal (Henri Beyle) 197
Stourm, René 87
Sutherland, D. M. G. 57

T

Taine, Hippolyte Adolphe 58
Tarasulo, Yitzhak Yankel 128
Tarlé, Eugène 70, 88, 128
Tersen, Emile 70
Thibaudeau, Antoine-Clair 48
Thiers, Louis Adolphe 58
Thiry, Jean 58, 162
Thomazi, Auguste Antoine 129
Thompson, J. M. 70
Thuillier, G. 88
Tone, John Lawrence 129
Tranié, J., and J. C. Carmigniani 129
Tulard, Jean 52, 71, 79, 105, 143 - 144, 162

V

Van de Walle, Etienne 136
Vandal, Albert 59, 183
Viennet, Odette 88
Villani, Pasquale 162
Villefosse, Louis de, and Janine Bouissounouse 79

W

Walsh, Henry Horace 173
Wehler, Hans-Ulrich 163
Weill, Georges 94
Weiner, Dora B. 98
Welschinger, H. 79
Whitcomb, Edward A. 80, 184
Williams, Pearce L. 94
Woloch, Isser 130, 136
Woolf, Stuart 163 - 164
Woronoff, Denis 88
Wren, Keith 105
Wright, D. G. 59

Y

Yorck von Wartenburg, Hans Ludwig
 Daniel Maximilien (Graf) 131
Young, Norwood 130

Z

Zaghi, Carlo 164

SUBJECT INDEX

A
Agriculture 52
Alexander I, Tsar 38
Arc de Triomphe 142
Austerlitz 110
Austria 62

B
Bank of France 44
Bankers 82
Battles 42, 108
Bavaria 115
Beethoven, Ludwig van 191
Belgium 155
Berlin Decrees 86
Black legend 39
Bonaparte, Jérôme 62
Bonaparte, Joseph 36, 61
Bonaparte, Louis 68
Bonaparte, Lucien 36
Bonapartism 56
Bourbons 76
Bourgeoisie 57
British Empire 124
Budgets 43
Bureaucracy 50, 80

C
Cadoudal conspiracy 188
Campaigns 63, 108
Canada 100
Censorship 79
Chateaubriand, François-René, vicomte de 187, 194
Church 71
Civil Code 132
Coleridge, Samuel Taylor 185, 188, 194, 196
Commerce 36
Concordat 153, 167
Congress of Vienna 53

Conscription 72
Constant, Benjamin 105, 187
Constitution, French 73
Continental Blockade 82
Continental System 64, 84
Coronation, Napoleon's 169
Correspondence, Napoleon's 45
Corsica 43
Council of State 48
Counter-revolution 58

D
Demography 79
Departments 49
Despot, Napoleon as 39
Dictator, Napoleon as 65
Dictatorship 58
Diplomat, Napoleon as 63
Directory 45
Dostoevsky, Fyodor 194

E
Ecole Normale Supérieure 95
Ecole Polytechnique 90
Ecoles centrales 89
Economy 82
Education 59, 89
Egypt 59
18 Brumaire 71, 168
Elba 42
Elections 75
Elites 91
Emigrants 41
Emperor, Napoleon as 41
Empire 59
Engineers 91
Equality 78
Equipment 114
Europe 52, 84

F
Factories 82
Feudal system 149
Finance 40
Foreign affairs 44
Foreign policy 42
Fouché, Joseph 41
French Revolution 54

G
General, Napoleon as 63
Germany 111
Gourgaud, Gaspard 104
Government 66
Grand Army 45, 111
Great Britain 52, 84
Great Sanhedrin 47
Guerrillas 112
Guilds 82

H
Hazlitt, William 185, 188, 196
Health 69
Herder, Johann Gottfried 190
Historiography 101
Holland 68
Hospitals 97
Hugo, Victor 188
Hundred Days 43

I
Ideologues 76, 79
Imperial Army 117, 121
Imperial University 89
Industry 81, 89
Institutions 48
International relations 183
Italy 117

J
Jacobins 69
Jefferson, Thomas 177
Judaism 166
Judicial system 148

K
Kingdom 66

L
Landlords 149
Las Cases, Emmanuel 41
Laws 34
Legion of Honor 133
Legislation 92
Legislative Body 74
Liberty 78
Louis XIV 78
Louis XVIII 172
Louisiana 149, 177
Lycées 92

M
Manufacturers 82
Marengo, Battle of 65
Marriage 133
Marshals 127
Marshals, Napoleon's 109, 127
Marxist historiography 65
Medicine 95
Memorial, Napoleon's 45
Merchants 82
Metternich, Clement-Wenceslas-Lothaire 42
Military 42
Modernization 157
Monuments 138

N
Naples 68
Napoleon III 43, 71
Napoleonic codes 50
Napoleonic legend 41
Nationalism 190
Navy, French 114
Nelson, Horation, Viscount 110
Newspapers 35, 79
Ney, Marshal 116, 127
Nobility 52, 112
Notables 49, 138

SUBJECT INDEX

O
Old Regime 73, 112

P
Painting 53
Paris 79
Peasants 52
Peninsular War 106
Piedmont 148
Pius VII, Pope 67
Poland 145
Police 35
Politics 54
Population of France 142
Portugal 115
Prefects 36
Priests 75
Proclamations 46
Propaganda 60
Protestantism 135, 166
Prussia 146
Psychiatry 96
Public opinion 38

R
Recruitment 112
Reforms 70
Religion 36
Republic 46
Restoration 74, 81
Revolutionaries 61
Rhineland 152
Roman Catholicism 166
Romantic era 102
Royalists 116
Russia 83
Russian campaign 108

S
Saint Helena 45
Satellite kingdoms 50
Schleswig-Holstein 87
Schools 90
Science 94
Scott, Sir Walter 64, 188
Second Empire 58
Senate 35
Ships 110
Soult, Marshal 127
Spain 156
Staël, Madame de 100, 132, 187
Stendhal (Marie-Henri Beyle) 188
Strategy 116
Switzerland 123

T
Taine, Hyppolyte Adolphe 47
Taxation 85, 112
Theater 185
Thiers, Louis Adophe 55
Third Coalition 110
Tilsit 87
Tolstoy, Leo 108, 194
Trade 86
Trafalgar 127
Treaties 34, 69, 87, 182
Treaty of Lunéville 70
Treaty of Tilsit 87
Tribunate 35, 74

U
Uniforms 124
United States 55

W
War 85, 89
Warsaw, Duchy of 145
Waterloo 109, 114
Weaponry 123
Wellington, Arthur Wellesley, Duke of 64, 107
Westphalia 62
Women 132
Wordsworth, William 185, 196

ABOUT THE AUTHOR

Leigh Whaley received her Ph.D. in modern French history from the University of York, England, and has taught in the history departments at the Universities of Saskatchewan and Toronto, where she also held a postdoctoral fellowship from the Social Sciences and Humanities Research Council of Canada. Her current position is Associate Professor of Modern European History in the School of Modern History at the Queens University of Belfast.

Dr. Whaley is a specialist in the history of the French Revolution and Napoleon. In addition to being the author of several articles on the politics of the French Revolution, Napoleon Bonaparte, and modern French historiography, she is currently writing a book entitled *The Politics of Terror during the French Revolution.*